ABANDONED

Arctic Regions, Showing Location of Circumpolar Stations, 1881–1883.

The Story of the **GREELY ARCTIC EXPEDITION** 1881–1884

ABANDONED

Alden Todd

with foreword by Terrence Cole
and introduction by Vilhjalmur Stefansson

University of Alaska Press
Fairbanks, Alaska

Library of Congress Cataloging-In-Publication Data

Todd, A. L. (Alden L.), 1918-
  Abandoned : the story of the Greely Arctic Expedition,
1881-1884 / Alden Todd with foreword by Terrence Cole
and introduction by Viljalmur Stefansson.-- 2nd ed.
    p. cm.
Originally published: New York : McGraw-Hill, 1961.
Includes bibliographical references (p.).
ISBN 1-889963-29-1
  1. Lady Franklin Bay Expedition (1881-1884) 2. Arctic
regions--Discovery and exploration. I. Title.

G670 1881 .G75 2001
919.804--dc21

                                        2001027295

Originally published in 1961 by McGraw-Hill, New York.
Copyright © 1961 by Alden Todd.
Foreword to the 2001 Edition by Terrence Cole © 2001 by the University of
    Alaska Press.
All rights reserved. First printing.
International Standard Book Number: cloth, 1-889963-53-4
                                    paper, 1-889963-29-1

Library of Congress Catalog Number: 2001027295

Printed in the United States of America by Sheridan Books, Inc.

This publication was printed on acid-free paper that meets the minimum requirements for the American National Standard for Information Science—Perma-
nence of Paper for Printed Library Materials ANSI Z39.48-1984.

Publication coordination and production by Deirdre Helfferich, University of
    Alaska Press.
Cover design by Dixon Jones, Rasmuson Library Graphics, University of
    Alaska Fairbanks.
Cover: Painting by Tom Lovell, gift to author.

Unless otherwise noted, all engravings and maps are from Augustus Greely's
    Three Years of Arctic Service.

Abandoned. The Story of the Greely Arctic Expedition, 1881–1884 is volume
No. 8 of the University of Alaska Press's Classic Reprint Series. This series
brings back into print highly regarded, classic works of enduring excellence.
For more information contact the University of Alaska Press, P.O. Box
756240, University of Alaska Fairbanks, Fairbanks, AK 99775-6240.

To the memory of my mother,
Constance Leupp Todd

The Rescue, June 23, 1884.

CONTENTS

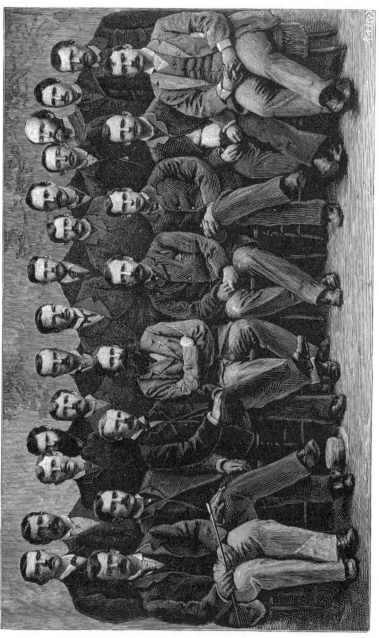

Engraving from a photo taken in Washington studio of Moses P. Rice, brother of expedition member George Rice. seated, left to right: Maurice Connell, David L. Brainard, Frederick F. Kislingbury, Adolphus Washington Greely, James B. Lockwood, Edward Israel, Winfield S. Jewell, George W. Rice. Standing, left to right: William Whisler, William A. Ellis, Jacob Bender, William H. Cross, Julius Frederick, David Linn, Henry Biederbick, Charles B. Henry, Francis Long, David C. Ralston, Nicholas Salor, Dr. Octave Pavy (not in the original photo), Hampden S. Gardiner, Joseph Elison.

FOREWORD

ALDEN TODD'S *Abandoned* tells the tale of the most disastrous chapter in the history of American exploration of the Arctic, the Greely Expedition of 1881–1884. Like the 1986 explosion of the space shuttle *Challenger*, the tragedy and suffering of the Greely expedition shocked the world. Launched with high hopes for establishing the northernmost station of the First International Polar Year, a ground-breaking multinational campaign of fourteen separate scientific expeditions simultaneously exploring the Arctic, Greely's expedition crumpled under bureaucratic bungling and miscalculations that would leave a frightful legacy of death and disgrace. One bitter early account complained the U.S. government's failed relief efforts to save Greely in 1882 and 1883 constituted "a flawless record of misfortune and blundering."[1] Altogether nineteen of the Greely expedition's twenty-five members died in the North. The starving six men who barely survived their rescue on June 22, 1884, including General A.W. Greely, would be haunted forever by charges of cowardice, cannibalism, and murder.[2]

While writing this classic account of the Greely disaster, originally published in 1961, author Alden Todd discovered numerous collections of private papers never previously examined, and explored the crucial questions at the heart of the calamity: Why did the U.S. government leave its official exploring expedition marooned in the Arctic? Why did only six of the original twenty-five survive? While absolute answers may never be possible involving human affairs, Todd's detective work demonstrates how a series of wrong turns by a multitude of officials resulted in the final catastrophe.

Shortly before his death, famed arctic explorer and scholar Vilhjalmur Stefansson read Todd's manuscript and wrote the introduction to the book. Stefansson claimed that in his mind *Abandoned* solved many of the longest-standing mysteries of the Greely party, and changed some of his opinions about what exactly took place during those three fateful years on Ellesmere Island in the early 1880s.

Looming always over the history of the doomed expedition was the unmistakable evidence of cannibalism from the mutilated bodies of some of the dead. "We who knew Greely talked of it in whispers," Stefansson wrote, "and fell silent if he, or another of the six, came within possible hearing."[3] In Stefansson's mind the final chapters of *Abandoned* proved that Greely and most of the other survivors were probably telling the truth when they swore they had not carved any flesh from the bodies of their dead comrades, and that ironically the guilty most likely included some of those who had died of starvation, succumbing to protein-poisoning from eating meat with no fat.

Stefansson explained that Todd's greatest virtue was his attempt to be impartial. "Everybody heretofore, including me," Stefansson wrote, "has been one of three things—for the General, against him, or leaning backward to be charitable, and therefore constantly out of balance."[4]

Freelance writer Alden Todd, the author of six books, became interested in A.W. Greely at a young age. Born in Washington, D.C., in 1918, his grandfather and the general were old friends, and Todd was ten years old when he met Greely on one memorable occasion in the late 1920s. Educated at Phillips Exeter Academy and Swarthmore College, Todd served as infantryman with the 101st Airborne Division during World War II. Following the war he became a freelance writer, and the story of the grand old arctic explorer he had met as a child became the subject of his first book.

The title *Abandoned* is a one-word summation of his thesis. "My story," Todd wrote, "is essentially one of the physical and moral courage displayed by a small group of men abandoned to hunger and cold in the distant, early days of arctic work."[5] Todd concluded that despite Greely's many critics, including some of the men who served under his command, blaming Greely for the deaths of his men is as irrational as blaming Greely for the weather or the size of the Arctic's ice pack.

The expedition had first set sail in summer of 1881 en route to Lady Franklin Bay on the northeast coast of Ellesmere Island, where the twenty-five-man crew established its permanent station known, as Fort Conger. During the first winter they compiled an impressive amount of scientific data and recorded numerous other accomplishments, including a sledging trip over the top of northern Greenland in the spring of 1882 that reached the farthest north point of any humans in recorded history, a record that would stand for more than a dozen years. After the expected relief ship failed to arrive in the summer of 1882, the two dozen men under Lieutenant Greely's command were forced to spend a second year on Ellesmere Island. Though bitterly disappointed at having to stay in their icy prison for a second winter, the well-supplied party faced no immediate danger. But when the relief ship failed to arrive yet once again in the summer of 1883, the situation became critical as they faced their third and final winter with dim prospects.

As their official orders from the War Department dictated, the Greely party began a long and arduous journey south through the ice-choked waters of the high Arctic—including one month stranded on an ice floe erratically drifting southwards through Kane Basin—hoping to find either the supply ship, or a cache of provisions that was supposed to have been left for Greely in case of emergency. They would find neither.

Much of *Abandoned* recounts the harrowing details of their slow starvation at Cape Sabine, where the Greely party holed up for the winter in October 1883, hoping to stretch a meager forty days' worth of food out over eight or nine months. They did this by limiting meals to about fourteen ounces per day, and calculating rations to as little as one-tenth of an ounce.

In arctic history the Greely story will perhaps forever be com-

pared to the greatest British tragedy in arctic exploration: the
deaths of the 129 members of the Sir John Franklin Expedition.
As their food supplies dwindled, the men of the Greely party
were haunted by the fear that they would share the fate of Franklin.
But unlike the British expedition which disappeared without a
trace, Greely and his men have left volumes of diaries, memories, and reminiscences, recounting the disaster as it unfolded
day by day. While we know almost nothing of Franklin's final
days, the struggles and mental anguish of Greely's men in their
living death are recorded in painful detail. Ironically, as a result
of this explicit record, history has tended to be relatively harsher
on Greely than Franklin, perhaps only because the complaints of
Greely's men can still be heard from beyond the grave, while
Franklin's legacy is nothing but silence.

In a sense, we know both too much and too little about what
occurred to Greely and his men that last winter. Certainly the
written evidence contains much criticism of the commander, since
naturally the favorite pastime of the party during their confinement seemed to have been constant complaining, about the
weather, the lack of food, and especially Lieutenant Greely, who
was called by some of his men, among other things, ignorant,
egotistical, stupid, a madman, fraud, lunatic, miserable fool, devil,
heathen, serpent, and brute.[6]

Like the story of any traumatic family quarrel, the truth about
the feuding members of the Greely party is difficult to recount,
in part because the nature of historical evidence so often tends to
amplify controversy; good news seldom makes headlines or in-
spires pages of scribbling in a personal journal. As Greely himself wrote in his 1886 memoir, he was embarrassed by the negative tone of his own diary because it "does not indicate sufficiently the kindly feeling and thought for others that was daily
and hourly testified in that miserable life. This was the rule, and
therefore was not dwelt upon. The reverse was exceptional, and
so noted; and, as I have before said, the rest must be read between the lines."[7] Despite Greely's stubborn personality quirks
which some of his crew found so irritating, such as his insistence

on the privileges of rank and ceremony—for instance, on the retreat he insisted on carrying his dress uniform complete with epaulets, sword and scabbard—he did manage to keep his party alive and well in the Arctic for two and a half years.[8] Despite chronic grumbling by Greely's men—one malcontent was executed for stealing food and insubordination—it was only in the third and final year, when their supplies were exhausted, that the crew truly began to suffer. All of the nineteen deaths occurred within the final six months of their captivity, including eleven men who died during the last four weeks before they were found, and one man who perished after their rescue.

Under Greely's leadership his men would simply outlive their supply of food, and their prolonged existence in the last camp at Cape Sabine was a living nightmare. "The constant gnawing of hunger almost drives us mad," Sgt. David Brainard wrote on November 4, 1883, eight months before the relief ship finally arrived. "I wonder if we will retain control of our minds throughout the trying period which seems inevitable."[9] Brainard would be one of the lucky six to survive the ordeal. Less fortunate was Lt. James B. Lockwood, and his diary is one of the saddest imaginable, the voice of a man losing his mind as he slowly starves to death. Obsessed by food, Lockwood could not restrain himself from continually talking about imaginary meals and delicacies he planned to devour when he returned home.

"We are now constantly hungry," Lockwood wrote, "and the constant thought and talk run on food, dishes of all kinds, and what we have eaten and what we hope to eat when we reach civilization. I have a constant longing for food."[10] Day after day the men talked "incessantly about food and dishes, restaurants and hotels, and everything in connection with eating."[11] Shivering and starving in the cold, Lockwood compulsively listed his favorite restaurants and their specialties, and any dishes that came to mind. "In fact I can think of nothing but eating," he wrote.[12] It was almost as if he believed that writing down names of foods he enjoyed, like "oatmeal muffins," *"Omelette soufflé,"* "Fig pie," "Cranberry jelly," "Pumpkin butter," or "Mrs. O'Shea's figs," was almost as good as actually eating. Vowing never to be hungry again, he wrote a list of "Things to be kept in my room at Washington for midnight lunches."

> Sardines, potted ham, smoked beef, smoked goose and eel, shrimps, anchovy paste, spice oysters, stuffed olives, Boston pilot bread, buttered crackers, Albert and Arundel crackers, soda and water, ditto ginger, nuts and cakes, can of butter and condensed milk, preserved peaches, strawberries, & etc. and blackberry jam, *fromage de Brie,* and Schweitzerkäse, sugar, beer, ale and porter, and cider, and *liqueurs,* and Virginia seedling wine, mustard, vinegar, pepper, salt etc., and Maryland biscuit, black cake.[13]

On the night before Thanksgiving 1883, Lockwood asked each man to compose a menu for happier days in the future, which the lieutenant scribbled down in shorthand, proposing that surviving "members of the expedition will adhere as closely as possible to the bill of fare on their next birthdays."[14] While the reality was that the emaciated men would soon be reduced to eating bird droppings, caterpillars, crumbs picked out of the vilest garbage, and their sealskin boots, pants, and sleeping bags, Lockwood filled his mind with delicious fantasies.

> I am to eat a cold roast turkey with Linn down at the farm on my return—turkey to be stuffed with oysters and eaten with cranberries. With Ralston, some hot hoe-cakes. With Ellis, spare ribs. With Long, pork steaks. With Biederbick, 'buffers,' old regiment dish. With my other neighbor, Connell, I am to eat Irish stew. Connell is to cook this himself. With Bender, a roast sucking pig. With Schneider, tenderloin. With Brainard, peaches and cream. With Frederick, a black cake, to be cooked by one of my sisters, with preserves. With Salor, veal cutlets and lettuce salad. With Whisler, flapjacks, with molasses. With Jewell, roast oysters on toast. With Rice, clam chowder. With Israel, hashed-up liver. With Gardiner, Virginia Indian pone (hot). With Elison, Vienna sausage. With Dr. Pavy, *pâté de fois gras.* With Henry, Hamburg beefsteak. With Kislingbury, hashed-up tur-

key, chicken and veal. With Lieutenant Greely, Parker House rolls and coffee, cheese, omelet, chicken curry, and rice, and preserved strawberries. The Parker House rolls are to the baked at his house, and I am to furnish the preserved strawberries.[15]

Lockwood would never eat any of those imaginary meals, however, as he died of starvation on April 9, 1884, the fourth of the nineteen men who would perish.

By the time that a crew from a naval relief ship finally reached the Greely party on the evening of June 22, 1884, the last of their tiny rations had been consumed five weeks earlier, and Greely and the other last six survivors were probably only hours away from death. The stunned and starving men, lying in their rags waiting to die, were almost oblivious to the fact that they had been saved. Like a crazed man, Sgt. Francis Long could only keep muttering over and over again, "a hard winter—a hard winter."[16]

A.W. Greely went on to enjoy a long and spectacular career as an author, explorer, scientist, and army officer. He became the first president of the Explorer's Club and the chief of the U.S. Army Signal Corps, retiring as a major general in 1908, an incredible achievement for a man who began his military service as a private in the Civil War. Shortly before his death at age ninety-one in 1935, A.W. Greely was awarded the Congressional Medal of Honor, only the second such award—following Charles A. Lindbergh—granted for peacetime service.[17]

Despite his many accomplishments, however, Greely's life was always shadowed by the tragedy in the Arctic at Cape Sabine so skillfully recounted in *Abandoned*. The general always honored the memory of the men he had lost on the expedition. Each year whenever possible on June 22, the anniversary of their rescue, he and other survivors would dine at the Army-Navy Club in Washington and share a dish from the menus that Lieutenant Lockwood had compiled, a quiet memorial to the cold and hungry days they had shared when they had been abandoned in the Arctic.[18]

—*Terrence Cole*
Professor of History, University of Alaska Fairbanks

1. David L. Brainard, *The Outpost of the Lost* (Indianapolis: Bobbs-Merrill Co., 1929), p. 110.

2. Seven members of the 25-man expedition were *alive* at the time of their rescue, however Private Joseph Elison died on board the relief ship on his way south.

3. page xv.

4. pages xiii-xiv.

5. page xix.

6. Echoing the negative view of Greely's leadership ability see: Leonard F. Guttridge, *Ghosts of Cape Sabine: The Harrowing True Story of the Greely Expedition* (New York: G.P. Putnam's Sons, 2000), pp. 154–155, 165.

7. Adolphus W. Greely, *Three Years of Arctic Service* (New York: Charles Scribner's Sons, 1886), Vol. II, pp. 330–331.

8. Guttridge, *Ghosts of Cape Sabine,* p. 153.

9. Brainard, *The Outpost of the Lost,* p. 130.

10. page 131. See also: Adolphus W. Greely, *Report of the United States Expedition to Lady Franklin Bay,* House Misc. Documents, 1st Session, 49th Congress, 1885–1886, (Hereafter cited as Lockwood Journal), p. 397.

11. page 139.

12. Lockwood Journal, p. 404.

13. Lockwood Journal, p. 401.

14. Brainard, *The Outpost of the Lost,* p. 150.

15. Lockwood Journal, p. 402.

16. W. S. Schley, *The Rescue of Greely* (New York: Charles Scribner's Sons, 1886), p. 227. See page 255.

17. For a brief profile of Greely see: Ronald T. Reuther, "First President of the Explorer's Club—Major General Adolphus Washington Greely," *The Explorers Journal,* Spring 1994, pp. 4–9.

18. page 314.

Next Page:
Aldolphus Washington Greely.

INTRODUCTION

THE HISTORY of North American arctic discovery has two great tragic figures: from Britain, Captain Sir John Franklin, and from the United States, Major General Adolphus Washington Greely. The Franklin tragedy of the 1840s has been told in dozens of narrative and analytical volumes, and keeps being rewritten as new material comes to light and new interests develop. But the Greely story of the 1880s is only now beginning to be retold.

Two years ago A. L. Todd brought us news that General Greely's family were releasing new material, as were the family of his chief assistant, Brigadier General David Brainard, and some others. Seeking further new sources, Todd came to Dartmouth's arctic collection; and we have helped him, as have other groups, notably the Explorers Club of New York, founded by Greely in the sense that he was their first president, and the National Geographic Society of Washington, with whom the General was associated for half a century and whom he chose as permanent custodians of his arctic library. Doubtless there will hereafter be found other sources of Greely information, just as there constantly are being found new ones on John Franklin, but meantime these have given us a fresh start in Greely scholarship that is more than promising.

The newly available material is documentary; and there still live men who knew the General, among them I who joined the Explorers Club during his presidency and who had the good fortune to become, decades later, their seventh and thirteenth president. So Todd, who as a boy of ten met Greely once, has asked me to write for his book a personal introduction. I agreed the more readily because I not only respected Greely as a scholar but had also felt from childhood that I shared the burden of his tragedy.

For at the age of five I heard my father reading the weekly country newspaper aloud, as he always did; and what he read during the late summer of 1884 must have been in part the Greely story, since in August of that year the press began to fill with dark hints as to why it was that only six men came back of twenty-five who had gone north on the three-year expedition. These press reports, as we can read them still in the files of old papers, were a blend of unsuccessful concealment and inadequate frankness, the charges and denials bewildering alike in the disclaimed malice of the attackers and the proclaimed benevolence of those who defended. As to why only six came back, I for one was still baffled fifty-one years later when Greely died.

And if my uncertainty persisted, whose would not? For, with what now seems like a premonition of destiny, I began in childhood to read books on polar exploration; though I did not reach Greely's two-volume *Three Years of Arctic Service* till college days. I had not yet had the chance to meet the General when in 1906 I resigned a teaching fellowship in anthropology at Harvard to become the anthropologist of a polar expedition, on the return from which I was invited to join the New York Explorers Club. In Washington Greely and I were fellow-members of another club, the Cosmos, and we met there frequently and lunched together occasionally. When in 1919 the National Geographic Society awarded me their Hubbard trophy they asked Greely to introduce me to their audience while Peary handed me the medal. Next day Dr. Gilbert Grosvenor, President of the Society, said it was a greater achievement for me to have maneuvered Greely and Peary into shaking hands in public than the achievements for which they had awarded me the medal.

For it was part of Greely's tragedy that he suffered many bitter enmities, most conspicuous the one between himself and Peary, though they showed it chiefly by avoiding each other—a strange situation between officers of comparable rank, Rear Admiral against Major General, easily the foremost American polar explorers. It still seems to me (though many of my opinions have changed as I read the manuscript of the book I am here introducing) that we on the sidelines were right in thinking this particular bitterness to rest on Peary's criticism of Greely as responsible for the sacrificed lives of his nineteen comrades who did not return from the Lady Franklin Bay expedition. Peary quoted such admissions as Greely's having said to his own men: "As you are aware, I myself know nothing about ice navigation, I am disadvantaged by having poor eyesight."

Peary, and many of the rest of us, said without adequate charity that a man so handicapped should not have commanded a polar expedition. We should have placed this blame on those who sent Greely north, as little equipped by training as by eyesight. In contrast, Peary himself was physically and mentally qualified for northern leadership. An engineer, an athlete, a rough-and-tumble frontiersman, he resembled George Washington not merely in having a gift for command but also in the physical prowess which made it possible for a youngster in Braddock's army to dash into the woods and meet the French and Indians on their own terms. For all I know, General Greely might have taken General Eisenhower's place adequately at the Battle of the Bulge; but I feel I know that Greely could not have filled Washington's shoes as an aide to Braddock. But Peary could have; he would have been at Washington's heels, if not ahead of him, in salvaging Braddock.

As said, I have changed my mind on many things the last few days, while reading the manuscript from which Todd's *Abandoned* is to be published. For this the reasons are many, some of them connected with Todd's having had before him sources I have never seen before, notably those furnished by the Greely and Brainard families. The over-riding superiority of *Abandoned*, however, is in its being truly impartial. Everybody heretofore, including me, has been one of three things—for the General, against him, or leaning backward to be charitable, and therefore constantly out of balance. But to A. L. Todd has been given the gift not to be for, against, or charitable, but just to tell everything that he has space for, if it is pertinent and interesting.

This introduction has space for only one illustration of how Todd's method has worked to reveal about the Greely mystery things that Greely himself evidently did not know, which were also things I never understood in my long association with the General, and perhaps ones the significance of which Todd himself may not realize till he sees this introduction to his own book. The illustration I take is that *Abandoned* solves, incidentally and in the course of mere truth telling, the problem Greely thought insoluble, of who were the perpetrators of the cannibalism of which the General himself knew nothing. I summarize briefly the solution which is given at length by Todd in its proper chapter:

When Schley reached Greely on June 22, 1884, eighteen men had already died and one lay dying. By August 12 the remaining six were steadily recovering health at the Navy Yard, Portsmouth, New Hampshire. For that date Todd says: "At great length *The New York Times* article asserted that the survivors of the abandoned party had eked out their existence by living on human flesh." General Hazen, Greely's superior, wrote him: "As to the talk of eating human flesh you can just say what you are prepared to." Todd reports, further on, that "the three surviving brothers of Lieutenant Kislingbury had signed an agreement [for] exhumation of their brother's corpse . . . large pieces of tissue had been cut from the thighs and trunk . . . Greely, shocked at the Rochester dispatch, then gave his side of the story from Portsmouth . . . 'I say that it is news, horrible news to me . . . I can but repeat that if there has been cannibalism, and there now seems no doubt about it, the man-eating was done in secrecy and entirely without my knowledge and contrary to discipline . . . Every man of the survivors has called upon me . . . each man solemnly swore that he was innocent of the deed. I cannot tell whether they told the truth or not, and doubt that any investigation will reveal who are the cannibals . . . I can but answer for myself.' "

It was the heart of the tragic Greely mystery that each man

could answer only for himself, and none knew whom else to believe. This was true not merely of what each survivor thought of
the other five but also of what everybody else—for instance,
Peary and I—thought of all the six. A tabu had been broken, the
severest our culture knows, the one against eating human flesh, to
which we attach an irrational horror. We who knew Greely talked
of it in whispers, and fell silent if he, or another of the six, came
within possible hearing. No one will probably doubt me when I
tell this of myself and of Greely's acquaintances and friends. But
in a way I can prove it, and shall now try.

Of all people, we anthropologists would be least likely to be
swayed by tabu, for it is our profession to study irrational human
conduct based upon irrational belief. Among the anthropologists
who knew Greely, and who knew each other well, were Elmer
Ekblaw and I. So, as I write this, it occurs to me that he and I
used to talk about the cannibalism on the Greely expedition, and
that Ekblaw is the author of the Greely sketch in the *Dictionary
of American Biography*. Recalling how we used to fall silent at
Greely's approach, I wondered how, in that encyclopedia article,
he had approached the topic. For Ekblaw would remember that
the Greely family would be among his readers.

I found, as I expected, that Professor W. Elmer Ekblaw, ge-
ographer and anthropologist of Clark University, has written
what is (within tabu limits) a frank and just account of a great
man whom he had known as a friend. In his article of three large
double-column pages the nearest he comes to mentioning cannibalism is: "Supplies gradually failed . . . The strength, health and
morale of the men were gradually broken by lack of food . . . until by mid-January the first death came, followed by six deaths in
April, four in May, and seven in June, all under harrowing circumstances." Thus, as if he had fallen silent on the General's approach, Ekblaw falls silent in his critical estimate.

Not till I read the final chapters of Todd's *Abandoned* did I
realize that since 1906 there had never existed, for me, even a
tabu reason to whisper furtively or to drop silent at the approach
of a Greely survivor. For almost as soon as I started north from

Edmonton upon my first arctic journey, traveling with fur traders and missionaries down stream along the Mackenzie, I began to hear of that "rabbit starvation" which is now to me the key to the Greely problem.

At first visualizing poor woodland Indians starving because they were unable to secure enough rabbits, I soon learned that "rabbit starvation" has an opposite connotation, referring to people who tried to live on nothing but rabbits, or on some other fat-deficient meat such as skinny caribou. It was explained to me that well-clad hunters in warm camps could live six or eight weeks wholly without food, but that if they ate fatless meat along with their water-drinking, they would die sooner, perhaps in three or four weeks. This belief was confirmed to me from numerous sources during ten arctic years. Many books contain such testimonies, among them several of my own where the relevant information is usually indexed as "rabbit starvation," though sometimes referred to as protein-poisoning.

That the deadliness of an exclusively fatless meat diet was unknown to the newspapers of 1884 seems obvious from their quoted charge that "the survivors of the abandoned party had eked out their existence by living on human flesh." Nor does Greely seem to have known, for he says in his reply to the Kislingbury charge: "Every man of the survivors ... solemnly swore he was innocent ... I cannot tell whether they told the truth." The General could not tell. But we who understand "rabbit poisoning" feel sure that his comrades, with possibly one exception, told the truth. For if they had been feeding on the flesh of men who died of starvation, then they themselves would probably not have survived long enough to be rescued by Schley.

But proving the innocence of almost all of those who lived also points to the guilt of some who died, especially those who, by Todd's quotations from the record, were notably strong till at the last, when their strength failed them suddenly. As to some of these we have corroborative evidence. One of the cannibals probably was the doctor, for some of the partly eaten bodies had been carved with the skill of a surgeon. Another may have been Kislingbury, for that exhumation of his body which demonstrated cannibalism to Greely also showed traces of human flesh in his digestive tract. It is a grim case of being hoist with their own petard that almost all those whose morale broke, to the extent of eating human flesh, were apparently not among the survivors.

By exonerating most of those who came back, A. L. Todd has made but one of his many contributions to history and to scholarship. By these contributions he has increased both the stature and the verisimilitude of Greely and of his men. Through telling more truth, more precisely, than previous Greely narratives, *Abandoned* contributes to the pride we feel in men who under the supreme test rose to moral heights. We think the better of humanity for these revelations.

Abandoned is a notable book; and the start, let us hope, of a new school of pioneer chronicles.

Vilhjalmur Stefansson, Consultant
Program of Northern Studies
Dartmouth College

AUTHOR'S PREFACE

WHEN I WAS ten years old, a call with my mother on family friends brought me face to face with General Adolphus Washington Greely, then in his eighties. He and my grandfather had known each other in Washington for some thirty years. To a small boy, General Greely's appearance and manner were Olympian. The white-whiskered face, the penetrating voice and gaze stuck in my memory later when my mother spoke in guarded terms of the Greely Expedition as a mysterious and tragic episode that had occurred during her childhood. Ever since that day I carried in the back of my mind the idea that I should like to pull back the veil of mystery and scandal from this affair of my grandfather's time.

In 1958, starting in earnest to investigate the story, I found to my surprise that the Greely Expedition, or more properly, the Lady Franklin Bay Expedition, had never been fully described in one volume. Although much was written about it in the 1880s, the facts became so obscured by wishful fantasy and sensational journalism at the very outset that the story has ever since been known only in distorted form—indeed, almost as a legend.

What emerged from my researches into the basic materials was a drama of the Arctic acted by living, breathing people, rather than by cardboard figures. Concealed by the distortions and omissions of the earlier writers I found the expedition members, and others with whom their fate was entwined, displaying the normal range of motives and passions—fear beside courage, weakness together with strength, and cowardice alongside heroism.

This new account of the Greely story draws heavily from unpublished material. It was made possible, first of all, by the kindness of Miss Rose I. Greely in turning over to me the extensive private papers of her father, to examine and use with complete liberty. Because General Greely had lost considerable property in the San Francisco fire of 1906, it was generally assumed that the documents of his three years in the Arctic were no longer available. But I found them, apparently complete, in Miss Greely's summer home in Center Conway, New Hampshire, just as Greely left them a quarter century ago. These Arctic papers, together with the rest of General Greely's papers—a collection stretching from the Civil War to the 1930s, have this year been presented by Miss Greely to the Library of Congress.

Elsewhere in private hands I turned up unpublished papers and diaries of Brigadier General David L. Brainard, Dr. Octave Pavy, and Sergeant George W. Rice, all members of the expedition. Further, I drew on copies of other unpublished expedition diaries in the National Archives.

The printed record on which I drew is scattered through many books and periodicals, each marred by errors, serious omissions, or restrictions of viewpoint. This is true even of the published writings of Greely and Brainard, since both kindly omitted certain material to spare the feeling of those with a personal interest in members of the abandoned party. Sufficient time has now elapsed that a full account of their behavior under stress can fairly be put in print.

My story is essentially one of the physical and moral courage displayed by a small group of men abandoned to hunger and cold in the distant, early days of Arctic work. As such, it makes no pretense of detailing the expedition's many scientific findings, all admirably presented by Greely himself in the 1880s.

Nothing in the following pages has been fictionalized, not even the occasional bits of dialogue. The characters in this drama speak for themselves through their letters, their diaries, and such of their remarks as were written down at the time. Although a few points that have been in controversy for seventy-five years or more have been left to the reader to evaluate, I have not hesitated to present my own judgments on others.

In addition to the thanks I owe Miss Rose I. Greely, I wish to acknowledge special help from:

Major General John Nesmith Greely, retired, of Washington, D.C., who with his sisters, Rose Greely and Mrs. George H. Shedd, patiently helped me to gather information about their father;

Mrs. Donald McVickar, of New York City, who furnished private papers, pictures, and personal memories of her stepfather, David L. Brainard;

Paul J. Scheips, of the Historical Division, U.S. Army Signal Corps, keen student of early Signal Corps history, for many courtesies;

Vilhjalmur Stefansson and his colleagues at Baker Library, Dartmouth College, for kind interest, advice, and the loan of papers;

the Board of Directors of the Explorers Club, New York, and Melville P. Cummin, Secretary, for making accessible private papers of Dr. Octave Pavy and George W. Rice;

and also Richard Blalock of the *Portsmouth Herald*, New Hampshire; Captain Carl A. Johnson, Commandant, Portsmouth Naval Shipyard; Richard F. Pourade of the *San Diego Union and Evening Tribune;* the Société de Géographie, Paris; and Miss Louise Wood of the Indiana State Library.

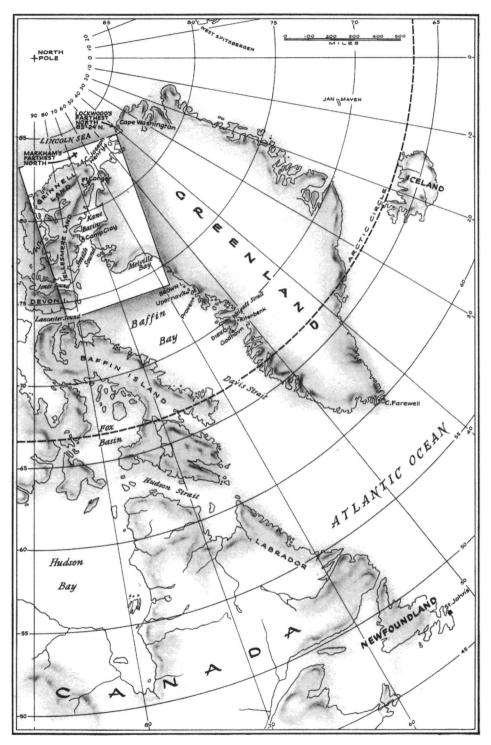

NORTH POLE

WEST SPITSBERGEN

MILES
100 200 300 400 500

JAN MAYEN

LOCKWOOD'S FARTHEST NORTH 83°24' N.
Cape Washington

LINCOLN SEA

MARKHAM'S FARTHEST NORTH

ICELAND

ARCTIC CIRCLE

GRINNELL LAND
C. Joseph Henry
Ft. Conger

Kane Basin

Camp Clay

ELLESMERE LAND

Smith Sound

Melville Bay

Jones Sound

DEVON I.

Lancaster Sound

GREENLAND

BROWN I.
Upernavik
Proven
Disko I.
Ritenbenk
Godhavn

Baffin Bay

Whale Strait

BAFFIN ISLAND

Davis Strait

C. Farewell

Fox Basin

ATLANTIC OCEAN

Hudson Strait

Hudson Bay

LABRADOR

CANADA

NEWFOUNDLAND
St. John's

— *from 1961 edition* —

Greely aboard the *Thetis* about two weeks after the rescue.
— *Greely Papers* —

1 AUGUST 26, 1881

A MILE OFFSHORE in the ice-choked harbor, the *Proteus* was inching out toward the channel and escape. Black smoke belched from her thick stack amidships, sending a cloud of soot up through her rigging to arch downwind and settle on the harbor ice.

Lieutenant Kislingbury saw that this time Captain Pike, after being penned for a week in Discovery Harbor, was making a determined try to break clear and steam for home. He took a new grip on his load of gear and broke into a stumbling run.

The self-esteem that had grown within Lieutenant Frederick F. Kislingbury through fifteen years of creditable army service, much of it on the Western frontier, and through his fathering of four sons, had suffered a terrible blow on this critical day of decision. A few months ago he had volunteered to join Lieutenant A. W. Greely on this expedition far into the arctic regions, and at that time he had wanted in every fiber of his being to go. Yet now he was running to catch the ship that would take him home before the great adventure really started. It was bitterly frustrating, humiliating, to quit. Yet he felt he could not knuckle under to Greely's unreasonable demands. Better to resign and go back to his infantry command than try to endure a full year under such a martinet of a commander.

Dismay stabbed Kislingbury's heart as he saw the ship's prow cutting more rapidly through the light pack, splattering bits of rotten ice aside as she steadily gained headway. Out before her

1

in Lady Franklin Bay stretched an expanse of dark, open water. The *Proteus* was getting away!

Frantically the officer waved, hoping that someone on the vessel would see him. His shouts mocked his ears with their futility. Still, something might happen to delay the ship again; the pack ice had turned her back several times before. Kislingbury hurried on down the shore with his burden, across the ice foot, where land met sea—running, staggering all the way to Dutch Island, the tiny dot of rock that stood just off the point a full two miles from camp. But as he hurried across the rubble to the little island, the *Proteus* was already a good two miles distant, steaming away into the sound, her stern pointing at him as if in disdain. Kislingbury threw himself down on the cold, bare rock, overcome with despair.

In January at Fort Custer, in Montana Territory, Greely's unexpected letter had lifted Kislingbury from the depths of his misery. He had answered it eagerly, pouring out to his old army acquaintance the troubles of his tortured soul. Only three years before, Kislingbury's first wife, Agnes, had been laid in her grave. Then his second wife, Jessie, had been swept away by typhoid fever at the post while he was in the field. He had been left alone, to raise four young boys. Surely his were the agonies of Job.

I must thank you again for your kind offer to take me with you [he had written Greely in the sweeping hand that reflected in its flourishes his intense, emotional nature]. It is simply a God-send to me just now, and I look upon it as a wonderful chance for me to wear out my second terrible sorrow. . . . With you, up there in the cold North, I can find relief. It will be like leaving a world that has been so cruel to me. I can find up there hard work and plenty of it—overland trips through snow and ice, and the kind of exposure that will do me good.

Ah, my friend, the future looked very dark to me and your good letter comes as a boon. It awakens me from a fit almost of despondency. . . . I feel that I shall come back a new man. I am with you heart and soul in the enterprise and you shall find no truer friend and more devoted servant. . . . We will not think of home, nor of turning towards the same, until the mission is accomplished.

The two men had been so close in spirit then; now they were at loggerheads. The dispute with Greely which came to a head today had at first seemed trivial. Whether officers should rise and eat breakfast at the same time as the men was not the kind of issue over which an expedition leader and his second-in-command should have a falling out. Yet Greely had insisted that his orders be obeyed without question, even though it meant telling a fellow officer when he must rise and eat breakfast. There would be no honor in giving in to him. The only self-respecting course, Kislingbury had thought, was to resign from the expedition.

But why had he not resolved the issue yesterday, when his visit aboard the *Proteus* made his suppressed longing for home well up within him? Or early this morning? Why had he taken time to write that long letter to Greely? Had he cut the formalities shorter, even by ten minutes, he would have been aboard the *Proteus* at this moment. Now she was gone, and he was part of an expedition for which he had lost all enthusiasm, under a commander he had come to despise.

As he watched Kislingbury picking his way back toward camp, Lieutenant Adolphus Washington Greely realized how awkward the situation had become. But the discomfort, he resolved, would be Kislingbury's, not his own. With the ship's departure he was stuck with an insubordinate second officer who had, in resigning, formally withdrawn from the expedition. A most regrettable way for the venture to start! Yet, if Kislingbury would play the soldier from here on, things would doubtless work out. That evening Greely summarized the situation in his journal:

August 26, 1881. Rose quite reluctantly at 7 A.M., having worked hard the day before and being very tired and sleepy. Lt. Kislingbury was up soon after but Lt. Lockwood was not until 7:40. Breakfast was delayed over half an hour and considering that the officers had been repeatedly requested to be up to breakfast at the same hour as the men, 7 A.M. Washington mean time (or 7:50 local time) Lt. Kislingbury surprised me by saying that he would not get up at such an hour but would remain in bed and do without his breakfast. I said promptly that in future he would get up whether he chose to eat or not . . . that it was a regulation of the expedition and must be complied with. He said that he would do so if it was insisted on. I said to him that this was no place for an officer to say that he would obey an order only if it was insisted on, that cheerful compliance was expected and when an officer could not yield it his usefulness as a member of the expedition was destroyed. He commenced discussing the question and I was twice compelled to say that I proposed having no arguments regarding it.

Greely had supposed that this would be the end of the matter, but at noon the expedition's doctor, Octave Pavy, had brought a lengthy letter from Kislingbury requesting his relief and accusing Greely of having stated that his second-in-command "had better go." The letter reiterated Kislingbury's disinclination to rise with the enlisted men. After dinner Greely called Kislingbury and Pavy outside the quarters to settle the issue for good. As Greely later recorded it in his journal, the discussion went like this:

I stated that I remembered no such words and that when I wanted an officer to go I should plainly say so, but I added that possibly it was a mere choice of words and I acknowledged having said that his usefulness was impaired and destroyed when he rebelled against my orders, and if he thought them (the orders) unreasonable I still thought so. He said that he did think the orders unreasonable and I then said "I will put it stronger than the language you said I used this morning and now say not that any officer so thinking and acting had better go but that he must go." I said moreover that I would prefer losing every officer and remain to do my work with enlisted men alone rather than be surrounded by men disposed to question orders given. I then asked Lt. K. if he wanted to go on such a basis. He said, "Yes since matters have gone thus far."

Greely at once issued the orders relieving Kislingbury, gave the lieutenant all the commissary stores he asked for, and made arrangements by letter to Captain Pike for his return home by the *Proteus*. But by the time Kislingbury reached the shore the ship had started moving.

THE LADY FRANKLIN Bay Expedition was one of two parties dispatched by the United States government to the arctic regions as part of an International Polar Year, the first time in history that a dozen countries were cooperating in a scientific venture. For many decades before 1881, explorers from Europe and America had been probing the polar frontiers at the frozen top of the globe. One attraction in sailing arctic waters was that elusive golden fleece, the Northwest Passage between the Atlantic and Pacific oceans. An even stronger magnet was the North Pole and the glory that would come to him who should first reach it.

Each attempt was dangerous; almost every expedition suffered losses, for the polar regions did not yield easily to penetration by man. The Arctic especially, in contrast to the more remote and therefore less tantalizing Antarctic, was scattered with the bones of explorers and the wrecks of their ships, dotted with unvisited frozen supply caches, with signal cairns in which many an urgent plea for succor scribbled with chilled fingers remained for years unread.

The long search for the English explorer Sir John Franklin, lost since 1845, drew one ship after another to the Arctic, each bearing with her the prayers of the courageous Lady Franklin, who would not give in to despair. Captain Edward A. Inglefield, Charles Francis Hall, Isaac Israel Hayes, Dr. Elisha Kent Kane, Karl Weyprecht, Sir George Nares, Lieutenant Commander George Washington De Long—these and others from many nations had tempted fate in the Arctic for some thirty-five years. Some returned safely. But there were those who either left their comrades in icy sleep or who were themselves lost pursuing their dreams. If the lure of the white North seemed strongest to the British, as shown by the frequency of their voyages, the Americans were not far behind.

In the mid-seventies, Karl Weyprecht of Austria suggested a new approach to arctic exploration. The pursuit of scientific knowledge, he urged, should be made primary to foolhardy striving for distance or endurance records in northern latitudes. Merely to sketch new terrain features into the map bearing the explorer's name, said Weyprecht, was a motive unworthy of serious men. But should polar-minded geographers of all nations act in concert to collect basic information on tides, currents, wind velocity, precipitation, barometric pressure, temperature, magnetic declination, and natural history over a sustained period, then explorers could use this detailed information to probe the Arctic with greater safety and to more worthy purpose.

Approved by his German and Austrian colleagues, Weyprecht's plan was presented to the International Meteorological Congress which met in Rome in April 1879. The Congress approved his idea and called an International Polar Conference at Hamburg in October of the same year; here the delegates agreed on a common program of simultaneous observations. The Arctic, they decided, would be ringed with a series of stations as far toward the top of the known world as they could be planted—in Siberia, Lapland, Spitsbergen, Greenland, the North American archipelago, and Alaska. A second international conference, held in Bern in August 1880, confirmed the Hamburg plans and put them in motion. After delegates decided on a one-year postponement to enable all parties to be fully equipped and staffed, the International Polar Year was set for 1882–1883, to last from summer to summer.

For a long time before these plans matured in Europe, Captain Henry W. Howgate of the U.S. Army Signal Corps had quite independently been carrying on a crusade in the United States to arouse interest in his own polar exploration scheme. A handsome Civil War veteran with a sweeping mustache and a winning way of speaking, Howgate eventually persuaded a number of moneyed men to back his plan for "polar colonization," about which he wrote enthusiastic and voluminous articles in military service periodicals.

Howgate deprecated dangerous one-season dashes into the polar seas, as well as wintering in the ice, because relying on a ship that could be crushed in the ice and sunk could bring a party to disaster. At best, a vessel could deliver explorers only part-way to their ultimate goal, the North Pole. Howgate saw no virtue in trying to cover great distances over the ice and being forced to haul all one's equipment. A chain, or ladder, of well-equipped permanent stations extending northward would enable explorers not only to live and travel safely at high latitudes but also by degrees to approach and conquer the Pole.

When Captain George Nares of the British Royal Navy returned from Grinnell Land in 1876 with word of an exposed coal seam near Lady Franklin Bay, Howgate found his clinching argument. This abundance of fuel at 81° 41′ North, at a point within 500 miles of the North Pole yet accessible in summer by ship, made this the logical spot on which to plant an arctic colony, he declared. Howgate wrote with assurance in the military monthly *The United Service:*

> With substantial frame buildings that could be carried in sections on shipboard and put together after reaching the colony, the party could be made as comfortable and as safe from climatic dangers as are the employees of the Hudson's Bay Company, scattered along the shores of Hudson's Bay and at the isolated posts extending through the interior of British America to the Arctic Circle, or as safe as the men of the U.S. Signal Service stationed upon Mount Washington or Pike's Peak.

Howgate's ideas were running in the same direction as Weyprecht's, and they began to catch hold with the exploring fraternity —and not only with the rich amateurs whom he had learned to cultivate. For Howgate also found an eager enthusiast in a lean, studious young New Englander detailed to the Signal Corps in Washington, D.C., from his regular outfit, the 5th Cavalry. Shortly after his first tour of Signal Corps duty in Washington in 1867, Lieutenant Adolphus Washington Greely fell under the spell of the older man when Howgate talked expansively of his plans to unlock the secrets of the North. Early in the seventies, when his Signal Corps detail became permanent, Greely took a room in the Howgate home. Living there for six years, he became almost a member of the family.

At this stage Greely was one of the officers striving to build a reliable national weather service from the reports of local weather conditions wired into Washington by Signal Corps sergeants who manned the military telegraph lines. During the seventies Greely was frequently sent into the field to inspect signal stations and construct telegraph lines and saw a great deal of Howgate, since the captain, as Corps disbursing officer, was the man through whom he ordered equipment. All the while Greely was drinking in the lore of the North from Howgate's compelling dinner-table conversation. In the great frontier region above the civilized world, it seemed to young Greely, a man could make a name for himself. Opportunity threw itself at an officer in wartime, but promotion came slowly in the peacetime Army, especially for a non-West Pointer. He would have to seek his own way to distinguish himself by extraordinary service.

By the time the International Polar Year took form, Greely had devoured every printed study of the polar regions on which he could lay hands. It was therefore no accident that Lieutenant A. W. Greely (he leaned toward the crisp initials) emerged in 1880 as the logical field commander for the Lady Franklin Bay Expedition being promoted by Captain Howgate. The U.S. government, through congressional action, was willing to back it to the extent of authorizing the loan of certain equipment from Army and Navy stores.

Although therefore actually quasi-official the projected 1880 expedition was known as "the Howgate expedition," as if it were the captain's private venture. The expedition never sailed. Navy inspectors condemned as unseaworthy the *Gulnare,* the ship chartered by the overeager promotor. Greely promptly withdrew from command, having no ambition to lead men to sea in a leaky vessel. He was a thorough planner who favored a well-equipped expedition or none at all. He could wait.

The engraving accompanying newspaper articles on the How-gate expedition in 1880 pictured Greely as a serious, academic-looking man who wore spectacles and somewhat severe black cheek whiskers. The picture did not belie the man. Born March 27, 1844, in Newburyport, Massachusetts, Greely was a typical product of the morally stern New England atmosphere of his immediate surroundings. The dominating spirit of his family and town was compounded of Puritan frugality, hard work, Christian duty, opposition to chattel slavery, and a firm respect for book learning, especially the English and American classics. At twelve, young Dolph Greely proudly carried a torchlight in a Frémont election parade; at fourteen he was seriously discussing the merits of the Lincoln-Douglas debates. Graduating from Brown High School in Newburyport at age sixteen, he led his class and de-livered the valedictory address in Latin, but with no funds to enter college this was the end of the academic road. His father had become a bedridden invalid, and his mother had gone to work in a textile mill. Greely undertook tutoring some cousins at Jack-son, New Hampshire, who were backward in their books.

The boy who had through his school years learned about pub-lic affairs surrounded by the intellectual ferment of New England in the 1850s could not be happy in the remote White Mountains while the drums of rebellion were rolling and great issues were poised for a clash amid smoke and steel. In April 1861 Dolph Greely returned home and got his parents' consent to join the Union Army. At first rejected because he was not yet eighteen, Greely finally pleaded his way into uniform in the 19th Massa-chusetts Volunteers and marched off to war. His four years' in-fantry service took him through Washington to Balls Bluff, the Peninsular Campaign, Antietam, Fredericksburg, and finally to Louisiana.

Near Antietam Bridge on September 17, 1862, in the bloodiest day's fighting of the war, Greely won his red badge of courage. During the height of the desperately confused encounter, while his command was trying to avoid being rolled up from the flank, a rifle ball smashed into Greely's jaw, knocking out four of his teeth. He fainted from the shock, but recovered just in time to escape capture where he lay. As he did so another bullet tore into his knee. A long stay in a hospital, where he recalled later seeing limbs "piled up like cordwood," brought the eighteen-year-old soldier a chance to reflect on the basic inhumanity of war. He went back to his Bible, searching for a morality that would explain how justice and right could be born from fratricidal hatred, and found himself deeply troubled by what a civil war was doing to him.

In 1863, home on leave, Greely accepted a commission as lieutenant of Colored Infantry, then being organized in Massachusetts under Colonel Robert Gould Shaw and other abolitionist officers. During the remainder of the conflict he rose to the rank of captain and finally, while serving in Louisiana, to brevet major. The final months of the war and two years of occupation duty after Appomatox found him commanding Negroes assigned to patrol New Orleans, a delicate assignment which proved a strenuous schooling in leadership and diplomacy for the young volunteer soldier from the North. By 1867, when he was mustered out from the Volunteers and decided to accept a second lieutenant's commission in the Regular Army, he knew far more of military administration and the art of handling men than most officers of twenty-three.

Keenly feeling the need for self-improvement, Greely did not permit his day to end at retreat parade. During his years as a junior officer in the Deep South, and later in the territories of the West, he left many an evening card game and whisky bout to his comrades of the regiment while he gave himself to his books, which he knew held the keys to his future. He found one such key in his study of telegraphy, the means of communication which had come of age in the war.

The Signal Corps of the U.S. Army, also at times called the Signal Service, had been organized early in the Civil War under the leadership of General Albert J. Myer. Experiments dotted its early history—carrying messages and spying out enemy dispositions by military balloon, signaling with flag and heliograph by day, dit-dotting by night with a lantern ducked in and out of a barrel. The war proved that electric signaling in code over a wire was the swiftest, safest way to transmit messages a great distance. Assigned to one post after another in Utah, Nebraska, and Wyoming territories shortly after the war, Greely studied signaling technique and qualified as an electrician. This led to his detail to the Corps headquarters in Washington for advanced signal instruction. Alternating between his cavalry regiment in the territories and duty under Myer in the capital, Greely found that his detail to the Corps had become a long-term affair. Here he fell in with Howgate.

The study of signaling to the processing of weather information to a serious study of meteorology was a logical progression for a young man of compelling intellectual curiosity. In his Signal Corps work Greely learned all he could absorb from such outstanding meteorologists as Professor Cleveland Abbe, Myer's highly regarded civilian consultant, a man known in later years as the father of the U.S. Weather Service.

The problems with which Abbe, Myer, and their colleagues were wrestling fascinated the young officer. What, they wanted to know—not guess—are the preconditions for storms in the populated areas along the Atlantic seaboard? How far in advance and how accurately can we predict weather? What new data do we need? How accurate are our instruments? Can we give St. Louis and New Orleans timely warning of floods gathering in the headwaters of the Mississippi–Missouri basin? Can we save more lives and prevent distress?

These questions became mingled in Greely's mind with the excitement Howgate brought to their after-duty discussions of the Arctic. An expedition, perhaps all the way to the Pole, would bring not only benefits to science but also the fame as a pioneer that could assist one's career. The captain was too old to lead an arctic expedition himself. He was content to remain the idea man, the promoter. To a young, ambitious lieutenant like Greely, who felt sharply the disadvantage of competing daily with West Pointers, an offer to command an expedition to the arctic regions was the chance of a lifetime, the gold of El Dorado.

In 1875 General Myer sent Greely to Texas to erect a military signal line across the state and up the Rio Grande to El Paso, at its extreme western tip. Raids on isolated settlers by Mexican bandits and marauding Indians made this task imperative. Furthermore, other parts of the military communications network needed repair in northern Texas and the Indian Territory (later to become Oklahoma). It proved a hard year's work, not the least difficult feat of which was to secure timber for poles in country devoid of trees. Greely, at thirty-one, carried out his assignment so well that Myer detailed him in 1877 to rebuild and restore the old military telegraph line extending from El Paso across New Mexico and Arizona territories to San Diego, California. Like the previous one, this job meant making executive decisions in the field, determining methods of construction, ordering equipment, and directing personnel. Physically it required weeks of tough, outdoor life, day after day in the saddle, taking meals by the campfire, and sleeping on the ground. Late in the year the line was in operation all the way to San Diego, and Greely that autumn found himself with the pleasant assignment of inspecting the San Diego signal office. In San Diego he met Henrietta Nesmith.

Since his early soldier days Greely had paid calls on young ladies and attended dances like any other young man with normal self-confidence. But a certain reserve, stemming from his Newburyport background, restrained him from taking liberties with women—so much so that his more cavalier comrades in arms may have considered him "slow." But now Dolph Greely had found a charmer who sent him into an emotional spin. Soft-spoken and well-read, with a grace of speech and manner which warmed his heart, Henrietta of the lustrous eyes and dark hair was reserved in Greely's presence but did not act the shy violet. In the mature way in which she cared for her invalid father and directed her household Greely saw a queenly poise.

When in November he decisively told Henrietta that he would have her and no other as his wife, she was both flattered and admittedly upset. Henrietta was not to be ordered about by a swain in uniform, nor would she be swept off her feet by a dominating male like a silly girl in a second-rate novel. She demanded that the young man show the seriousness of his intentions. They should separate for some months, she said. He should return to his Washington duties and woo her by letter. She promised to reply faithfully and tell him everything that was in her heart. If the separation drew them closer together, she would agree to marriage; if their affection should wane with the miles between them, they would both be better off to learn it this way.

Hanging over their relationship like the sword of Damocles was Greely's ambition to lead the polar expedition he had discussed countless times with Howgate. Greely was frank with Henrietta about it from the start. Now, in 1878, after years of promotion by Howgate, the venture seemed to be shaping up. Certain members of Congress were pushing a bill to bring it government support. In writing Henrietta of his yearning for the North, Greely was torn between the conflicting appeals, which he tried to resolve, of his ambition to go to the Arctic and his desire to be close to her, in the warmth of her love:

> There is no such danger as is painted. Modern appliances, the use of steam ships, the experience of other expeditions all forbid it, and the mortality among Arctic explorers for the past 20 years has really been less than the percentage among the same number of men remaining at home.
>
> Did I not believe the plan a feasible one, and that I am quite certain of returning to your arms safe and sound, I should not desire to lead it. We are not certain that I can attain to the command. There will be enough anxious and striving. The command alone means a certain degree of fame. . . .
>
> You are somewhat inclined through your fears to exaggerate the danger and suffering. Could any such trial ever come to you from the expedition as came into Lady Franklin's life I would never go. Doubt as to my fate cannot exist and we cannot be abandoned nor cut off for ships are to visit from year to year.

When Henrietta suggested that perhaps they might wait to marry until his return, Greely's pen cried out his anguish:

> I could not think of going without you were my wife. I should suffer untold agony while gone in thinking of you. All manner of doubts would come to me, no matter how my heart might go out

to you. I *could* not endure it! You must say that we will have a few months of happiness and of each other.

The arctic project was both a matter of honor and of self-fulfillment, he declared:

I could have withdrawn without loss of honor when I spoke to you, but even then had I turned back, even with your concurrence and at your entreaty, I should always have feared the might-have-been would some day rise up to stand before us. You decided wisely and well. . . . It will be hard—hard, but can be borne by stout hearts and strong wills.

As Greely kept one eye on his Signal Corps duties and the other on Capitol Hill where the fate of the polar bill hung in the balance, Henrietta poured into her letters the torment of a woman in love with a man called to duty amid dangers:

If you go, while you are absent I dare say I can bear it and live, most unhappily I have no doubt. But if you should not return, in what condition should I be after two or three years of watching, waiting and suspense to sustain your loss? . . . Are not your ambiton and pride guiding you to the exclusion of all other thought? I know it is as much for me as yourself that you think, but oh! my love, I would rather be your wife as you are, than your widow as the most revered man that you could become. I am *not* a Lady Franklin. My spirit may be willing, but my flesh is weak. I realize that you will be terribly disappointed in me, dear, but remember that I do not even *suggest* that you stay. I want you to go. I feel that perhaps we should never be so happy if you gave up the opportunity for you would always think of what you had missed. I love you too well to mar your life, to interfere with your life dreams.

The interference came instead from an indifferent Congress, which failed that year to pass the bill for which Howgate and Greely were lobbying. On hearing the news Henrietta took up her pen and confessed to her far-off lover:

For your sake I suppose I should be sorry. For my own, how can I help giving thanks? It means I can have my husband with me instead of drearily living apart for years with my mind full of anxious, painful thought for him when I need so much his loving care and strength to hold me up. For I *do* need them. Do you know, dear, you are intending to marry a very weak woman?

The defeat of the polar bill in March 1878 lifted the cloud that had hung over the pair. They were married in San Diego in June and returned to Washington. But the best construction officer of the Signal Corps drew more field duty, married or no. Since Sitting Bull's massacre of Custer's forces two years earlier, the Indians in the Dakota Badlands on west through Montana Territory were harrying settlers with increasing boldness. Greely was ordered to connect the signal office at Bismarck, Dakota Territory, with the Columbia section in Washington Territory, by way of the upper Missouri and Yellowstone rivers. When he objected to General Myer that he had served for many months in the field and had been promised Washington duty after his marriage, Myer told Greely that congressmen were insisting that the Northwest be made safe for settlers. Greely had to take on the job—and finish it, as the Chief Signal Officer put it, "before the snow flies."

Once more, by prodigious effort, Greely completed the task promptly, but during his final inspection tour over the line in November, the snow flew into a blizzard which nearly froze him and his three-man escort to death. The one compensation, Greely noted, was that the weather was too cold for hostile Indians to molest them. When he reached the safety of a cavalry escort at the Powder River, he counted the experience a sort of training test of the Arctic adventure he hoped was to come.

Congress passed no polar bill in 1879, and in 1880 the Howgate expedition collapsed with the Navy condemnation of the *Gulnare*. The vessel did limp as far as Greenland, bearing the parts for the expedition's winter house, and left the party's surgeon, Octave Pavy, and secretary, Henry Clay, there to contract for sledge dogs and certain supplies for the group which would follow the next summer. The maturing of the Weyprecht plan in Europe led the outgoing Congress, early in 1881, to assume the entire project as a government undertaking. On March 3, 1881, as the Hayes administration retired and James A. Garfield became President, Congress voted $25,000 for the Lady Franklin Bay Expedition, and made it an official venture to be carried out under direction of the Chief Signal Officer. The arctic party was to carry on meteorological work for two years, the second of which (from August 1882 to August 1883), was to coincide with the International Polar Year.

Neither Garfield nor his new Secretary of War, Robert Todd Lincoln, was interested in the project. To them the War Department's main tasks were to account for every dollar and to protect western settlers from the Indians. Exposure of wholesale corruption in the department in recent years led Garfield to place it under Lincoln, a sound businessman with a revered name, but never a soldier. Although the Secretary of War cared nothing for America's participation in the International Polar Year, which fell under his department's responsibility, it meant a great deal to the new Chief Signal Officer, General William Babcock Hazen, who had become Signal Corps head a year before upon the death of Myer. A driving personality, Hazen by nature seemed to prefer a fight to conciliation in the frequent disputes in which he became embroiled. He had already made high-placed enemies by instigating the charges of corruption that had forced the resignation of William W. Belknap, Grant's Secretary of War.

Hazen was intensely interested in the meteorological research party to be sent to Lady Franklin Bay, and he worked hard to prepare it. Head and shoulders above all other candidates to lead it, and there were few, stood Lieutenant Adolphus Washington Greely. Hazen could see in him the one man in the Corps with the right combination of qualities for the post: physical toughness, experience in command of men, scientific background, and the executive capacity to direct the work of specialists. Above all, Greely obviously felt the inward call to the Arctic which few Regular Army officers shared. In Hazen's eyes Greely was the reliable professional with the zeal of the amateur.

Greely and his Henrietta had long since settled the issue of separation that had tormented their courtship three years earlier. The marriage had been happy; they had golden-haired Antoinette, now nearing her second birthday, and were expecting a second child. Once the decision was made, Henrietta turned her thoughts with enthusiastic loyalty to helping her husband prepare. Lovingly she sought out gifts and tokens to diminish his sense of distance from home and make his arctic stay more comfortable. She made warm, embroidered slippers, a rug, and a large afghan decorated with the initials HNG and AWG. She stimulated other army wives to donate presents for the men's Christmas, to strengthen the party's ties with their home and country. She packed away china for the officers' mess, bought cigars and plum pudding for the entire party as a holiday treat, and sewed a bright-colored silk flag on the thirteen-star Betsy Ross pattern for her husband to fly over points of land not before touched by the foot of man.

Secretary Lincoln, the amiable but unaccomplished and unimaginative son of the war President, did not make life easy for Greely. For weeks he neglected to sign expedition papers that required his authority. Without them Greely could not select his personnel or contract for equipment he could not just walk down Pennsylvania Avenue and buy—arctic footgear, ice boats, sledges, pemmican and other preserved foods, windproof lanterns and cookers, chronometers, scientific instruments, and many other items which the expedition leader had listed on page after handwritten page.

Finally, in exasperation, Greely called on the Secretary and advised him that if he were not given swift executive authority to carry out his duty to prepare the expedition, the will of Congress would be frustrated. Lincoln, fuming at the temerity of the brash lieutenant, whom he considered a nobody, signed the necessary papers. For the rest of his life he was to remember Adolphus Washington Greely.

The executive weight of the project rested heavily on Greely's shoulders. He was bogged down in detail—hunting out the best price among food processors whose bids to supply beef pemmican ranged between 50¢ and $1.25 a pound, seeing that chronometers were overhauled and calibrated, that a specially built New Bedford whale boat was equipped to resist ice, that buffalo sleeping bags and robes, tents, wool socks, mittens, and stove pipes of the right size and quality were bought in sufficient number at the best possible rates. Three fourths of the $25,000 appropriation was needed to charter the steam sealer in St. John's, Newfoundland, that would transport the party to Grinnell Land, so there was no extra money to waste. Greely quickly found that his fellow officers, Lieutenants Kislingbury and Lockwood, while eager to brave the rigors of the Arctic, had slight management capacity. He carried most of the task himself. At the height of his preoccupation Henrietta, after difficult and anxious labor, gave birth to twins. The boy died, but the girl survived and Henrietta named her Adola for the husband she was about to give up to the Arctic. Although Greely was well acquainted with little Antoinette when it came time to kiss his family good-by, it seemed as if he had just a brief, passing knowledge of his tiny namesake.

After many minor crises in the procurement of supplies and equipment, the Lady Franklin Bay Expedition finally assembled in St. John's early in July. This was the home port of the sealers and whalers, the only ships afloat that could dare the arctic ice. Some 350 tons of expedition supplies were stowed aboard the *Proteus,* now sailing for her eighth season into the icy regions under the command of a veteran ice hand, Captain Richard Pike. On the afternoon of July 8 she hoisted anchor, slid through the narrows of St. John's harbor and plowed her way out into the rough North Atlantic. To Henrietta, Greely wrote that evening from his cabin:

> There was not the slightest interest manifested in St. John's over our departure, and except by the U.S. Consul's family none at all during any time except by those who have a direct or prospective pecuniary interest in our movements.

Aboard the *Proteus,* as throughout the United States, concern was repeatedly expressed for President Garfield, who was fighting for his life in his White House bed after being critically wounded by an assassin's bullet. As the expedition cut its last tie with home, a week after the shooting, the latest dispatches said that the President appeared to be recovering.

St. John's was the jumping-off point for arctic waters, reached through the North Atlantic, Davis Strait, and Baffin Bay, where few but hunters of whale and seal ever ventured. The *Proteus* crossed the Arctic Circle (66° 20′ North latitude) stopping later in July at the tiny Greenland outposts of Godhavn, Ritenbenk, and finally Upernavik, northernmost of the three. Dr. Octave Pavy, who was to have been surgeon of the Howgate expedition, was taken aboard at Godhavn, signing as contract surgeon and naturalist of the Greely party. At Ritenbenk, Henry Clay, grandson of the distinguished Kentucky politician, joined the party in the status of civilian Signal Corps employee. Left by the *Gulnare* the summer before, he had spent the year studying Greenland and the people of its western coast while awaiting the 1881 expedition.

At Upernavik Greely bargained with the Danish royal governor for sledge dogs, dog food, and items omitted from his incomplete purchase of proper arctic clothing in the United States. He also engaged two Greenland sledge drivers and hunters living in the coastal settlement of Proven, both men highly recommended by the governor. One, Jens Edward, was a full-blooded Eskimo; his companion, Frederik Thorlip Christiansen, was a half-breed born of a Greenland Eskimo mother and a Danish father. Neither spoke a word of English.

As the *Proteus* steamed on toward her goal in early August, past the redoubtable Baffin Bay "middle pack," which prevailing currents swirling around Greenland churn into a crushing graveyard for ships, the newcomers marveled at the stark beauty of the ice. Floating bergs, dazzling white above the water when the sky was clear, at other times somber, brooding gray to match lowering skies, revealed an endless variety of deep blues merging into greens as the eye followed them deeper below the water.

Greely's first run-in with Kislingbury, the man he had invited to join his party on the strength of an interest in the Arctic expressed in their telegraph-line days in Dakota, occurred this early in the journey. An enthusiastic sportsman, Kislingbury was eager to try out the shiny Remington rifle given him by a member of the famous arms firm. When the *Proteus* came upon a polar bear resting on a nearby ice floe, Kislingbury jumped into the small boat that several men had lowered to go after the beast. Here was novel, formidable game, often pictured in books but rarely seen heretofore by Americans. Kislingbury's shot was the one that brought the bear down, and the lieutenant claimed its magnificent pelt as a trophy. Greely pointed out that it was an expedition capture and therefore official rather than personal property. Kislingbury's petty annoyance over this rebuff, in Greely's eyes, was not a sign of soldierly character.

There had been minor difficulties with other members of the party. Private Ryan, drunk while on duty with the supplies at St. John's, was insubordinate on several occasions at sea. More serious to Greely was the antipathy of unknown origin which Dr. Pavy felt toward Henry Clay, so violent that Greely saw that one of the pair must return home with the ship. By the time the *Proteus* cautiously entered the narrows of Smith Sound, gateway to the polar sea—"Lincoln Sea" on the maps—Greely had already decided to make certain personnel changes.

Discovered by the Elizabethan adventurer William Baffin in 1616 and named after one of his patrons, Smith Sound had long been known as the "Northern Pillars of Hercules" because it was believed the most likely route to the Pole. From both north and south it resembled a bottleneck. Baffin Bay extended below it, washing Greenland's mountainous coast on the east. On the west shore was Ellesmere Island and, to the south, Baffin Island, which looked to imaginative map-readers like a fantastic clawing animal turned on its back.

North of the bottleneck the shoreline on a map resembled an antique flower vase with a bulging body and a long neck. The body was Kane Basin, some 120 miles across at its broadest point. The long neck, Kennedy Channel, was a scant 25 miles across, leading north and slightly east between Grinnell Land and Greenland, past a swollen joint—Hall Basin—into the even narrower Robeson Channel. This in turn led directly into the unexplored Lincoln Sea.

Lady Franklin Bay, the spot chosen for the expedition to winter, was an offshoot of Hall Basin to the west, its mouth on a clear day within easy view of the Greenland shore. Thus the colony was planted where the land of two hemispheres reached out to touch in the narrow top of the world.

According to plans worked out in Washington with General Hazen, Greely's party was to be visited by a resupply ship in the summer of 1882 and repatriated by ship in 1883. On the way north, Greely laid down several supply caches above Smith Sound against future contingencies and visited others left by the British before him. Captain Pike had a hard time of it bringing the *Proteus* through the pack ice that choked the long, sleevelike Kennedy Channel and Hall Basin. But after a full week of delay, drift, and searching for a lead of open water, the wind shifted and the vessel could maneuver close enough to shore at Discovery Harbor in Lady Franklin Bay to permit unloading. The preceding winter had been unusually mild and the summer had arrived early, the Danish governor in Godhavn had told Greely. Although only six other vessels were known to have penetrated Smith Sound in all the previous years of exploration and only three had reached Lady Franklin Bay, the promise of the season caused Greely and Pike to be optimistic. Their northward journey had been completed safely. This much, at least, of the mission had been accomplished.

Now, on August 26, the stores had all been landed and construction of the winter house was well along. The *Proteus* was steaming down the ice-strewn ribbon of water that led out of the Arctic toward home. On board, in addition to her crew, she carried Henry Clay. He had told Greely a week before that his incompatibility with the doctor dictated his reluctant resignation. The medical man, Clay generously acknowledged, was essential to safety and success, whereas he himself had no essential talents to offer. Also being repatriated were two enlisted men: Ryan, with a case of asthma on his record as the cause for release, instead of insubordination as Greely had planned; and Corporal Starr, who had been the victim of periodic epileptic fits since departure from St. John's.

Dr. Pavy, thought Greely, had already proven a bit difficult. He had surprised Greely after the landing by presenting an ultimatum: the commander must choose between him and Clay. Greely faced Dr. Pavy down and forced him to amend his ultimatum to a respectful presentation of a complaint. Greely was inclined to believe that in time the doctor's self-assertion, his seeming to flaunt, by hints and digs, his status as a civilian-specialist, could with patience be fitted into the scheme of a military command. With Ryan and Starr gone, the entire party appeared physically fit and of sound character.

In the United States, about the time the *Proteus* broke free from Discovery Harbor, a nameless cavalry officer made a disturbing discovery in the pages of *Harper's Weekly*. In the group photograph of the Lady Franklin Bay Expedition reproduced in the magazine, a face caught his eye. That hulking fellow in the back row—why, the man had served under him in Custer's command before the massacre, and he was a convicted forger and thief. A thorough scoundrel who had killed a Chinese in a barroom brawl in Deadwood, Dakota Territory, the man had obviously re-enlisted in the Army under a false identity, since now his middle and last names were transposed. Word of this discovery was passed through army channels and soon reached the attention of General Hazen.

Meanwhile, a scandal close to the expedition was being aired in the Washington papers. For two years General Hazen had been investigating the loose way in which Signal Corps money had been handled, a condition he discovered soon after the death of Myer had brought him to Washington as Chief Signal Officer. Hazen and a handful of tight-lipped assistants found that some $200,000 had been embezzled during the previous decade. The trail led directly to the Corps disbursing officer, Captain Henry W. Howgate. So secretive was Hazen's check that Greely caught no hint of it; the *Proteus* had been at sea for a week when his friend and patron was arrested, charged with embezzlement and fraud, and confined to jail in Washington to await trial. But all this was a long way from Discovery Harbor.

Now the *Proteus*, plumed with black smoke, was disappearing down the bay, the slanting sun shining on her masts. To Lieutenant Greely her retreating silhouette was a welcome sight. The nightmare of preparation under forced draft, with no help from his department head, was over. His command, twenty-five in all, were at their posts, every man in good health and eager to get on with the work. They were in a world of their own—vast in its wild expanse, but in its human community intimately close. They would see no other face or have any further tie wiith home until the resupply ship arrived next summer.

The *Proteus* in Discovery Harbor.

2 FARTHEST NORTH

*Behold, how good and how pleasant it is for brethren
to dwell together in unity! . . .*

The 133d Psalm of David, Greely told his listeners before he
read it to them, seemed to strike precisely the right note for their
close association. This last Sunday in August, after three weeks
of unremitting toil to unload the *Proteus* and erect their house,
was their first day off. The men were all seated before and around
him now, perched on the mess benches and bunks in the barrack
room where Greely had assembled them to set the tone for their
future observance of the Sabbath and to inculcate an *esprit de
corps* that had been lacking aboard the *Proteus*.

Henceforth, the commander stated, every member of the expedition would attend psalm-reading at ten o'clock on Sunday
morning, unless he had conscientious scruples against listening.
There would be no sermon. Only the most necessary duty would
be performed on Sundays, and no games would be permitted.

A wanderer coming upon the colony at Discovery Harbor
would have had no trouble discerning which among this hardy-
looking lot was its leader. Nearly six foot one, Lieutenant Greely
towered above most of his command—not merely physically.
There was something dominating about him—the lean, wiry
frame, the eyes enlarged by spectacles and the black beard jutting
to a point in front. When Greely spoke, his firm delivery com-
municated a determination of purpose compelling attention and
respect. The men had already learned how serious he was about

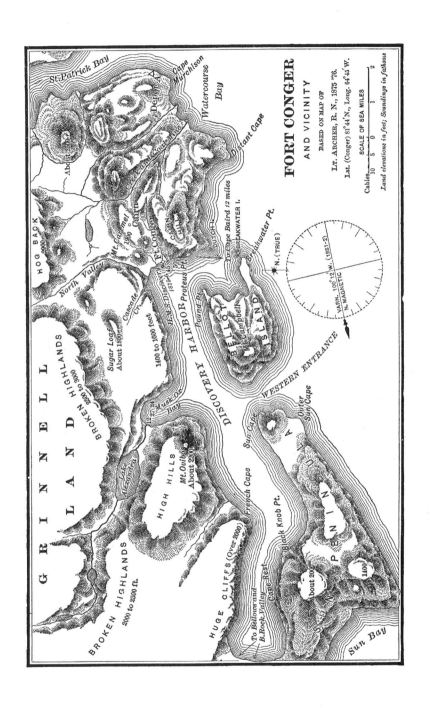

FORT CONGER

AND VICINITY

BASED ON MAP OF

Lt. ARCHER, R. N., 1875 '76.

Lat. (Conger) 81°44'N., Long. 64°45'W.

SCALE OF SEA MILES

Cables 10   5   0   1   2

Land elevations in feet; Soundings in fathoms

N. (TRUE)

VARN. 100°12'W. (1881-2)

N. MAGNETIC

St. Patrick Bay

Cape Murchison

Watercourse Bay

Distant Cape

Depôt

Cape Wm. Cook

Cairn

Mt. Carmel

Mt. Ovibos

CAIRN HILL

BUGH.

To Cape Baird 12 miles

BREAKWATER I.

Breakwater Pt.

HOG BACK
3000

North Valley

Cascade Cr.

Sugar Loaf
About 1800

1400 to 1000 feet

H. M. S. Discovery
1875-76

Mt. Carmel
1190

Ft. CONGER

Proteus Pt.

Point P.

DISCOVERY HARBOR

Campbell

BELLOT ISLAND

Mt. Musk-Ox

GRINNELL

LAND HIGHLANDS
2500 to 3000

BROKEN HIGHLANDS

Lake Alexandra

HIGH HILLS

Mt. Ovibos
About 2300

HUGE CLIFFS (Over 2000)

To Balloons and
B. Rock Valley

French Cape

Cape Rest

Black Knob Pt.

Sun Cape

WESTERN ENTRANCE

Outer Sun Cape

BROKEN HIGHLANDS
2000 to 2500 ft.

about 200

S U N   P E N I N S U L A

1400

Sun Bay

Lieutenant F. F. Kislingbury.

Lieutenant James B. Lockwood.

carrying out the objectives of the International Polar Year as defined by the Hamburg conference and augmented by the orders of the Chief Signal Officer. With him, by choice, they had joined in one effort, each impelled by his own motives. As many springs and rivulets lead to the river which flows to the sea, these twenty-five had been led from lives widely divergent in character to this rocky point on a lonely arctic island.

Facing Greely were two infantry officers, Lieutenants Frederick F. Kislingbury and James B. Lockwood, both experienced veterans of the western frontier, recommended as industrious, competent, sober, and worthy of trust. Because their schooling had been military, they were trained to execute orders in the army tradition and to handle men. Neither had a college education or knew much more than the rudiments of meteorology or other branches of natural science. Both had promised Greely they would study instrument work deligently, yet already Kislingbury had proved a poor choice for the disciplined teamwork required in the Arctic. Lockwood, four years younger than Kislingbury and unmarried, was now second-in-command by virtue of Kislingbury's resignation. Personable and gifted with wry wit, he had grown up in Annapolis, where his father was a Naval Academy instructor who during the Civil War had risen to general's rank. Lockwood, Greely knew, would strive hard to bring nothing but credit to the name of his family, whom he deeply loved.

The surgeon, Dr. Octave Pavy, was a civilian with officer's rank under contract at $100 a month. He had first studied medicine in Paris and then completed his training at Missouri Medical College. He had also known bohemian life and had traveled widely. His high, broad forehead and constant pipe-puffing bespoke the thinker. In a formal sense he was the best-educated member of the party, and his grasp of arctic lore was the equal of Greely's.

The two Eskimo sledge drivers hired in Greenland had already shown themselves quiet, obliging, and dutiful in their care of the dogs. Smiling most of the time, Jens and Fred had been almost childish in their attempts to anticipate the commander's wishes through the language barrier.

Since the unlamented departure of Ryan, Greely thought the nineteen enlisted men had become a willing, able crew. The ranking non-com, who acted as both first sergeant and supply chief, was David L. Brainard. A veteran, at twenty-four, of the Sioux wars, he had received his share of wound stripes and commendations. Brainard had taken like a disciplined soldier the one dressing-down Greely had already given him over a matter of fresh meat issued to the men without the commander's authority.

Four of the non-coms were really civilian specialists temporarily in uniform, each of whom had accepted an army sergeant's rating in order to be part of the expedition. Winfield Scott Jewell, chief meteorologist, had been a member of the Signal Service crew through the winter on the stormy peak of Mount Washington in New Hampshire, back in the seventies, and he had put on his old uniform again for this venture. Sergeant Edward Israel, the astronomer, had been plucked from the senior class of the University of Michigan on the recommendation of his astronomy professor. He ranked as the beardless boy of the party, the youngest at twenty-one, and its only Jew.

Sergeant William H. Cross, one of the eldest, looked the angry patriarch behind his bushy, black beard (the only one in camp save Greely's) and his ever-frowning countenance. A machinist at the Washington Navy Yard, he had enlisted as engineer of the expedition's steam launch. Sergeant George W. Rice had also been recruited in Washington, D.C., though he had originated in Nova Scotia. The expedition's photographer, Rice had studied law for a year at Columbian Institute before going to work in the studio of his brother, Moses P. Rice, photographer of Capitol Hill notables.

Excepting Jewell's two assistant observers, Sergeants Gardiner and Ralston, the rest were men who had about their tanned, mustached faces the rugged look of the frontiersman. The East had lately become familiar with their type in the color prints pro-

Sergeant Rice and Greenland Eskimo.

Fort Conger, Grinnell Land, May 20, 1883.

duced by Messrs. Currier & Ives. The eight German-born members of the party had been molded into the American pattern by their years in the infantry or cavalry, and to a man their commanding officers had recommended them to Greely as tough and dependable. The enlisted men were all volunteers. If three or four could not read English fluently or figure up to the standard of the elementary school certificate, they had mastered among them a dozen essential mechanical trades.

Greely had named the post Fort Conger, in honor of Senator Omar D. Conger of Michigan, sponsor of the bill that had brought government backing to the Lady Franklin Bay Expedition. Certainly the loneliest post under U.S. Army control, Conger consisted of one long barracklike house, a few outlying shacks sheltering the scientific instruments, and lean-tos adjoining the house for the supplies and dogs.

The carpenters had taken over as soon as Greely had chosen the site for the building, and within a few days (or work-shifts, for there were no nights) they had raised the rafters for the long house, measuring sixty by seventeen feet. While one crew hauled cargo from the ship, the other was furiously hammering on flooring and sheathing boards, fitting windows and doors, installing the kitchen range, stoves, boiler, bathtub, bunk frames, and shelving. By the end of August the house was nearly finished.

The four officers shared a room at one end. Adjoining was a hall leading outdoors and to the kitchen. Near the center of the structure was the observers' workroom and the common washroom. The remaining space, about half the building area, comprised the enlisted men's room, with double-deck bunks around the walls and mess tables in a line down the center. The entire house was insulated by a double thickness of tarpaper, and it was comfortably warmed by a large coal stove in the big room, a smaller pot-bellied stove in the officers' quarters, and the kitchen range.

While daylight still remained, Greely set the men to work on a dozen outdoor projects. At a latitude above 81° North, from May through August the sun was constantly above the horizon, circling the compass in the course of a day. About September 1 it would dip, near midnight, below the northern hills; through September and October there would be the day and night which, Genesis reports, Jehovah created as the standard order of things. The expedition members were startled by the rapid increase in the length of the autumn nights. By the second week in October the sun cut only a tiny arc in the southern sky near midday. On October 23 Greely described to Henrietta, in a letter that was to be sent home by the supply steamer the next summer, the beginning of the winter night:

> Mr. Sun has not put in an appearance since Oct. 14 although he did not go below the horizon until Oct. 16. He reddens yet the southern sky, painting the clouds with the loveliest reds and yellows you can imagine. At the same time, or shortly after, we have in the northern heavens the most exquisite tints of violet running into the deepest blue, such as give character and, as it were, personality to Arctic scenery.

The long night would reach its turning point on December 21, the winter solstice, and the sun would reappear toward the end of February, bringing in its train the rapidly lengthening days of March and April. Next year again there would be a summer of twenty weeks without a sunset. The full yearly cycle, therefore, included a scant twelve weeks with daily sunset and sunrise, as contrasted with one long twenty-week day in summer and a winter night of similar length. Greely knew that upsetting the cycle of nature's light would in a subtle way try the nerves of men from the temperate zone who had not experienced it before, as the record of earlier expeditions had proved.

While the observers concentrated on their meteorological work, Greely broke the rest of the party into sledging and trail-making. Several parties sledged five miles east along the coast, between the rugged headlands and the rubble ice, to the coal mine at Watercourse Bay. Hacking bituminous coal from the outcropping, they hauled it back to Fort Conger and to depots

Lieutenant Greely's Corner at Fort Conger.

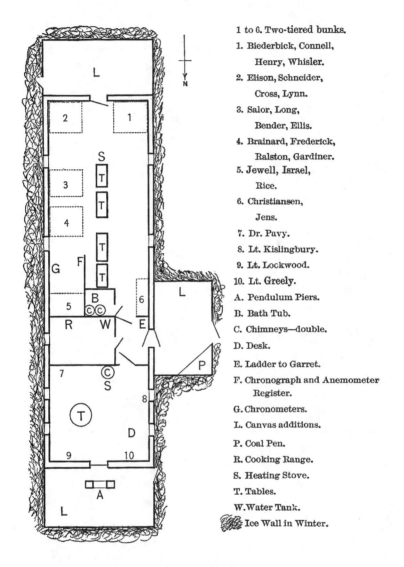

1 to 6. Two-tiered bunks.
1. Biederbick, Connell, Henry, Whisler.
2. Elison, Schneider, Cross, Lynn.
3. Salor, Long, Bender, Ellis.
4. Brainard, Frederick, Ralston, Gardiner.
5. Jewell, Israel, Rice.
6. Christiansen, Jens.
7. Dr. Pavy.
8. Lt. Kislingbury.
9. Lt. Lockwood.
10. Lt. Greely.
A. Pendulum Piers.
B. Bath Tub.
C. Chimneys—double.
D. Desk.
E. Ladder to Garret.
F. Chronograph and Anemometer Register.
G. Chronometers.
L. Canvas additions.
P. Coal Pen.
R. Cooking Range.
S. Heating Stove.
T. Tables.
W. Water Tank.
Ice Wall in Winter.

Plan of House at Fort Conger.
Scale: 16 feet to the inch.

up the coast to the north, which Greely was stocking against the exploration trips he planned for the coming spring.

Although the Eskimos, Fred and Jens, drove the sledges at first, the Americans soon learned to manage them fairly well. But mastering the wily Greenland sledge-dogs was another matter. It was a long while before the soldiers could coax from the half-wild beasts the work the Eskimos could command with a quick cry and a rifle-report crack of the whip.

Almost daily the more enthusiastic hunters of the group were out seeking musk oxen; shaggy-haired bovines with massive heads and curled horns. They had been found grazing near Conger when the party landed. By the time darkness ended the hunting season, the bag of twenty-six musk oxen provided enough dressed meat to allow each man a pound a day until spring. Together with more than a hundred eider ducks shot in Greenland, this made some three tons of fresh meat for the party, plus nearly an equal amount of offal for the dogs. The table meat had to be hung from high poles to secure it from the dogs, who from the outset challenged their masters in a war of stealth to seize whatever meat they could, by whatever means.

From the first week Greely had parties in the field exploring the area in all directions: by sledge, steam launch, and over the mountains on foot. The maps he had brought showed little more than the coastline, and he wanted to fill in details. Fall sledging was a tricky business, he soon found. As new ice formed, the tides created great pressure which heaved slabs on edge, toppled them over on the adjoining surface, then, receding, dropped the supporting water from below. This constant motion, the steady decline in temperature, the vagaries of the winds and the piling snow created a rough surface over which the sledgers moved with difficulty. In some places the going was easier on shore, above the line where the harbor ice was pushed into a jumbled mass on the beach. But most of the coast was rocky, overhung with cliffs beneath which giant boulders lay as if tumbled from the heights in ages past by some arctic Cyclops.

From his reading of arctic literature the commander knew that man's greatest winter enemy is boredom; he sought by every possible means to postpone the shutdown of outdoor work, which would force the men into idleness. Sledge parties stayed out on the trail well into November in the deep twilight of half-day, and frequently under the bright moon, which permitted a view of hills twenty miles away. From this night work the men gained self-confidence to venture forth whatever the hour. The instruments were purposely placed some distance from the house so that the routine of visiting them for readings offered relief from monotony. Late in October and into November most of the party took turns as ice-brick makers and masons to build a six-foot wall a foot thick all the way around the long house, to seal it from the winter blasts. The space between the ice wall and the tarpapered wooden walls was packed with light, dry snow for insulation. Regarding the comfort of Fort Conger, Greely reassured Henrietta:

> Up to the present time, although we have had a day whose mean temperature was more than 25 degrees below zero, we have not suffered from cold in any way. The temperature in the enlisted men's room, about 20 feet from the stove, generally ranges from 55 to 60 degrees and at times reaches 75 degrees.

Later, however, he was to note that in midwinter a drop of water spilled on the floor froze where it fell, despite the warmth closer to the ceiling. It was not surprising that heavy socks and thick moccasins were in fashion at Conger most of the year.

When storms and darkness finally ended all outdoor work but routine post duties, Greely's chief concern became morale. At first he permitted the men to take long rests on their bunks during daytime hours, because the rigors of outdoor work made the warm, soft embrace of bed loom up as an earthly paradise. But he soon issued an order that no one but night observers off duty could sleep between breakfast and dinner-time—an odd reversal of his practice back in August of ordering the men to turn in at 11 P.M., while it was bright daylight.

Musk Ox Killed Near Fort Conger.

Schneider Hauling Ice with Puppy Team.

Birthdays brought a break in routine for the celebrant, who was relieved from all duty and given the right to choose the dinner from among the entire list of stores and delicacies on hand, plus a quart of rum from the expedition supply. Private Whisler, the first man to be given this welcome treatment, set a precedent —maintained through the stay at Fort Conger—of passing the bottle around among his comrades until the bottom was dry.

Early in the darkness Greely consulted Top Sergeant Brainard on methods by which the men other than the meteorological observers could be kept busy outdoors at least an hour daily. Understanding the need perfectly, Brainard developed a mixture of necessary work, recreation, and made-work, subtly conceived, that filled it. For himself there was no problem, since his duty as both orderly sergeant and supply sergeant kept him fully occupied assigning work details, making regular trips to the supply piles, issuing food to the cooks, and keeping records of tobacco and extra clothing drawn by each man. In addition, Brainard consistently maintained a diary.

Nor was there difficulty about outdoor exercise for Private Roderick Schneider, the last man Greely chose for duty with the expedition, selected because of his several years' experience as a seaman. What led Schneider out of doors every day that first winter was his care of the Eskimo puppies born to two of the bitches bought in Greenland. Dropped in the snow beside the trail while one of the sledging parties was many miles from camp, the first litter of three puppies was in peril of being shot as an unwanted burden until Schneider sounded such an ardent plea to save the frisky little fur-balls that his companions relented. The puppies were carried back to camp aboard the sledge, snugly wrapped in a deerskin. From that point on, all puppies were saved (sometimes fairly snatched from the fangs of their cannibalistic parents) and turned over to trainer Schneider. Later on, Schneider and Private Whisler tamed a number of other animals, including several musk-ox calves, a raven, and several owls.

For a short while in early winter a patch of ice in the harbor was smooth enough for skating, and a few men there played the most northerly game of shinny on record. There were no skis in camp, but several pairs of snowshoes brought out a group to practice on milder days. It was not long before Brainard and several others were getting the knack of flopping along in the snow, despite the ice hummocks and the lack of normal light-and-shadow contrast that made the going treacherous.

Inside the big house the men passed long days playing checkers, backgammon, parchesi, and cards by the light of kerosene lanterns. Imposing his Newburyport Puritan standards, Greely permitted no gambling for money—only for tobacco. An occasional chess game found Dr. Pavy and Sergeant Israel or Greely sitting silently across the board from each other. The more studious found plentiful reading matter—including encyclopedias, general scientific works, and some seventy-five volumes on the Arctic. For lighter reading Greely's collection held close to a thousand novels and other books, as well as magazines.

Thanksgiving Day was the first holiday celebration. After a short psalm-reading session at 9:30 A.M. the entire party bundled up against the crisp 33-below cold for sporting contests on a terrain lighted by stars and lanterns. There were races on foot and on snowshoes and a dog-sledge race between the Eskimos, with plenty of tobacco changing hands among the betting fraternity.

The novelty of the day was a marksmanship contest at twenty-five yards, with the regulation paper target pinned inside a box facing the marksmen. The flame of a lighted candle burned directly in front of the bull's-eye. Private Charles B. Henry, a husky German-born cavalryman, the biggest man in camp, was the winner with a perfect fifteen out of fifteen, Jens defeating Cross for second in a shoot-off. In the evening Sergeant Rice, the recognized live wire of the party, decked himself out in a makeshift swallow-tail coat and distributed the prizes like a veteran master of ceremonies. Trophies were preserved peaches, rum, tobacco, extra towels, and fancy bath soap, all of which Greely and Brainard had drawn from the supply pile.

The Thanksgiving dinner was the grandest on record at Fort Conger, introduced with a menu listing oyster soup, salmon, eider duck, boiled ham, asparagus, deviled crab, lobster salad, peach and blueberry pie, raisin and jelly cake, vanilla ice cream, dates, Brazil nuts, figs, and coffee. Greely ordered an issue of twice the usual Sunday serving of rum and the jollity continued far into the night.

This and other events were duly recorded in the *Arctic Moon,* a post newspaper reproduced by hectograph, which Rice and Henry started in November as a pastime. The pair found a willing fellow wit in Lieutenant Lockwood, whose sketch of Fort Conger-by-the-Sea, complete with crescent moon and floating ice, graced the masthead. A semimonthly destined to last only two months, the *Arctic Moon* opened its first editorial with a spoof and a flourish:

> With this issue of the *Arctic Moon* a new luminary dawns above the literary horizon. . . . "A guide by day and a light by night," the *Arctic Moon* will shine for the public good. In politics conservative, our influence shall always be used in supporting the established policy of Grinnell Land, which has withstood the mutations of centuries of time. In no case shall its traditions be disregarded. We shall earnestly endeavor to cultivate friendly relations with our neighbors over the water. To make Greenland our ally in all steps of progress and advance would be doing much for the future of the North Pole.

The paper carried serious pieces from Greely's pen, reminiscences, tongue-in-cheek items, and a sprightly column of such short notices as:

> The Anti-Swearing Club held their first monthly meeting last week and concluded to permit the Chinese to emigrate to this country.

> Schneider's interesting batch of infantile canines is progressing favorable. Were it not for the increasing appetite of some of the elder dogs for the young puppies, quite an extensive family could be raised.

> In endeavoring to fill a lighted gasoline lamp in the Carpenter Shop on Nov. 10, Joseph Elison severely burned his hands and face by the fluid ignition. The Alarm was sounded from Box 1,

and both Fire Companies responded promptly, battled with the fire fiend and succeeded in extinguishing it without loss of property. This was the second fire from the same locality.

A "didn't know it was loaded" gun went off Monday last in the quarters. Nobody killed.

A longer story, mentioning no names, recalled a camp laugh at the expense of Lieutenant Kislingbury, who was in the habit of taking a daily walk to Dutch Island and return, accompanied by Dr. Pavy:

> We would call the attention of those philosophers who are continually preaching of the degeneracy of the times and looking to the days of Chivalry and Ancient history for the heroes and the exhibition of great courage, to the following circumstance which occurred recently in our own community. No bright page in the history of Rome or Greece can dim its lustre.
>
> A few days ago a small party were taking their daily constitutional over the two mile course to Dutch Island. They had not proceeded far when by the dim, uncertain light they saw a pack of ferocious looking animals emerge from the spectre-like hummocks of ice and approach at a terrible rate. The situation was taken in at a glance. Each member of the devoted little band saw a terrible death staring him in the face, for the horrible ferocity of a pack of hungry wolves is well known, and resolved to sell life as dearly as possible. One is at once reminded of the little Spartan band at old Thermopalae. Our party had no suitable arms but its Leonidas, in stentor-like tones shouted:
>
> "Draw your jack-knives and resist the terrible onslaught!"
>
> With blenched face but stone heart each man produced his insignificant weapon and braced himself for the hand-to-hand encounter. A moment of terrible suspense, during which you might have heard a gum-drop, and then "Gypsy," "Cooney," "Old Major" and others of our four-footed pets were fawning about them.
>
> The brave party had forgotten that the Esquimaux, with a troop of dogs, had started out in advance of them.

December 13 nearly brought tragedy to Fort Conger. At breakfast-time Eskimo Jens was missing. Private Long, the cook, said he had seen Jens rise and wash himself as usual an hour earlier but had no idea where the Eskimo had gone. Immediately after breakfast Rice picked up the fugitive's tracks and took off in pursuit toward Dutch Island with Brainard, Private Whisler, and Dr. Pavy, who drove a sledge. Back at the station, Greely recalled that both Jens and Fred had fallen lately into moodiness that resembled descriptions of midwinter depression among Eskimos in the reports of Kane, Rink, and other arctic authorities. Though the Eskimo is accustomed to a long winter darkness, the length of the night at Conger was far greater from that which they had known at Proven.

Jens, Greely reasoned from his study of the man and Eskimo ways, had become obsessed with the idea of turning himself into a Kivingtok—one in league with Tornarsuk, the Devil. By taking up his abode far from other men he could, the superstition held, by solitary suffering learn to communicate with wild birds and beasts. For a couple of weeks Greely had tried to cajole Jens from his blue mood, and apparently he had failed. He had proferred figs, nuts, and smoking tobacco as gifts—even showed him pictures of Antoinette and Adola as a fellow father who understood Jens' longing for his wife and three children at home in Proven. Over the Eskimo's protestations, the commander kept assuring him that he was "all right" and "good man." However, Greely recalled, Jens had several times asked Rice and other soldiers to kill him or beat him because, he asserted, he was "bad, no good."

With great relief the men at Conger welcomed the five figures who pulled into camp out of the darkness at 3:30 P.M. The doctor and Brainard had made a total journey of nearly twenty miles. They had found Jens only a half-mile short of Cape Murchison, far around the coast to the northeast. When apprehended, Jens had had nothing to say and returned meekly behind the sledge.

Once he had heard about Jens, Greely learned of the close brush with death experienced in the past few hours by Rice and Whisler. On the outward journey, about six miles from Fort Conger, Rice had been following the sledge through a narrow gap when he missed his footing in the gloom and crashed heavily onto the jagged ice. Dazed for a few moments, he could not cry out for aid until the rest of the party were out of earshot, and he found himself alone in the near-obscurity with a badly twisted shoulder that rendered his left arm useless.

Rice managed with difficulty to light a stub of candle and stumbled forward after the sledgers. When he caught up, some distance ahead, Dr. Pavy saw immediately that Rice should return to the station. He sent Whisler too, since the man had set out without proper protection for his face against the wind and was already showing signs of frostbite. The search party could not spare the lantern. Whisler, a strong man, was told to lead Rice carefully, to spare the injured man another fall. The pair had not groped their way much past Distant Cape on the return trip when Rice saw that his guide was failing from the cold and was reeling into pitfalls himself. Rice thereupon was forced to take the lead. A half-mile farther on he was alarmed to hear his companion complain of wanting to sit down and rest, a fatal step for any chilled hiker on an unsheltered trail.

The doughty photographer threw his good arm about Whisler and led him on, coaxing and urging him to keep up courage. But the heavier man continually tripped and repeatedly both fell painfully. Letting go at last, Rice resorted to verbal whiplashing, alternating his stinging words with glowing descriptions of the comfort of Fort Conger, the dinner awaiting them, the warm fire, the glass of rum.

By sheer persuasion the spirited Canadian pushed and cajoled Whisler to within a mile of the house. Then the big man whined piteously that his legs were frozen stiff and he could go no farther. The doctor, Brainard, and Jens, preceded by the yapping dogs, came upon them to find Rice nursing his shoulder, which he thought broken, and urging on the reluctant Whisler, now dancing in the snow beside the path without taking any forward steps. The medical man commanded the woebegone soldier to get into the sledge.

"No! In sledge he die!" It was Jens breaking his silence. "He run behind sledge—keep warm!"

Whisler, moaning his protests, shuffled into the sledge path and

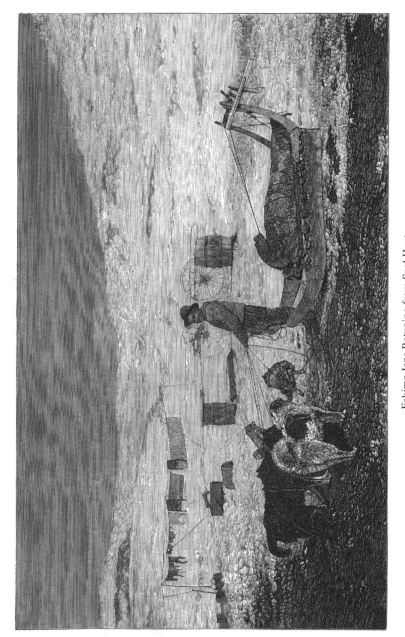

Eskimo Jens Retuning from Seal Hunt.

Dr. Pavy and Jens Skinning Seal. (Fort Conger, May 1882.)

stumbled a couple of hundred yards, falling several times. Finally Dr. Pavy, thinking he might not rise from another fall, put him on the sledge a quarter-mile out and drove as fast as he could into camp. Although he complained bitterly of aching leg muscles, which he insisted were frozen, Whisler had suffered nothing worse than acute soreness plus a touch of facial frostbite. Rice's injury turned out to be a severe sprain, not a fracture. From that day on the toughest among these Indian fighters looked with a new respect on the plucky Rice, who had shown great good sense and devotion to his companion for several trying hours at nearly 40 degrees below zero.

Jens' walkout was not the last of Greely's problems with the winter-touched Eskimos, but it was the worst. Two days after Jens' escapade, Fred rushed into the officers' room to grip first Greely and then Dr. Pavy by the hand.

"Good-by," he said solemnly, bobbing his head in salute, "good-by."

It appeared that now Fred had taken it into *his* mind to go off into the snow and become a Kivingtok. Only a long, persuasive talk from Greely and Dr. Pavy, who could speak some of the Eskimo dialect, convinced Fred that he was wanted, needed, appreciated here at the post. Thenceforth Greely called in the two natives from time to time and tried to communicate with them about home and family, plied them with figs and tobacco, and finally induced them to work on a kayak which, he assured them, only they could provide for the expedition. The enlisted men were warned not to make any jokes which either Fred or Jens might regard as a slight.

During the long darkness everyone had time to contemplate his choice of this arctic adventure. Greely found himself writing a double record—an official journal for the Chief Signal Officer and his ever-mounting pack of letters destined for Henrietta. In the latter he found an outlet for sentiments he did not care to share either with his chief or his subordinates:

It would never do that the commander should show signs of homesickness. He of all men must have the least to say and betray the fewest signs of ever thinking of it. . . . When I get back to you, you can have no fear that I shall ever be willing to leave you again. One such separation is enough for a lifetime. I do not actively think of you more than I can help. It is too much strain on me. . . .

I count all these dreary months and realize that I am well near to ending the eighth month of long, sad separation from you. I miss you so much, my darling, and want you so much, and yet with all my yearnings and inward sighings for you I cannot bring myself to regret coming. . . . I shall at least have made my mark in the world and shall go down in history as one of the Arctic leaders who has met in a measure with success. . . .

To do what one has set his ambition on causes a vast deal of pain, sorrow and privation. But did we all withdraw our hand from the plough share, what would be the harvest for coming generations? I am sure you approve of all done in this matter by—

Your husband and lover, *A.W.G.*

The calendar-markers of the party had for weeks been creeping their pencil marks closer to the winter solstice, December 21. On this day, when the invisible sun reached the point farthest from view and began his comeback, the tide of morale at Fort Conger seemed to turn. Now, everyone agreed, they were "over the ridge." It was downhill from now on, and spring was on the way. Lieutenant Lockwood exulted in his journal, which he kept in shorthand:

The sun now begins his journey to the north; the backbone of the winter is broken! . . . Walking out at noon today I was just able to see the hands of my watch by holding it close to my eye. The profound silence of this region is quite striking, and almost as disagreeable, as the darkness. Standing still, one can almost hear his heart beat. The sense of solitude is sublime.

For Brainard, December 21 was not only the solstice but also his twenty-fifth birthday: "Relieved of all duties and made out bill of fare for dinner. Another welcome offering—a quart of rum for the birthday punch."

The following evening Dr. Pavy lectured to the party on Africa, the men appearing as much interested as they had been in Greely's two lectures, one on the North Pole problem (how to reach it), the other his reminiscences of the battle of Fredericksburg. The lecture program, Greely hoped, would become a weekly event to break the long after-dinner hours. He had counted on Lockwood for help, but after giving one talk on arctic sledging Lockwood permitted his diffidence to prevail. Dr. Pavy promised several times to follow up his talk on Africa but did not do so the rest of the year. Kislingbury did not volunteer. Greely therefore continued largely without help.

Rum flowed again on Saturday evening, December 24, as the bunkhouse boys helped Corporal Salor liquidate his thirty-first year. Greely had a large bowl of hot eggnog set out for a Merry Christmas Eve celebration in the big room, which Rice and Brainard had decorated with pennants and bunting. Cup by cup the drink disappeared as presents from home were opened and the boisterous crowd rolled dice for a lap robe originally destined for the departed Ryan. While voices were joyous and the singing spirited, Greely confided to his journal his long thoughts of home:

> The evening passed off very pleasantly. I doubt not though that amid the merriment it was with some others as with me, that their hearts and minds were far away across the barren wastes of snow and ice, far beyond the rolling waves and dark forests, among the dear ones who were making merry in their own land and by their own firesides.

Lockwood, too, felt the tug of Christmas nostalgia, mingled with speculation about what the year ahead might hold. Greely had already notified him that he would lead a sledge party north in the hope of setting a new world record for latitude:

> The day with me [Lockwood wrote] suggests alternately the past and the future. Will next Christmas find me here, with everything around as auspicious as now, and shall I then be able to look back with satisfaction and self-complacency on my labors along the Greenland coast? Or will the future bring a record of dreams unsatisfied, of efforts unproductive, of labor in vain?

The big Christmas banquet, which outshone and outlasted the Thanksgiving production, wound up with the plum puddings packed by Henrietta, cigars given by one of her friends among the Washington military ladies, and bonbons courtesy of Huyler's in New York. Because Christmas Day fell on the Sabbath, Greely restrained secular celebration until the 26th. As the chronometer hands touched midnight the men shook off the restraint of the holy day to greet the holiday with mirth. About 3 A.M. they were still roaring repeated choruses of:

> We won't go home until morning!
> Till daylight doth appear!

followed by guffaws of laughter at the new twist which their arctic situation gave the old refrain.

The Christmas variety show, in rehearsal for a week, came off at 8 P.M. under the direction of the irrepressible George Rice. According to the hectographed PROGRAMME (*Arctic Moon*, print.), the show was a production of the

> Lime Juice Club at Dutch Island Operahouse (one night only). Geo. W. Rice, Manager. Dress Circle—1 lb. Tobacco, Admission—½ lb. Tobacco, Hayloft—free. Dog chariots ordered at 10 P.M. Doors open at 7:30 P.M.

The bill was played to the hilt. It featured an Indian Council and War Dance, with laughs at the expense of Tesumse (Freeze-to-death) Whisler and other "braves"; impersonation of an Eskimo belle by the smoothly shaved Schneider, who popped Eskimo puppies from "her" embroidered jumper at the blackout; dialect songs by Henry ("Some Dings I No Off Amerika"); and close-to-the-line "Imitations of a Well-Known Milty. Character" [unnamed—Sherman? Grant? Greely?] by Private Maurice Connell. The actor brought down the house with his mock commiseration over a poor private who had shot himself and was carried by on a stretcher: "A very sad case, indeed—very sad!—Charge him with two cartridges, Sergeant!" Jewell, the chief observer, closed the program with an announced "select reading," for which he advanced to center stage, opened his case with a flourish, pulled forth an aneroid barometer, hung it on the wall—and read it!

Brainard noted in his journal that "Everybody enjoyed the show and it terminated happily with a liberal allowance of Yankee dew."

Nor did the festivities drop off for another week. Brainard noted on January 1, 1882:

> A Happy New Year! We stayed up till 3 A.M. for the passing of the Old Year. Sang and danced and at midnight honored New Year with several volleys from the post arsenal; also with music from a tin pan orchestra. It was a lively celebration, with the added luxury of cigars, the gift of Lieut. Kislingbury.
>
> The revelry proved too much for Sgts. Linn and Ralston who early this morning were ordered to Mount Campbell to read the instruments. They tramped for several hours about the island and then returned to the station without having located the instruments—or the mountain, for that matter.

But all the jollity of the rum-spiced turn of the meteorological and calendar years did not melt the ice in the officers' room. Unhappy in his limbo status, Kislingbury was technically, as his orders read, "temporarily at the station awaiting transportation." Greely had expected that his disenchanted second officer would sulk for a while and then apply for reinstatement to duty so as to make normal an embarrassing situation. But Kislingbury did not do so. Feeling he had been wronged, he closed himself in a shell of self-pity. He considered he was standing on his dignity as a gentleman in sticking to his decision of August 26 to resign. Greely, in like manner, considered it beneath his status as commander to sue for an amicable peace—even though peace was needed to bring a measure of common sense to their relationship, and perhaps to lead to better feeling between them. So Kislingbury remained in the status of a guest. He ate, slept, took his walks and hunted—but undertook no responsibilities and was given none. Both in the fall and again early in the spring he occasionally asked Greely if he might accompany a one-day sledging party.

Greely acceded to keep the man occupied and give him no further cause to sulk.

As the winter wore on, Greely found the doctor a more complex character than he had at first thought. It became clear that Octave Pavy considered himself, not Greely, the one who should have been placed in command of the expedition. Yet all his erudition and his supercharged ego did not fit him for leadership. He was keenly intelligent, and a cracking good physician, as the health record of the party proved. But he misused equipment and was downright sloppy with his paper work. In his squandering of time he proved a sluggard. He lacked punctuality even in handing over his monthly medical report, which he could prepare in an hour, had he a mind to. Pavy resented discipline coming from an army lieutenant without higher education and in his smoldering discontent, fed by his jealousy toward Lockwood over their rivalry to set sledging records to the north, he found a natural ally in the unhappy, marooned Kislingbury. Almost daily the two walked down the shore to Dutch Island for exercise and a chance to talk out their mutual concerns.

James Booth Lockwood was far more of Greely's stripe; in fact, he resembled many of the junior officers the commander had known from the Civil War onward. Turning twenty-nine in the second month at Fort Conger, Lockwood was eight and a half years younger than Greely. Intelligent but without Greely's firmness of purpose, Lockwood had drifted through his army career searching for the elusive rainbow of self-fulfillment. He sketched tolerably well, but only for amusement, and he had learned shorthand. A more determined man would have pushed on from sketching to cartography, or perhaps from shorthand to a career in military law, but Lockwood did not have this kind of drive. His journals and letters reflected warmth of spirit, a keen eye for color and humor strangely combined with a Poelike penchant for morbid reflection, of which his Christmas Day thoughts were but a mild sample.

By nature a solo performer, not an organizer, Lockwood was at his best on the trail with one or two trusted comrades, in the

Arctic or on the prairie, where his wide-brimmed hat would have been set at a more rakish angle, his scarf brighter, his buttons shinier than those of his companions. A man of such temperament chafed at the winter confinement of Fort Conger, and long before the first light of spring pointed its shafted fingers into the sky Lockwood was itching to be off for the Greenland coast and derring-do—to set a record for the Farthest North, over a trail no man yet had trod. Even before the autumn sledging had closed down, Lockwood had minuted his impression of the stifling atmosphere in the officers' quarters:

> Surely this is a happy quartet occupying this room! We often sit silent during the whole day, and even a meal fails to elicit anything more than a chance remark or two. A charming prospect for four months of darkness, such gloom within, and penned up as we are in one room! I have doubts of getting over the straits (to the Greenland shore) but I must be off as soon as possible, for I find relief in getting away.

Toward winter's end, Greely described for Henrietta the opening of a typical day in quarters:

> At 7:30 the breakfast comes on the table. I am (except perhaps once a month when five minutes late) ready but no one else is. The Dr. is ready perhaps twice a week, and five times a week say five minutes late. We two sit down. Lt. K., after being very deliberate in his dressing and brushing out his whiskers &c. sits down *regularly* from 10 to 15 minutes late—just late enough to annoy me but not late enough for me to make trouble about it.
>
> Lt. Lockwood is called the 2nd or 3d time by the cook at 7:30 or 7:35 after everything is on the table and hurrying his toilet he is regularly from 15 to 20 minutes late, always when taxed with it pleading inability to wake up and get up. However, I have some consideration for him as I know that he lies in his bed for hours every night before he can get to sleep.
>
> Lt. K. has hardly been at the table two minutes when he gets up, goes and changes the calendar and winds up the clock. That procedure is gone through six times a week and occasional weeks seven times. . . . Lt. K. having finished breakfast washes and then

brushes his whiskers with great care. They are his pride and I have known him to brush them six times in a single day.

The onrush of spring brought relief as the party began busily preparing for the season's sledging while the sun gave light but before its warmth melted the heavy winter ice. The enlisted men's room was turned into a multiple workshop for sledge overhauling, tent-stitching, tinsmithing on the cooking equipment, leatherwork on boots and mittens. Greely at his desk drew up supply lists, Lockwood traced and sketched maps, and together the trail parties studied records of previous expeditions—those of Markham, Beaumont, Hall, Kane and the rest. Official orders were drafted for Dr. Pavy and Lockwood, who were to head the main parties to the north. Most of the other men would drag sledges in support for the first few marches. Israel gave a quick course in astronomical observation to the assault parties; Brainard busied himself with the supply breakdown; Jens and Fred exercised their teams.

The doctor was to travel with Rice and Eskimo Jens around the Grinnell Land coast east and then north to Cape Joseph Henry in an attempt to surpass the northern record set by Lieutenant Markham of the Royal Navy. Six years earlier the Englishman had left the coast behind and traveled out over the frozen Lincoln Sea to set a new Farthest-North record—83° 20′ 26″. Lockwood, scheduled to set out some days after Dr. Pavy, was to cross Robeson Channel to the Greenland coast and proceed northeast along the shore as far as he could consistent with weather conditions, supply, and his party's endurance. Brainard was to be Lockwood's trail companion, with Fred as sledge-driver. The sledge itself had been christened *Antoinette* after the commander's three-year-old daughter.

Both parties, but especially Dr. Pavy's, were to scour the coast for any sign of Lieutenant Commander George Washington De Long, who had disappeared into the Polar Sea in 1879 aboard the *Jeannette,* and in whose fate every arctic enthusiast was deeply interested. Greely and De Long, a Navy man, had known each

Dr. Pavy's Party Starting North, March 19, 1882.

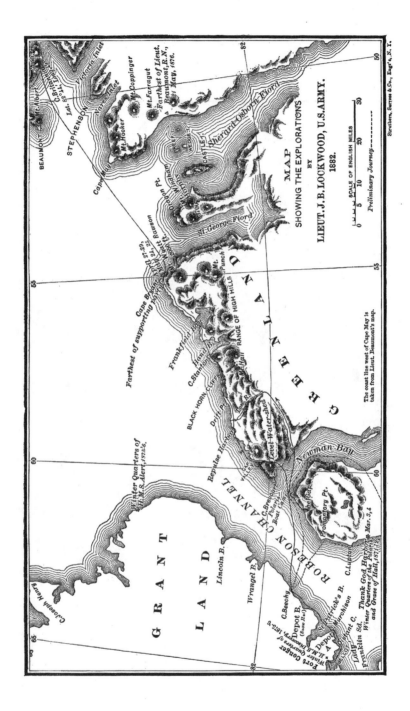

MAP

SHOWING THE EXPLORATIONS

BY

LIEUT. J. B. LOCKWOOD, U.S. ARMY.

1882.

SCALE OF ENGLISH MILES

0   5   10   20   30

Preliminary Journey----------

The coast line west of Cape May is
taken from Lieut. Beaumont's map.

Struthers, Servoss & Co., Eng'r's, N. Y.

GRANT LAND

GREENLAND

ROBESON CHANNEL

Newman Bay

BEAUMONT
STEPHENSON
Mt. Albert
C. Britannia
Lat. 83° 24' ½
Frederick Inlet
Mt. Hooker
Cape May
Mt. Coppinger
Mt. Farragut
Farthest of Lieut.
Beaumont, R.N.,
May, 1876.

Shergard Osborn Fiord

St. George Fiord

Cape Britannia
Wyatt Rawson
Stephenson Pt.

Farthest of supporting party

Lat. 27'-29'
Lat. 24', 25'

Mt. Punch

RANGE OF HIGH HILLS

Frankfield Bay
Hand Bay
C. Stanton
BLACK HORN CLIFFS
Drift Pt.
Repulse Harbor
Level Water shed

Winter Quarters of
H.M.S. Alert, 1875-6.

Lincoln B.

Wrangel R.

C. Beechy

Depot B.
(Snow Hut)
Distant C.
Fort Conger
Winter Quarters of
and Grave of Hall, 1871.
Thank God Harbor, Mar. 3, 4
Franklin Sd.
Repulse Harbor
C. Brevoort
Polaris
Boat Camp
Promontory Pt.
C. Lupton

C. Joseph Henry

other well back in Washington, and Mrs. De Long had gone so far as to entrust a letter for her lost husband to Greely's care.

On March 19 Greely bade farewell to Pavy, Rice, and Jens, accompanying them a couple of miles at the start and wishing them godspeed. But that evening he had to confess in a letter to Henrietta his gnawing anxieties over the medical man:

> I have not quite as much faith in the Doctor as formerly. I am satisfied that he has deceived me in many things and that he is an arrant mischief-maker. He has, I understand, been sowing seeds of dissension and discontent among the men, to no avail, however. I have been too just and fair to the men and they are too intelligent to be easily affected. I have no positive proof of it and possibly may never have, but am morally satisfied it is so, and Lt. Lockwood has been so informed. . . .
>
> I think that Dr. P. has done much to put Lt. K. in his present unenviable frame of mind. . . . Although I know he has done everything he can to destroy Lockwood's chances and work, and is eaten up with jealousy, yet he goes out to do important work. While despising the man and his methods I most heartily wish him all luck and a safe and speedy return.

But the doctor seemed plagued by ill-luck on the trail and never reached his goal. Open water at Cape Joseph Henry blocked his efforts—an unexpected frustration for Greely, who commented to Henrietta that the doctor appeared to be "quite a Jonah." Lockwood might have equally bad luck, he thought, but as the days passed and the support parties returned reporting firm ice at the start of the Greenland trip, his hopes rose. If only the ice would hold fast through May, so that Lockwood might return safely across Robeson Channel, then the thaws could come with a vengeance so the supply ship, with its new personnel and the mail, might steam up to Discovery Harbor in July or August.

With Lockwood away, the social climate was frosty for the commander:

> Lt. K. behaves like a spoiled schoolboy, and I hardly exchange 50 words a day with him. I treat him with the most uniform

civility and have tried to make his stay here endurable. He has low tastes, however, and has for months spent hours daily playing cards with the enlisted men, whom he treats as equals in every way, putting himself exactly on their footing. . . .

I should be tempted to quit this world at once were I doomed to pass my life under such conditions and with so small-minded a man as my only companion. The doctor too is the same—a tricky, double-faced man, idle, unfit for any Arctic work except doctoring & sledge travel & not first class in the latter. He is certainly an excellent doctor so you may rest easy on that score. He is too much of a Frenchman to be uncivil or impolite to his commanding officer. . . . He and Lt. K. consort entirely together —when not with enlisted men—united by the common wish and desire to break down the commander but not daring to openly act to that effect.

On Wednesday, June 1, Greely's vigil for Lockwood was over. The lieutenant, Brainard, and Fred, exhausted, suffering from snow-blindness but tremendously excited, came sledging into camp with a new record. They had extended the known coast of Greenland by eighty-five miles and had beaten Markham's Farthest North, an honor held by one British explorer after another for close to three centuries. The American eagle fairly screamed in triumph as Greely penned his exultant message of victory to Henrietta:

I write you a line to say that Lockwood returned at 2 P.M. having reached a point about 70 miles NE of Cape Britannia. He beat the latitude of Markham (and the world) *on land* by two miles or more. He could have gone a few miles north on ice but it was not needful. Land still ran on 15 miles to the NE and how much farther no one knows.

I am of course delighted beyond measure at this result, which places our expedition at the head of all others as regards the highest latitude and the discovery of the most northerly land known on the globe.

Tomorrow is dear Toinette's birthday and it was her sled that made the wonderful journey. Your flag, too, beats all others which will more than repay you for the work bestowed on it. The

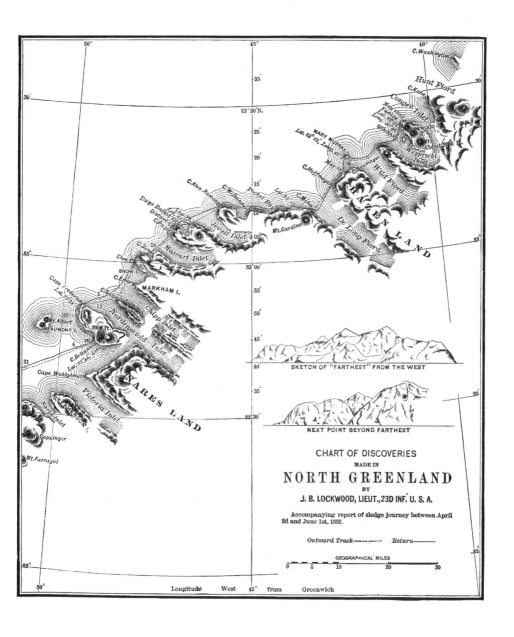

SKETCH OF "FARTHEST" FROM THE WEST

NEXT POINT BEYOND FARTHEST

CHART OF DISCOVERIES
MADE IN
NORTH GREENLAND
BY
J. B. LOCKWOOD, LIEUT., 23D INF. U. S. A.

Accompanying report of sledge journey between April
3d and June 1st, 1882.

Outward Track -------- Return ———

GEOGRAPHICAL MILES

0   5   10   20   30

Longitude   West   45°   from   Greenwich

Lieutenant Greely and Party Starting for Exploration of Grinnell Land, April, 1882.

men all come in with excellent health. Three lives paid for the English discoveries. We beat them and lose none.

Now the pressure was off. Anticipation of the supply ship's visit became the major concern at Fort Conger. In June and early July Greely and Lockwood led exploring parties to the interior of Grinnell Land on foot, where they mapped new lakes, mountains, glaciers, and rivers, collected ancient Eskimo relics, and observed an unexpected variety of wildlife. But their trips away from the station were not of long duration. By the second week in July anxious sentinels mounted the hills to watch the bay. With the ship, Greely anticipated getting rid of Kislingbury and two enlisted men who did not measure up to standard—one for petty theft and the other for general unreliability.

Everyone awaited letters, packages, and newspapers from the United States. Most of all, perhaps, after their year together they longed for the sight of new faces.

So EASY HAD BEEN the *Proteus'* cruise to Discovery Harbor in 1881 that General Hazen looked on the resupply mission of 1882 as a more or less routine operation. Accordingly, he put it in the charge of his private secretary, William M. Beebe, who had been an army major but was now a civilian. To deliver a shipload of supplies, after all, one did not need to organize an arctic expedition. Secretary of War Lincoln had thought about the Lady Franklin Bay party so little that Hazen was obliged to remind him early in May that since Greely expected a resupply mission it was high time to authorize one. Grudgingly, protesting that "I know of no such understanding," Lincoln forwarded Hazen's request to President Arthur, and Congress acted just in time for a St. John's whaler to be chartered.

On July 8, a year and a day after the *Proteus* had cleared St. John's, Beebe sailed aboard the *Neptune* with supplies, mail, and additional men to replace those who might have fallen ill or proved unsatisfactory. Five days out the *Neptune* ran into heavy gales, then into thick pan ice 135 miles west of Cape Farewell,

the southern tip of Greenland. The going became so heavy that
the stout vessel was slowed to three knots, and by nightfall on
July 13 visibility was so poor that she was moored to a convenient
ice pan until the weather should clear. In view of the *Proteus'*
fairly easy passage the year before, the outlook was unexpectedly
discouraging. It was only the beginning of weeks of frustration
and delay for Beebe.

Pack ice alternated with drifting bergs. High winds and stinging snows assaulted the vessel as she inched northward. By July
29, off Littleton Island in Smith Sound, the *Neptune* was brought
to a dead halt by an unbroken ice barrier, ranging from twelve
to twenty feet thick, blocking the sound all the way to the northwest horizon.

Crossing to the Ellesmere side, Beebe waited for a turn of luck,
which a new gale springing up from the southwest seemed to
promise. But when the ice broke to the north on August 7 the
ship entered the icefield only to become helplessly caught. Beset,
her timbers creaking ominously under the strain, the *Neptune*
drifted helplessly for three days. The most northerly latitude she
attained—79°20'—was some 200 miles short of Fort Conger.

Breaking clear at last, the ship zigzagged back and forth in the
lower Kane Basin and Smith Sound until, after three weeks, Beebe
realized he might not reach Greely this year after all. A storm
from the north broke over the sound on August 29, threatening
to drive the *Neptune* south into Baffin Bay, and Beebe hastily
landed a part of his stores near Cape Sabine, an emergency
measure that had been agreed upon the year before. At one
o'clock the following morning Beebe ripped a page from his
pocket notebook and scribbled a message for Greely:

> Whaleboat and cache just above high water mark N by W
> magnetic. Cannot by any possibility get further northward now.
> If we cannot get further or return here (for we cannot hold on
> here now on account of ice) will leave other whale boat on this
> shore—if possible at Brevoort Island or in sight, marking spot
> with tripod.
>
> *Beebe*

Late in the evening of September 5, having made no forward progress and with new blasts threatening the ship, Beebe and the ship officers concluded that further effort to reach Greely this year would be fruitless.

As the *Neptune*'s prow turned toward St. John's after thirty-nine days within Smith Sound or above it, the vessel carried in her hold three quarters of the supplies that had been destined for the party at Lady Franklin Bay.

3 BLOCKADE

THROUGH THE long daylight of July and August Greely's party kept an anxious watch for the ship that never appeared. At times the men could see clear water extending for miles down the coast. More often the channel was choked with pack ice which, driven by the wind or the rising tide, surged into Lady Franklin Bay—the ice blockade.

Realizing that no ship might get through in either of the two following summers, Greely had equipped his expedition with sufficient stores to last three years if necessary. At least there would be no hardship. On August 25 the commander recorded his disappointment:

> Artificial light will soon be needed. I have quite given up the ship, as, indeed, have most of the men. I hope against hope, and defer going on an allowance of our remaining stock of vegetables until September 1. . . . We must live much more simply than in the past year.

To the men, the final realization that there would be no supply vessel was a cruel blow. There would be no break in the monotony of their confinement, no letters from home. They faced another long, dark arctic winter. It would not be an adventure the second time, but an ordeal of dull existence. To Kislingbury, who had been expecting to leave for home, the prospect was especially bitter.

Sergeant William Cross, the dour, dark-bearded engineer, sought to drown his unhappiness in spirit-lamp fuel, which he stole from the supply kept in the motor launch *Lady Greely*. A long-married, childless man, slightly older than the commanding officer, his last name fit him as if he had stepped from the pages of a novel by Charles Dickens. Swigging the alcohol alone, he drank himself into a stupor and fell from the deck of the *Lady Greely* into the frigid harbor water. Sergeant Brainard was close enough to haul him out, getting a chill soaking in the process. The shock of his ducking brought Cross sufficiently to his senses to dread the wrath of the commander. Summoned to the house, the frightened drunk tried to hide in the supply tent. Greely, with the help of Private Biederbick, the medical orderly, at last shoved him indoors bodily and forced him to strip off his sopping clothes.

Greely did not break Cross to the grade of private, as he at first contemplated. The unstable man, alas, was his only engineer. Further, as Cross was one of the two enlisted men in the party who had left wives at home, the commander could understand how the unfulfilled longing of the summer for the ship which never came would have been harder on him than the others. But while he treated Cross with lenience, a few weeks later Greely acted with vigor to curb insubordination from Sergeant David Linn, second-ranking man to Brainard and a veteran cavalry non-com whose conduct should have been a model to the others.

Upon the sudden appearance of a bear near the station Greely had dispatched another man to overtake Linn, who was at a distance with a hunting rifle, take the weapon and pursue the bear, since he had observed the direction in which it was heading. Linn, apparently feeling he had been slighted, stalked angrily into Greely's quarters demanding in an insolent tone:

"Lieutenant, did you order that I should give up my gun?"

"Yes," replied Greely.

"Well, I don't think very much of it!" the sergeant burst out.

The commander drew himself up straight. "Sergeant Linn, do you realize what you are saying?"

Linn turned his back on his superior and muttered: "Yes, and I still don't think much of it."

To the strait-laced New Englander insolence from a subordinate was intolerable.

"Sergeant," he said curtly, "I shall reduce you to private, and if you are not careful try you by court-martial on our return."

That evening at dinner he read the reduction order to the men and announced the promotion of Private Maurice Connell to sergeant in Linn's place.

Born in County Kerry, a man who never neglected to uphold the cause of Ireland in barracks arguments, Connell had come to the expedition highly recommended by his company commander, and had even accepted a reduction from sergeant to private in order to go. During the past year he had proved himself an excellent sledgeman—"one of our best men," Greely had noted approvingly in his diary.

At the end of October, Private Bender told the commander that as a Roman Catholic he objected to attending the Sunday psalm-reading. A semiliterate soldier given to outbursts of ill temper and foul language, Bender had sat uncomplaining through Greely's reading of the Sunday psalms for fourteen months. Greely was inclined to look on the incident as a manifestation of winter irritability rather than the result of prayerful consideration of theological duty, but he at once agreed to excuse the man. Bender, a tinsmith by trade, more than carried his weight in the party as a general handyman who emerged as an ingenious and industrious Mr. Fixit. He could be allowed his declaration of faith for the sake of maintaining harmony.

The tedium of the deepening winter was not appreciably lightened by the wailing of Private Roderick Schneider's violin. The only musician of the group, Schneider seemed to his listeners to have a one-tune repertoire consisting of the music-hall ballad "Over the Garden Wall," which told how a young swain first wooed his girl over the wall, then spirited her away by night by the same route, foiling the classically hostile father:

> Over the garden wall, the sweetest girl of all,
> There never were yet, such eyes of jet,
> And you may bet I'll never forget

> The night our lips in kisses met,
> Over the garden wall.

Though the men of Fort Conger may have sung the chorus lustily to Schneider's scraping the first winter, it palled on them through the second.

About 5 A.M. on November 17 Observer Gardiner ran excitedly into the house and called for everyone to come out and see an exceptionally brilliant aurora borealis. Sergeant Israel, rushing out the door with his eyes half open, was so blinded by the vivid light and by surprise that he sprang back and banged the door shut.

"By heavens!" he exclaimed. "I thought the aurora was going to strike me in the face!"

The men laughed at the astronomer's hyperbole. But they later agreed that the lights appeared so close they had the sensation of being almost able to reach out and touch them. The diarists felt no restraint describing the sight. Thus Brainard:

> The heavens were one luminous mass of blazing light with colors of varying blues, yellows and white. The aurora was of no definite formation, but extended to all parts of the sky, arches, streamers and patches blending harmoniously into one huge sheet. . . .
> A streamer would leap from the horizon, pass through the zenith and reach the opposite horizon with the quickness of thought. Receding it appeared to swoop downward almost to the earth taking new forms, coiling and twisting convulsively like a gigantic serpent.

Several of the accounts mentioned patches of white light and compared them to puffs of smoke rising as from a giant locomotive somewhere in the distance. Private Charles B. Henry, who had once worked in a print shop and before leaving the U.S. had distributed cards identifying himself as "Special Correspondent of the *Chicago Times* with the Lady Franklin Bay Expedition," threw away the grammar book and let his prose run free:

The aurora defies description by words, and is not to be pictured by painters' skill. Arches with every shade of red, from the palest pink to crimson, and every shade of yellow, from brilliant orange to delicate primrose, now dazzling and resplendent, now gently glowing in humbler effusion, and suddenly shooting thousands of narrow radiant streaks and bars of light in a semicircle toward the zenith. Streamers of every shade of green, from the softest apple or pea to the dark invisible green of the hemlock pines, harmoniously blend the lovely tints of lilac and purple with the celestial blue of the canopy, and shining here for an instant and then playfully skip to another portion of the sky.

At the instrument shack the observers noted that the magnetic needle was violently agitated for three days, revealing an extraordinary disturbance.

For several days after the aurora faded, the party moved about in the light of a moon so brilliant that it almost rivaled sunshine. Yet even this extraordinary show brought excitement for only a short time. The dull routine resumed. Thanksgiving came and went, the men merely going through the motions of celebration without the spirit of the year before. On December 5 Brainard was recording:

> The monotonous routine of our life is felt more keenly every day. . . . Our time, after the usual hour's work in the morning, is spent in reading, writing or discussion. . . . Nothing seems to hurry the flight of time. . . . Everything annoys and aggravates us. We give way readily in any situation with a burst of unreasonableness, rather than bolster up our will-power.

Christmas 1882 was a pale ghost of the previous one. There was no enthusiasm to put on a show this year; a few leftover presents were distributed on Christmas Eve, the men greeting Christmas Day itself with songs at midnight. Private Francis Long, the fiery-haired chief cook, seemed to have more zest for celebration than most and outdid himself in preparing a splendid dinner, amusing the enlisted men's table by serving with his halo of red hair dusted with flour. Yet, Brainard chronicled,

The enthusiasm of the party for these occasions has diminished considerably and a celebration, no matter how we strive to make it otherwise, becomes nothing more than a mockery. The men grow more captious daily.

Part of the reason lay in Greely's order that no man was to go more than a half-mile from the station without permission, a rule put in force early in the winter after bear tracks had been found several times near the house. Within the radius allowed, the men, like prisoners—well fed, idle and bored—covered every square foot of ice and snow many times over. The continual repetition took away most of the pleasure they had sought in fresh air and outdoor walking. Indeed, they found this arctic zoo strangely ironic—the polar bears roamed at will outside while the men felt themselves caged.

Alone at his desk on Christmas Day, Greely faced the photograph of his serenely beautiful Henrietta, gold-haired Antoinette, and tiny Adola. His pen spoke his hopes for good times to come, of the worst of their separation being over:

> I trust we shall be happy enough in the Christmas of 1883. It is a long time to look ahead. The New Year comes in a week, and our darkest day—Dec. 21 the sun was farthest from us—has already passed 4 days since. In a few days we will be studying the face of the southern horizon watching for the gradual brightening arch of noonday twilight. With the sun there will come to us new life and strength. Courage we always have here. I have never yet been inclined to look on other than the bright side of matters here and while providing for the worst as far as practicable, feeling assured of a happy issue.

On January 16, a careless room orderly smashed the last of the four dozen glass lamp chimneys brought to the Arctic. Bender, the ingenious tinkerer, set to work and produced a number of excellent chimneys from empty bottles. When to everyone's delight they passed a test brilliantly, Brainard noted: "If a vote were taken today, Bender would be the hero of the expedition."

As the winter darkness stretched on, Greely became increasingly concerned over Kislingbury's fraternization with the enlisted men, as if he were systematically currying favor with them. This conduct was entered in the commander's journal for the later consideration of General Hazen:

> He has habitually consorted with the enlisted men for over a year, regularly playing cards with them—whist, casino, etc. He at first did it in the observers' room, out of view, with the observers. But this room was abandoned and he played anywhere and with anybody. I did not interfere with him. I wished to give him no pretext for claiming this command, which I firmly believe would be most unfortunate, in case of fatal disability to myself.

When Greely discovered that the detached officer was playing poker for money with the men, it was more than he could stand, although he wanted to play his own disciplinary hand with caution. Quietly summoning Brainard, he ordered the first sergeant to pass the word in the enlisted men's quarters that no one, from this point on, was to play betting games with Lieutenant Kislingbury. The word was enough, and the games for stakes stopped.

With Dr. Pavy it was a series of petty annoyances. The doctor had no conception of his duty to speak officially as a responsible physician in a military command. He would only hint, opine, or suggest, as in the case of the sauerkraut:

> *Jan. 17, 1883.* The Doctor spoke about the sauerkraut today which the men with but few exceptions do not eat. I asked him if it was not good I wish he would say so, and of course that would settle the matter. He said that all he was willing to say was that it was old—which goes without saying! He said that freezing might have injured it, but he could not say it was improper food. I ate of it as usual. I have never liked it, but eat it because we have it and it is served generally. Of course I shall discontinue the issue of it.

But if the officers continued as difficult to get along with as before, Greely noted a mild improvement in Cross' behavior:

Jan. 20, 1883. Cross' 39th birthday. I offered him a glass of wine which I was glad to see him refuse, and a quart of rum was issued to him which he gave to the men, drinking none himself.

Life continued as usual in the animal kingdom, the commander observing, "One of the bitches in heat today, which appears remarkable—at such a season of the year and at such temperature (40 below zero)."

So frequent were Greely's points of vexation with Dr. Pavy and Kislingbury that on February 1 he analyzed their behavior as almost a studied campaign to thwart him:

> It appears to me to be a continual effort to "make a record," as the soldier says, on me. I have exercised all patience and perhaps have been too lenient, but I have thought it more dignified and better to avoid quarrels, bickerings and squabbles. I deem this work and the success and lives of this party too valuable to be induced to endanger either by harsh, violent or unjust words or measures. Indeed, my experiences here have been, as I doubt not have those of most Arctic commanders, a veritable network of anxieties, annoyances and vexations. Naturally of a somewhat irritable disposition I have carefully restrained myself and cannot recall an instance in which I have not so done. I have mentioned a number of these matters to Lt. Lockwood, who naturally and by instruction succeeds me in command, that he may be informed as to them in case of injury or disability to me.

With the approach of spring Dr. Pavy shifted his tactics in the battle of personalities. Almost daily he revealed his obsession with preparing for retreat by the launch and boats to Smith Sound, should that become necessary in case of failure of relief by ship. There should be no long spring exploration trips, he counseled, either north or to the interior of Grinnell Land. The only parties sent out should be those preparing a line of caches southward down Kennedy Channel. As the doctor pushed this line of argument, Greely suspected that part of his motive was his ill-concealed jealousy of Lockwood, who was scheduled to try again, with Brainard and Fred, to better his Farthest-North record, and possibly to prove the insularity of Greenland.

Greely did not know that Dr. Pavy had already tried to cajole, then to browbeat, Private Whisler—physically one of the strongest of the men but definitely not one of the smartest—into a plan to steal the best of the sledge-dogs for a trip Pavy planned to make with Rice. Had Whisler fallen in line, Dr. Pavy would have sledged off to snatch glory with a northward push from Cape Joseph Henry, and Lockwood's journey would have been effectively sabotaged. To his credit, Whisler resisted the surgeon's blandishments, and when Dr. Pavy displayed extreme anger at him the loyal soldier drew his pistol to show the plotter he meant business. Having failed in this, Dr. Pavy abandoned his scheme and resigned his course to preparing retreat.

Greely would brook no suggestion of giving up his plan to send out exploring parties or to delay preparing the supply line for Lockwood, as Pavy counseled. The commander chronicled, March 9, 1883:

> To abandon the laying out of depots (for Lockwood) until *perfectly safe* weather for traveling would be to abandon the geographical work in north Greenland. As Dr. Pavy reports officially that the men's health has been better during this winter than in 1881–82, I should feel I was doing an unsoldierly and unmanly act in abandoning the work.... It has been all retreat with him ever since last autumn.... That was the first proposal to abandon all work and seek only personal safety regardless of duty or honor.

When Kislingbury on March 15 proposed a harebrained plan to send a sledge party all the way south to Littleton Island to leave notice for a ship, or to remain there to guide the vessel, Greely flatly turned the idea down, noting in his journal:

> He was very vehement about my plans and said that the voice of one man ought not to weigh against 24, that he was confident the men were depressed over their foreshadowed fate, &c. He said Lt. Lockwood thinks about the same but *says* he (Lt. L) can stand it if I (Lt. G) can.

This suggestion of appeal to a town-meeting type of democracy within an isolated military command caused Greely great uneasiness. In effect, it was a hint at mutiny. He decided that he would have to give up the journey he planned to the interior of Grinnell Land via Archer Fiord during Lockwood's absence. It would never do to leave two such disaffected men as Kislingbury and Dr. Pavy to depress the party or to stir them up while he was gone. Greely was ready to retreat to Smith Sound by boat if need be, he wrote in his journal. But he would depart in order, not in flight:

> If no vessel comes I consider our chances desperate—God help us. If one does come, we cannot well miss reaching it. With provisions at Craycroft, Carl Ritter Bay, Cape Collinson & Cape Hawks we must be able to make Cape Isabella. Whale boats and small depots should be there now on this western coast.

In April Lockwood, Brainard, and Fred set out again to break their Farthest-North record of the year before, but were stopped by open water. Undaunted, Lockwood determined to make yet another assault. His new plan, which he proposed with boyish enthusiasm to Brainard, contrasted strongly with the gloomy foreboding of Kislingbury and the counsel of retreat with which the doctor had assailed Greely. It would be an ambitious overland push with two sledges, both Eskimo drivers, and more dogs. The first sergeant caught in his diary Lockwood's yearning to round the tip of Greenland:

> With a new idea tucked beneath his heavy fur cap, his spirits were joyful and very soon his imagination had us standing on firm ice at the 84th parallel of latitude, gazing along the coast of Greenland as it tended away toward the southeast. In these enthusiastic moments the Lieut. is delightful and his spell irresistible.

The game was not to be played, however. When Lockwood returned to the station Greely ruled there would be no more assaults on the northern mark. He had already dispatched Sergeant George Rice, his best trail leader in the absence of Lockwood and Brainard, with a detail across Robeson Channel to bring back on the largest of the sledges the twenty-foot iceboat cached there in 1876 by Lieutenant Beaumont of the Royal Navy. Working like Trojans under the inspiration of Rice's contagious good humor, the men delivered the boat to Fort Conger without the slightest damage after a journey of thirty miles over rough ice. Rice had taken advantage of the wind by hoisting the sail and permitting the breeze to help his straining crew move the boat over the ice hummocks.

In early summer, tension in the camp mounted. When would the channel ice melt and the ship arrive? Not a man but was ready to have done with this arctic loneliness and sail for home. The July 4 holiday provided a slight psychological break, according to Brainard:

> We no longer have the imagination necessary to provide enter-tainment for these holiday occasions. Our lone ceremony was the unfurling of the flag. Lieut. Kislingbury caused a little excitement when he presented the only cigars remaining in Grinnell Land to be contended for in a shooting match. Ellis won. We had a game of baseball afterward with Lieut. Kislingbury and Sergt. Gardiner the captains. Gardiner's team won by a run; score, 32–31. The natives participated, causing much laughter.

In July the ill-feeling between Dr. Pavy and Greely moved swiftly to a crisis. Consistent with his habitual tardiness in making medical reports, the doctor had neglected his duties as expedition naturalist, even though he took pride in his knowledge in this area. The commander saw that he must take some action to prepare the collections for shipment, be it by steamship or in the small boats. He ordered Lockwood to relieve Dr. Pavy as natu-ralist and put the collections in order. To his great dismay, Lock-wood found that Pavy had jumbled stuffed birds, animal skins, pressed flowers, ancient Eskimo artifacts, and geological speci-mens in a hopeless mess, largely unlabeled and carelessly packed. Totally untrained for this new task, Lockwood did his loyal best, but a great deal of data had already been lost.

On the heels of this cause of friction, Dr. Pavy early in July informed Greely that with the expiration of his year's contract on July 20, he intended to terminate his official obligation to the U.S. Army. Although he did not intend to sign another contract when the present one should expire, he would, of course, extend his medical skill gratis for the common good until the party should return home—a matter of just a few weeks. In this he was being a good fellow, he insinuated, because he really was not legally required to render any service after his contract ran out. In reply, Greely wrote Dr. Pavy a strong objection, which wound up:

> Ship or no ship, retreat or no, you joined this expedition under a moral obligation to serve during its continuance, and you well know that the Surgeon General never would have sanctioned your contract had he surmised even the possibility of your quitting, under any circumstances, a command situated without the confines of the civilized world.

As the doctor persisted in his legalistic stand for the freedom to contract or not as he pleased, Greely ordered him to turn over all the expedition's medical stores to Lockwood—as well as his diary, in a sealed package addressed to the Chief Signal Officer. By diary, the commander specified, "will be understood all notes and observations written during this expedition, as well as memoranda of current events." Each member of the party had been informed in writing in 1881 that the journal books handed out to them were to be submitted to the C.S.O. on return. Personal letters and notes would, of course, not be turned in. No one should have been surprised, but Dr. Pavy nonetheless refused to obey Greely's order. On his final day under contract, July 19, he protested to Greely in writing:

> My journal, destitute of any official value, is a mere record of events, hypothesis, and reminscences, closely mingled with personal and intimate thoughts synthetized from detached notes and reduced into letters of an entirely private character, for the only use of my family.

Angrily Greely faced the Frenchman in the officers' room: "I give you until six o'clock to turn in your journal, or consider yourself under arrest."

"It is not necessary," protested Dr. Pavy. "I told you in this letter that—"

"Very well," rejoined Greely, "you remain in the service and I place you in arrest."

Pavy turned defiant: "I do not consider myself in the service, and I do not accept arrest!"

Greely bristled. "You do not accept arrest? Then call Sergeant Brainard!"

Pavy could hear determination in the commander's tone and retreated behind a metaphysical distinction in meanings: "Oh, I want to say that physically I may accept, yes. But morally I do not accept it. I will, of course, obey all rules and regulations, but if some accident happens I will not be responsible for it."

Thus the doctor might be physically present, in arrest, but the skill of the surgeon was not to be coerced. Let this high-school lieutenant ponder that!

Greely turned his back on Dr. Pavy and busied himself at his desk. Later in the day, through a messenger, he served a formal charge on the doctor for disobedience of orders. The specifications: that Dr. Pavy twice refused to hand over his sealed diary to Lieutenant Lockwood and that he refused to accept arrest until the commander called a guard to enforce it. Greely's stiff note ended ominously:

> The legal results of this action prevent the termination of your service with this day as contemplated by you, but retain you in the Army awaiting trial by general court-martial.

In the contest of wills and legal technicalities, the *diplomé* of the University of Paris had met his match in the self-educated graduate of Brown High School, Newburyport.

Back in 1881 it had been clearly understood between Greely and General Hazen that if a ship should not reach Fort Conger in the summer of 1883, the party should make its way by launch and small boats to a rendezvous at Smith Sound. As it looked now, a ship might still come through to them, but Greely nevertheless put the party to preparation for the retreat by boat. The meteorological records, fruit of two years' observations, were sealed in watertight tin boxes, along with the instruments which were to be checked for accuracy in Washington. Food, fuel, tools, tents, and other accessories were packed and methodically moved down to the boats. While lookouts kept a sharp watch for a ship, day after day passed with nothing new on the horizon. This summer, as in the preceding one, the channel would be partly free from ice for an hour or more, then choked with floating white at the whim of wind and tide. It was indeed a formidable route, Kennedy Channel. As summer wore on the men began to comprehend that this was its normal aspect and that the conditions in 1881 had been exceptional. On July 28 Greely posted a general order setting a deadline for action:

> In case of the non-arrival of a vessel by August 9, this station will be abandoned and a retreat southward by boats to Littleton Island will be attempted. Sixteen pounds of personal baggage will be allowed each officer and eight pounds to each man.

On August 4 the floating ice at the entrance to Lady Franklin Bay appeared fairly open; water holes and small lanes marked the entire surface. But on Sunday, August 5, Greely returned from Cairn Hill, northeast of the station, with the disquieting news that Kennedy Channel was again choked—no water in sight. The pack ice, he said, was evidently moving north with the tide. The barrier remained on the 6th and 7th, but on the 8th an opportune high southerly wind sprang up about 2 A.M. and continued to blow all day, at times reaching twenty-mile velocity. By the evening hours the lead in the floating ice near the entry of Lady Franklin Bay had increased to a mile in width. Now it looked as if they could safely embark.

On the morning of August 9 most of the party moved to Dutch Island on foot, the boats ready in the water with their full loads aboard. Sergeant Edward Israel, the astronomer, remained at the post to take final observations, begun there exactly two years before. Brainard was securing the supplies left behind and closing up the house, and Long was cooking dinner against the possibility that the party might be forced to return. At 2:30 P.M. Brainard, watching through his spyglass, saw Greely signal the three to follow. Israel swiftly boxed the precious chronometers for the journey. Long gulped several mouthfuls, filled a food container to take to his comrades, then closed the stove dampers, leaving the half-prepared dinner simmering on the stove. Breakfast dishes lay scattered, unwashed, on the mess tables; bunks remained just as the men had left them when they crawled that morning from their blankets.

A final sad duty for the three men was to overturn several barrels of seal blubber, pork, and hard bread for the Eskimo dogs and puppies. All the men hated abandoning their faithful sledge-dogs, but it was a case of necessity. Should they find their retreat by boat blocked and be forced to return to Fort Conger, the dogs would prove invaluable in a later attempt to reach Smith Sound by sledge. But should the party fight its way to safety in the south, these animals must revert to a fully wild state or starve.

As the growling dogs gorged themselves on the feast suddenly spilled out for them, Brainard's hammer drove home nails securing the door to the big house. With the last of his ringing blows a strange quiet descended on Fort Conger, abandoned now to the arctic wilderness—to wind, snow, and solitude.

IN SEPTEMBER 1882, Henrietta Greely was in California with her two daughters when General Hazen's terse wire arrived:

> Failed to reach Lady Franklin Bay. Vessel returned safely.
> *Hazen*

Beebe's failure in the *Neptune* deeply disappointed Henrietta, but because she knew the expedition was equipped for three years, and that the men were engaged in scientific work at Fort Conger, not challenging the mysteries of the North Pole, she did not at first feel great concern over their safety.

In the following months, while Henrietta often reached out in thought and prayer toward her husband, she was sufficiently practical to lend the Divine Power a helping hand. From the day

Beebe's failure was known, she was in regular correspondence with General Hazen and other Signal Corps officers, as well as with General and Mrs. Lockwood, parents of Lieutenant James B. Lockwood, at their home in Washington—quietly, determinedly lobbying for a more carefully planned relief mission to be sent the following summer. During these weeks she read deeply in the arctic writings of George Kennan, veteran traveler of the Siberian Arctic, in the reports of Drs. Kane and Hayes, and other volumes on which her husband had founded his own knowledge of the North, so that she might be better equipped to make practical suggestions to the men who made the decisions in Washington. Of the sex too gentle to voyage to the Arctic, she nevertheless absorbed more knowledge of it than most of the officials responsible for her husband's safety.

In their exchanges, Mrs. Lockwood gave way to more emotion over the absence of her son than did Henrietta over her separation from her husband. It was as though Mrs. Lockwood, the mature wife of a general and mother of an experienced junior officer, leaned upon the younger Henrietta for strength. Indeed, to her family and the host of friends who sent her messages of sympathy and moral support, Henrietta seemed the model military wife, radiating confidence, stoically calm as she knew that her husband was living with danger in the frozen Arctic. Doubtless she felt a certain responsibility for all the families, as wife of the expedition commander. But Henrietta confessed in a letter to Mrs. Lockwood that her outward appearance was in part a mask worn for duty's sake:

> I have always been able to simulate calmness and while this probably gives me the credit among outsiders of not feeling very deeply, it at all events prevents my making those about me or in communication with me unhappy, on my account.

To Henrietta the older woman poured out her mother's worry —and her faith:

> You are young, and perhaps naturally more buoyant than one of my age. I hope you are. My dear boy is ever in my thoughts— in the darkness and in the light—when the cold wind blows and

when it is calm. But I know that you remember as I try to, that there is One whose watchfulness never slumbers nor sleeps, Who can do much more than we ever can for those we love. Let us try to put our trust in Him.

Henrietta Greely and General Lockwood soon resolved that the *Proteus* and Captain Pike, having proved themselves in 1881, were the ship and master they should obtain for the summer of 1883. Their spirits soared when the friendly interest shown in the mission by Secretary of the Navy William E. Chandler brought the offer of a naval escort vessel, the *Yantic*, to accompany the relief ship. In place of the obviously incompetent office-man Beebe, Hazen informed them in January, a thirty-year-old West Pointer with Signal Corps experience, Lieutenant Ernest A. Garlington, would head the next party. The general described his choice to Henrietta as "a man I would send above all others in the Army—sober, persistent and able. I am confident everything will go right." Late in the spring Hazen went to St. John's himself to pin down the details with the firm of I. & W. Stewart, owners of the *Proteus*. It seemed to Henrietta and the Lockwoods that every possible step was now being taken to bring their men safely home.

Secretary of War Lincoln was more interested in the success of the relief mission than he had been the previous year, but for a different reason than Henrietta's. Even in his absence this fellow Greely had given him no peace. Lincoln was annoyed at the adverse publicity his department had received from the failure of the *Neptune* mission. And he was forever being badgered by the press over his department's failure to locate that thief Howgate, who had escaped from custody not long after his arrest and was still at large. Howgate had asked permission, as an officer and gentleman, to pack some of his clothing at his Washington home, and while his guard waited in the front room the deposed disbursing officer had skipped out the back and disappeared. Lincoln had hired the Pinkerton Detective Agency to track Howgate down, but despite its efforts the man continued to elude the law, to the Secretary's annoyance. To him all this business of Howgate,

Greely, and the *Neptune* was one distasteful mess. He longed to wind up this costly, pseudoscientific wild goose chase into nowhere, wished on him by a lame-duck Congress, and get back to his main concerns of running the Army and subduing the Indians. His orders were: Get to Greely and bring him back!

The presence of the naval escort *Yantic,* skippered by Commander Frank Wildes, would enable the *Proteus* to take greater risks than if she were alone. Not heavily sheathed for bucking the pack, the *Yantic* could go up to the danger zone, while the sealer could continue into the ice. The *Yantic* would serve as a supply carrier, message ship and, if need be, a rescue vessel.

"On every hand I hear such praise bestowed upon you that I feel the relief of my husband's party is in very earnest hands," wrote Henrietta to Lieutenant Garlington early in June as he prepared to sail. Garlington had every reason to feel confident, having the pick of the St. John's sealing vessels under the command of the veteran skipper who had brought her unscathed to Lady Franklin Bay and return two years before. His confidence rose even higher when Navy Lieutenant John C. Colwell of the *Yantic* prevailed upon his superiors to shift him to the *Proteus* for the northern cruise. The move came as an impulse on Colwell's part, but was most welcome to Garlington, who was completely innocent of seamanship. Should the two vessels separate in the northern waters, an experienced American sailor under military discipline would now be at his side as an advisor. Surely, last year's ice in Smith Sound must have been exceptional. This time, as she had back in 1881, the *Proteus* would make the run to Lady Franklin Bay without great difficulty.

From St. John's Garlington wrote Henrietta:

> You may rest assured, Madame, that every effort possible will be made to reach Fort Conger with the *Proteus* and enable Mr. Greely to come out this season. Capt. Pike has a very favorable view of the probability of reaching Lady Franklin Bay with his ship, and I am sure will contribute all his energy to that end. If the ship does not get through to him, I most assuredly will by means of sledges. You may feel perfectly secure that if it be

within the reach of possibility he will have relief. . . . I sincerely trust that you will have the happiness of seeing Mr. Greely back safe and well before the coming of another winter.

It was with such resolve in all hearts, beneath a beautiful summer sky, that the *Proteus* and *Yantic* under steam and sail cleared St. John's harbor at four o'clock on the afternoon of June 29, bound for Godhavn, Greenland, and then Lady Franklin Bay. Though her primary mission was to bring Greely and his party home, the *Proteus* carried supplies to last them through another winter at the Cape Sabine rendezvous point should ice conditions prevent their meeting before the ships would be forced to leave the ice zone. Also aboard were mail sacks bulging with packages and letters from the party's loved ones at home. And Garlington took along a magnificent Newfoundland dog, Rover, which he had bought in St. John's.

The ships touched at Godhavn, where Garlington purchased winter skin garments against the bare possibility, as he saw it, of the need to resort to sledges for a link-up with Greely. Fog rolled in and floating ice was encountered frequently as the ships moved up the Greenland coast. At Upernavik Commander Wildes discovered that he had to hold his vessel there for a few days to make repairs to the *Yantic*'s ailing boilers. He arranged with Garlington to follow the *Proteus* to Littleton Island as soon as repairs and ice conditions would permit.

The sealer moved cautiously ahead, her pace slowing as the ice became more dense in Melville Bay. Backtracking and zigzagging in his search for open leads in the pack, Pike managed to inch his ship around Cape York, the corner point of the waterway north to Smith Sound. By midafternoon of July 21 the *Proteus,* now clear of ice, reached the Carey Islands, which stand as a sentinel 125 miles below Smith Sound. The Careys were the most northerly point commonly touched by sealers plying these waters. Here Garlington and Colwell found that the record left in the cairn by Lockwood in 1881 had not been disturbed. They copied it, left an account of their own visit, and by 7:30 P.M. the *Proteus* was sailing north once more with no ice in sight. So excited had Garlington become at the prospect of an ice-free run that as the ship poked her prow around Cape Alexander to enter Pandora Harbor on the Greenland shore of Smith Sound, he wrote an enthusiastic message to be placed in a cairn for Commander Wildes:

> No ice met between Carey Island and this point, and none to be seen to the north from the crow's nest with the aid of a powerful telescope. Weather perfect; if it continues I will go directly north and not stop at Littleton Island to leave a record, for it takes but a very short time to change the aspect in these regions.

The final paragraph of General Hazen's instructions to Garlington had emphasized speed:

> Nothing in the northward movement must be allowed to retard the progress of the *Proteus*. It is of the utmost importance that she take advantage of every lead to get to Lady Franklin Bay.

At 9:45 A.M. on July 22 the *Proteus* steamed slowly past Littleton Island without halting. The coal pile left there by Beebe could be easily discerned, apparently undisturbed. The lookout in the crow's nest called out the all-clear. Yet by ten-thirty, some ten miles northwest a warning cry rang out from the foremast:

"Ice dead ahead!" By eleven-thirty the *Proteus* lay longside an unbroken front of ice that barred her from further passage north. Without hesitating, Garlington ordered a course west across the sound to Cape Sabine on the Ellesmere side.

In midafternoon the ship rounded the cape and pulled close to shore at Payer Harbor, an indentation near the tip of Cape Sabine. A quick inspection of the cache Beebe had left before his hurried flight convinced Garlington that most of the stores were still in good condition. Visiting bears had done minor damage to the whaleboat and shredded a tarpaulin to get at some of the food, but this was all.

While the damage to the boat and supply pile was being set right, Garlington noticed that the tide in Buchanan Strait, the body of water immediately to the north, seemed to have turned, with a loosening of the ice. Hastily summoning his men to finish and return to the ship, Garlington hurried back to the *Proteus* and banged on the door of the master's cabin, where Pike lay asleep.

When the ship's captain, half awake, poked his head from the cabin door to ask what Garlington wanted, the young lieutenant insisted that they should take advantage of the open water ahead. Just a shift in the floating ice caused by the tide, Pike protested; it would not last. It was still too early in the season to push through to the north, as he had already seen from the conditions today. Garlington grew more insistent.

Pike knew that nothing in the contract between the owners of the *Proteus* and General Hazen covered the possibility of disagreement between him and this cavalry lieutenant, who had been a kid playing marbles when the Newfoundland Board of Trade gave Pike his master's license. He could not be required to take his ship farther north than Lady Franklin Bay—that was specified in the contract. It provided further that if he and Garlington should agree, after consultation, that ice conditions, lateness of the season, or any other unsurmountable obstacle made it impracticable to reach Lady Franklin Bay, he might turn her home from Smith Sound, but no earlier than September 1. But in a situation where his good seaman's sense, his loyalty to the owners, and his concern for the lives of his crew (which included his own son) might tell him "No," while the landlubber might shout "Sail on!" —on this the contract was silent.

Against his better judgment, Captain Pike ordered the vessel turned north into the broken, swiftly churning ice of Buchanan Strait, setting her course for Cape Albert. The rugged headland loomed some thirty miles ahead in the pinkish pearl of the low northern sun. Weaving his ship among the floes, Pike managed to butt her out of packs three times during the evening and night hours of July 22–23. In the morning the ice closed in, some four miles off Cape Albert, and checked any progress for two hours. She emerged in the early afternoon, then was once more caught in a mighty vise—on one side floes reaching solidly out from the

Proteus First Stopped by Ice.

Ice Foot and Pressed-up Ice, Cape Murcheson, Robeson Channel. Engraving from a photograph taken midwinter, 1881–1882.

cape and on the other the large pans surging into the strait on the incoming tide.

At 2:45 P.M. the ship was brought to a dead halt within 400 yards of open water; movement in any direction was impossible. Almost at once Pike was horrified to see the ice in front of and behind his ship begin to show signs of enormous pressure, as the irresistible force of the incoming floes ground their way into the fixed barrier of shore ice. Huge cakes of hard, blue ice eight to ten feet thick were tumbled on top of the grounded floe. Garlington realized, as did Pike, that the *Proteus* was in mortal peril.

To the veteran ice pilot, the squeezing of a ship was euphemistically known as a "nip." When a vessel was nipped hard in the ice, the fates alone determined whether she would survive or go down. No masterful plan of ship design, no possible maneuver on the captain's part could save her. Impelled by action of wind, tide, and current, the ice could crush her oak ribs, splinter her heavy cedar planking like matchwood, and rip her copper and iron sheathing as if it were tinfoil. Pike pondered his chances. Should the pressure of ice upon ice immediately ahead and astern somehow lead to a deadlock of forces, the *Proteus* might get through. But if the full force of the frozen mass continued to press inward on her hull, or if a ramming prow of hard ice backed by the momentum of countless tons penetrated her hold below waterline, there would be no saving her.

In a panic at the sudden turn of fortune, Garlington shouted to his men to bring their equipment and stores to the deck. Part of his group rushed to the forepeak to remove the supplies that had been destined for Greely's relief caches along the route north, while Garlington clambered down into the midships hold to supervise the removal of the main body of provisions. An hour's desperate work—and then a loud crunching sound of splintering wood. The starboard rail gave way under the force of piled-up ice alongside. At this point Colwell called down the main hatch to Garlington that the bulwarks had given way, but that he thought perhaps the ship might stay afloat.

"Get the boats ready!" Garlington shouted back. Even as he did so, he heard a grinding crash below. A huge prong of ice had driven through the ship's side into the starboard coal bunker. Water poured into the hold.

Garlington called to his sweating men to follow him topside, where he found the deck planking had already begun to buckle, the seams opening out as if the ship were going to split a hundred ways beneath his feet. The lieutenant set his little band to throwing provisions overside as rapidly as possible, while Colwell tried to free the boats from their balky davits. Meanwhile, Garlington could see that the crewmen, not concerned with saving anything for Greely, were occupied with their personal duffle, preparing themselves and their own ship's boats for the emergency. Soldiers and crewmen rushed to salvage what they could from the deck— boxes, blankets, clothing, canned goods. Everything was dumped indiscriminately over the rail, and much of it disappeared into the dark water beside the ship.

In the agonizing hour during which they were acting out the final scene in this fiasco of an arctic rescue, Garlington and Colwell could imagine with horror and shame the fate that awaited Greely. The safety of his party, represented by the *Proteus,* was gone. Her cargo of food stores, the building materials that might have reinforced their shelter, the coal that might have heated them through the winter, all were settling down beneath an ice-covered sea.

Yet who among them could tell whether Greely, or the world, would ever know their fate? Though their mission had been to relieve the expedition at Lady Franklin Bay, they now wondered whether they could even save themselves.

4 ADRIFT

LAUNCHED AT Dundee, Scotland, in 1874, the *Proteus* had been built to last a half-century or more in the sealing trade. In her eighth season she had dared the northern ice and beaten it; now, in her tenth, the ice was taking revenge. At 6:50 P.M. a series of sickening shudders ran through her. The men still aboard clambered down the sides to safety. Colwell was the last to leave.

As the *Proteus* settled lower into the water on an even keel, Garlington, Colwell, and their men frantically tried to retrieve every box of supplies in danger of being carried under. Then they could only stand by to watch. At 7:15 P.M. the vessel slowly went down, a huge cloud of steam pouring from her stack, the waves rolling over her deck, her three proud masts standing straight to the end.

Almost as if acting on orders, the twenty-two men of Captain Pike's crew and the fifteen in Garlington's party behaved like two entirely separate commands. They had even left the ship over opposite rails, each group tossing gear down to their own friends on the ice below, and now they found themselves separated by a lead of water strewn with debris from the vanished ship. Under British maritime law the *Proteus* seamen at this point owed no duty to master or shipowners, since their contract and wages had gone down with the vessel. The army party, however, had a leader with authority and a mission to save everything possible for Greely.

Getting ashore with their equipment and stores was obviously the first concern of all thirty-seven men. Five small boats had been saved from the wreck—three belonging to the *Proteus* and two whaleboats brought north by Garlington. While between the two parties the number of men per boat was thus fairly even —seven being assigned to each of three craft and eight each to the two others, the civilian and military parties were by no means equal in ability to handle them. Pike's crew of Newfoundlanders had grown up around boats. The Americans, all landlubbers but Colwell, scarcely knew how to fit an oar into a rowlock.

Quickly sizing up the situation, Colwell, with Pike's help, persuaded four *Proteus* crewmen to help him ferry one whaleboat full of stores to the nearest land, which lay due south. There, at a point three miles west of Cape Sabine facing Buchanan Strait, close to the cache that he and Garlington had put in order a scant thirty hours before, Colwell stacked the boatload, hastily estimating the lot at 500 individual rations—largely hard bread and bacon, with some tea, canned goods, tobacco, lemons, and a few sleeping bags. He covered the pile with a tent fly, weighted it down with rocks, and left.

By 2 A.M. on the 24th, Colwell and his crew were back on the floe with the others. The chances for moving the entire party to solid ground had become more favorable since they had been borne closer to the tip of Cape Sabine by the ebbing tide. Should they wait, there was danger of being swept into Smith Sound and south into Baffin Bay. Mustering all their reserves of energy, the shipwrecked men worked their boats through the ice and in late morning touched shore at the rocky tip of the cape. The last boatload barely made it, for the current, picking up speed at the junction of Buchanan Strait and Smith Sound, carried off the last load of food boxes left on the floe. Regretfully the castaways watched them disappear amid the jumbled mass of ice gliding inexorably toward the open sea.

Exhausted, the men lay down on the rocks of Cape Sabine for what seemed their first rest in many hours. Fog had rolled in during the morning, followed by a chilling rain, and the end of this first day without warmth or shelter was thoroughly miserable for all. To add to the physical discomfort, Captain Pike contemplated with chagrin the loss of the fine vessel he had grown to love during the nine years he had been her skipper. Still, he had followed his orders. Not a man in St. John's could blame him for the disaster.

But for Garlington, who was responsible for more than a ship, there was no comfort in repose. What should he do, he asked himself in a torture of indecision. Should he camp here and wait? According to his 1881 orders, Greely was supposed to leave Lady Franklin Bay no later than September 1, in case a ship should not arrive, and proceed down the east coast of Grinnell Land and Ellesmere Land to Sabine. This meant that Greely, with the best of luck, might reach here six or seven weeks from now, possibly much later. If his own party should remain, thought Garlington, they could only pass on news of the wreck, which could be accomplished just as well by leaving a message. Further, anyone staying here would be eating into the few supplies they had saved.

Should he send a party up the coast to intercept Greely? Garlington dismissed the idea almost at once. A fool thing to attempt! Either by the shore route or by boat, they would never get through. Even if they did, the two parties might pass one another in a fog. At this point the confident words he had written to Mrs. Greely must have flooded back into Garlington's mind: "You may rest assured, Madame. . . . If the ship does not get through to him, I most assuredly will by means of sledges." The sledges were at the bottom of the strait, and all but one of the dogs had run off onto the ice, defying efforts at capture.

Garlington concluded that his only course was retreat to the *Yantic*. With good luck, he told himself, he should meet the tender along the Greenland shore as she moved up toward Littleton Island. And yet Wildes was a very cautious fellow. Garlington realized that he might not even risk the pack in Melville Bay. In order to meet the *Yantic* they might have to travel south almost to Upernavik, 500 miles. Should Wildes get through, Garlington could leave a big depot for Greely at Littleton Island and then the *Yantic* would return to St. John's for help, but should the *Yantic* not cross Melville Bay, the quicker they all got back to her the better.

The *Proteus* crew had their own stores and were in no mood to share them. A quick inventory of the army supplies showed only forty days' rations on hand for Garlington's party of fifteen. The lieutenant weighed the odds, thought about the cache already left for Greely, then decided he should take all his food supplies with him. After all, Greely might never come as far south as Sabine. The boats would be loaded heavily, true enough —but better safe than hungry in the Arctic.

The commander stripped his men's duffle down to one change of outer clothing plus two suits of underwear and gathered all the winter garments that could be assembled from the supply that his own men and the Newfoundlanders had picked up during the confused hours of the disaster. A large pile of buffalo overcoats, fur caps and gloves, arctic overshoes, uniform clothing, and underwear was cached for Greely in a crevasse in the rocks and covered with rubber blankets. On a tip of rock just offshore, Brevoort Island, Garlington raised a conspicuous marker and beneath it placed a record of the *Proteus'* fate and the location of the two caches. After phrasing his hopes for obtaining help in terms as optimistic as he could bring himself to write, Garlington concluded sadly:

> It is not within my power to express one tithe of my sorrow and regret at this fatal blow to my efforts to reach Lieutenant Greely. I will leave for the eastern shore just as soon as possible and endeavor to open communications.
>
> E. A. Garlington,
> 1st Lieut., 7th Cav., A.S.O., Commanding.

As soon as the little flotilla of five boats set out across Smith Sound on the afternoon of July 25 snow and rain set in, continuing throughout the night. In the dim light the boats were gripped by the swirling current and spun crazily apart from one another. Garlington's and Colwell's managed to reach a small cove near Littleton Island about midnight. After stopping at

Littleton Island to leave a second message in the coal pile, Garlington and Colwell pushed on to Pandora Harbor, where they
were happy to find Pike's three boats. So far so good; the Smith
Sound crossing, thank God, was behind them.

Relieved, the leaders of the two parties agreed on certain
measures for common safety—the shift of a few experienced
boatmen to the army boats and efforts to stick together afloat
while maintaining their separate authority and supplies while
camping ashore. Thereafter, although tempers sometimes flared
between the soldiers and civilians, the physical separation of the
two groups kept disputes to a minimum.

Moving cautiously down the coast toward Cape York, 250
miles from Littleton Island, the shipwrecked men played hide-
and-seek with ice and fog. High winds tossed the cockleshells
dangerously, wet snow stung the mariners' faces as they rowed
and sailed from island to headland, keeping on the lookout both
for the Yantic and for the Swedish steamer Sophia, which they
had been told in Upernavik was scheduled to cruise this coast in
August. At frequent stops Garlington left rewrites of his original
disaster message until they stretched out behind him like lonely
clues in a giant game of paper-chase.

By August 1 the boats were at Cape Parry. Twenty miles out
in the broad bay lay the Carey Islands, a message point arranged
with Commander Wildes. Garlington and Colwell considered the
choppy sea. Their heavily laden boats showed a scant eight to
ten inches of freeboard even in calm water. To venture so far
out would be too hazardous, they concluded. So it was that on
the afternoon of August 2, while the small boats were drawn up
at Saunders Island under a shroud of fog, the Yantic crept stealth-
ily past in the murk, some fifteen miles out, and touched at the
southeast Carey Island rendezvous they had bypassed. Had the
fog lifted for an hour, they could have signaled Wildes with
smoke or heliograph. But they never had the chance.

Not until the next afternoon, August 3, did one of Wildes' men,
hunting in the coal pile on Littleton Island, discover Garlington's message of July 26. The Proteus, it informed him, had gone

to the bottom. Garlington was retreating down the coast with his fourteen companions after having left 500 rations and some clothing for Greely.

For a few minutes Commander Wildes hesitated; Garlington gave no word of Pike and the *Proteus* crew. He stated only that his army party had all been saved. Across the channel Frank Wildes could see Cape Sabine plainly—just twenty-six miles away, according to the chart. The water was clear; he could reach it in three hours or less. Although Wildes' orders from the Navy Department directed him under no circumstances to go north of Littleton Island, he thought he should venture the few miles north of west to Sabine to make certain that the *Proteus* hands were not stranded there.

Just as Wildes was about to give the order to stand for Cape Sabine, one of his men came running to the bridge with a message from Pike's party found at Pandora Harbor, just south of Littleton Island. So Pike had made the Smith Sound passage after all! No need to cross to Cape Sabine now: the victims of the disaster were all moving south in their small boats under sail with an eight-day start.

As Wildes cleared Pandora Harbor his one intention was the rescue of his companions of the *Proteus,* who had left St. John's under his protection. His duty was to Garlington; reaching Greely was an affair of army logistics in which the Navy was not concerned. Futhermore, Garlington had not suggested by as much as one word in his message that Wildes should strip his ship's stores to do the job with which the *Proteus* had been charged. Leaving the waters of Smith Sound in her wake, the *Yantic* bore in her hold 7000 lbs. of bread, seven full tons of salt beef, pork, and other preserved meats, plus large supplies of other foods. Altogether some 50,000 individual rations had been carried into Smith Sound last summer and this—aboard the *Neptune,* the *Proteus* and the *Yantic.* A scant thousand had been left for Greely—just forty days' food supply for twenty-five men.

For a full week the *Yantic* cautiously poked her prow into bays and channels searching for the *Proteus* survivors. By August 10

Wildes could see that new ice was forming every night, and that his coal supply was running low. The time had come for him to bypass Cape York and run straight for Upernavik, across the long leg of the Melville Bay triangle. The small boats were doubtless skirting the coast, but he could no longer spend his days looking for them. He would wait for them at Upernavik as long as he dared. Wildes passed Cape York forty miles out in the bay, and in so doing again missed the object of his search. Had his course been diverted a few points to port, the reunion might have taken place that very afternoon near Cape York.

Reaching Upernavik August 12, Wildes held the *Yantic* there for ten days, during which he anxiously looked for sails on the northern horizon. By August 22 he realized that the short summer of this high latitude had come to an end. Knowing the autumn gales were likely to set in at any time and that the first one of any severity would put his ship on the rocks, Wildes left a message for Garlington at the settlement and turned south to Weigatt Strait, a sheltered haven between Disko Island and the mainland, where his black gang could fill his bunkers with coal mined from an exposed seam.

Meanwhile the victims of the *Proteus* sinking were working their way, one bitter, freezing mile after another, toward rescue. Storm and fog at times forced a layover of a day or two; at others, they snatched opportunity from wind and fog to run for many hours while the weather held. Backs had long since grown weary and hands were blistered from pulling on the leaden oars. Sleep was fitful in the hard boats and on the rocky shore. Clothes were soaked and throats sore. Bellies were tortured by ill-prepared food which was often wolfed down only to be heaved overside in fits of nausea.

Just east of Cape York, on August 16, the miserable group decided that Colwell should take one of the whaleboats and make a lone dash for help. Thanks to the Navy officer's skillful, daring seamanship, Colwell and his crew reached Upernavik in seven days, and hardly pausing for more than a meal and a quick nap, continued in chase of the *Yantic* down the coast past Proven and through Weigatt Strait. At Godhavn Wildes welcomed the hardy mariners aboard.

Colwell and his men had been thirty-nine days in the open, either in their small boat or camping ashore. They had covered 900 miles through one of the least familiar and most treacherous stretches of icy, foggy sea known to sailors. Yet, in spite of the hardships through which they had just passed, Wildes later reported to the Navy Department, Colwell and his crew of six "looked well and hearty, though somewhat thin and weather-beaten."

The trip back to Upernavik, some 275 miles north, required only a day and a half. There it was found that Pike and Garlington had pulled in, all hands safe, shortly after Colwell had left. The survivors were quickly taken aboard the *Yantic*, whose skipper considered September 2 already much too late in the year to tempt fate in Melville Bay, especially with a ship not built for work in the ice. Early next season a proper ice ship might be able to reach Smith Sound in three or four days from Upernavik. Now the only course was home. With Garlington's full assent, Commander Wildes put on steam for St. John's.

The trip was not a happy one for First Lieutenant Ernest A. Garlington. Reporting to Washington the loss of the *Proteus* and the failure of his mission was going to be a dreadful task. As he agonized over the wording of the telegram he would have to dispatch to General Hazen from St. John's, young Garlington could already sense the criticism that would be leveled at him for having so boldly volunteered to reach Greely and having so miserably failed.

WHEN THEY turned their backs on Fort Conger on the the afternoon of August 9, the men of the Lady Franklin Bay Expedition for the first time in two years were completely out of their element. Private Schneider, it is true, had been an ordinary seaman before joining the Army, and Rice had a certain familiarity with boats from his boyhood in Sydney, Cape Breton Island.

Launch *Lady Greely* in Discovery Harbor, August 1883.

A Wonderful Lead Through a Split Floeberg.

Lieutenant Lockwood had done a bit of sailing on the Chesapeake Bay when his father had been an instructor at Annapolis. But none of them, not even Lieutenant Greely, knew how to pilot a boat in the ice.

The steam launch *Lady Greely* was the lead vessel. Shaped like a whaleboat, strongly built with oak frame and double cedar planking, she was powered with a Herreshoff condensing engine. By some incredible blunder at the Washington Navy Yard, the launch had first been equipped with a boiler that could use only fresh water, but Greely had had this stupidity rectified before she was hoisted aboard the *Proteus* in 1881. Forward there was a small engine compartment. A canvas weather cover extended over the cockpit. The *Lady Greely* was twenty-eight feet long, had a seven-foot, eight-inch beam, and with her heavy load of coal, supplies, and men drew close to five feet of water. She was fitted with three keels designed to act as runners when she was dragged on the ice. Since she weighed close to ten tons empty, sledging her was completely out of the question.

The launch chugged steadily ahead, consuming coal at a tremendous rate as she towed the three smaller boats in a string. In the bow of each a man sat by the painter ready to cast loose at the first sign of danger. First among them was the *Narwhal,* a whaleboat built in New Bedford to Greely's order. Then followed the English jolly-boat *Valorous,* which the expedition had picked up in 1881, just north of Cape Hawks, enroute to Fort Conger. Last came a small Whitehall boat filled with supplies and requiring for crew only one or two men.

Crossing Lady Franklin Bay southeast to Cape Baird, the boats wove their way among the floating pans, the men often using the oars to push away from the ice. By midnight, when they had made camp on the far shore, they felt a moderate degree of confidence at their auspicious start. Here they picked up the English iceboat *Beaumont,* which Greely had cached weeks earlier against this day of need, and Sergeant Connell was put in command of her. Greely, with the two other officers and Dr. Pavy, traveled in the launch, Cross working the engine and Private Julius Frederick acting as fireman. A five-foot-two roly-poly of deadly earnest disposition, Frederick shared with Long the distinction of being the best cook at Fort Conger, as well as chief leatherworker. Greely knew him as conscientious almost to a fault. Brainard commanded the *Narwhal* and Rice steered the *Valorous*.

At Fort Conger Greely had relied on his key subordinates to carry out duties for which they were especially trained, but here in the ice he could not delegate. He knew the burden both of his responsibility and his ignorance of how best to proceed. The ice of Kennedy Channel was in constant motion and in every variation in the wind and ripping of the currents lurked danger for the boats. Small wonder, then, that the raw edges of Greely's nervous system were exposed, that the officer who at Conger had been the picture of self-confidence and efficiency should appear now to his command in a far less admirable light. They had come to rely on him to answer almost every question and now discovered that he no longer had the answers. He was feeling his way, and the men knew it.

As the party was preparing to leave Cape Baird, Greely inexplicably flared up at Brainard over a minor infraction of his orders on launching the boats from shore—then as quickly calmed down.

"We were all surprised by his extensive vocabulary and the fluent and forceful manner in which he delivered himself," Brainard noted that evening in his journal, dismissing the incident. But other diarists and whisperers in small groups were less understanding of their overwrought commander, as their fear of the journey mounted and their bones ached from having slept away from the soft bunks of the abandoned fort. Their view was short, their desires elemental. They could, at this moment, only focus on their discomfort.

The exhausted party was resting on shore the third morning out from Fort Conger when a sudden cry of alarm roused them from their sleeping bags. The launch, tied to a large grounded floeberg at high tide, had been left stranded under serious strain as the tide ebbed during the early morning hours. All hands were quickly summoned to lighten the craft and refloat her. Cross, the engineer, was supposed to have paid attention to her during the night and ease her off by degrees, but he was not in sight.

"Cross!" Greely shouted toward the engine room, where the man made his bed. "Come out here!"

There was a sound of stirring, then a grunt. Greely raised his voice and cried through the canvas topping:

"Cross, God damn your soul! Come out here so I can see you when I want you!"

The bearded engineer staggered out into the cockpit—dead drunk, mumbling that he hadn't known he was wanted.

Greely seethed with anger that this man should imperil the lives of the whole party by drinking stolen alcohol and nearly wrecking the launch. Now, on top of it, insolence!

"Shut up, or I'll put a bullet through you!" he roared. All eyes went to Greely's belt, where he carried a revolver.

Yet even in his rage the commander knew he was bluffing. Cross knew more about handling the engine than any of them. He would have to pull the fellow along with patience and somehow keep an eagle eye on him and the alcohol.

On the 13th the party found their passage down Kennedy Channel blocked by a huge floeberg running a mile out from shore, but on closer examination they discovered it had grounded and split, leaving a narrow cleft scarcely twelve feet wide and more than a hundred yards in length. As the boats passed through the center of the weird, imposing mass of blue-green ice, which extended some fifty feet above them leaving only a bright ribbon of sky overhead, not a man was left unawed by its cold grandeur. Greely estimated that it had probably formed through a thousand years of arctic snow, accumulating flake by flake, until it had attained such weight and thickness that it was transformed to ice. Through the ages this huge bulk must have slowly moved seaward. Broken from its parent mass, it had floated southward from the Polar Sea until it had become stranded here.

Chafing under the restrictions of his anomalous position—an

officer in social rank yet on this voyage just a supernumerary without any authority—Lieutenant Kislingbury could not restrain himself from proffering advice to Greely on how to navigate. Most of his counsel was caution—stick to the shore. The commander listened coldly and disregarded what he heard.

Rising to the occasion like a giant was Rice, who quickly proved the inspiration of the entire party. Standing on the slippery stern of the *Valorous,* the Canadian-born photographer seemed to have a nose for leads in the ice like that of a hunting dog searching out wildfowl. In the first six days Rice tumbled overboard four times from his tricky perch, yet he took it all with laughter. Willing hands pulled him aboard, and after squeezing the water from his drooping mustache he would strip off his soaked clothing, crack a joke about taking more baths than the rest of the men combined, then patch together a new outfit from his own bundle plus borrowed clothes. His wet garments were strung over the launch boiler to dry, in readiness for his next plunge.

Rice was a very foolish man, Kislingbury told himself, but terribly brave, and he excited in the officer's breast a fierce admiration which Kislingbury confided to his journal:

> I have a pair of extra footgear and some extra drawers, and I gladly helped him out by letting him use them. I would willingly strip myself and crawl into my sleeping bag than to have him do so because he is without doubt the most indispensable man we have.

Greely's patience with Cross came to an abrupt end on the morning of August 15, when Brainard reported finding the engineer drunk again aboard the launch. The commander at once ordered Cross transferred to Rice's boat crew, put Private Frederick in charge of the engine, and told him he was not to let the irresponsible Cross even approach the engine again.

Brainard had become concerned over Greely's distraught frame of mind, in which his irritations with the launch—the least maneuverable of their craft—played a central part. Were it not that they might need to sail as far as the Carey Islands, Greely had suggested once, he might abandon the launch, pull the smaller boats up on the ice pack in midchannel, and try to float with the southerly current down the strait. He had even hinted that had they taken such a step earlier they might already have passed Cape Lawrence and reached the Kane Basin. To Brainard this idea seemed sheer madness.

On the day of Cross' demotion, Brainard was approached with what he described years later as "a strange proposition." Exactly who spoke to him will never be known, but the proposal was made on behalf of Kislingbury, Pavy, and Rice. Lieutenant Greely, he was told, had obviously slipped over the verge of sanity and was no longer normal. Surely Brainard had heard his wild, profane language these last few days? And Greely's idea of floating south on the pack—did not Brainard agree that it was unsound? And now, should the lives of all be risked by a commander who had gone crazy?

Before Brainard committed himself, the proposition unfolded: Dr. Pavy would submit Lieutenant Greely to a medical examination and render a formal opinion that he was out of his mind. The command would then go to Lieutenant Kislingbury, the second-ranking man. If Brainard would join, among the four they could definitely command the allegiance of all the enlisted men. Lieutenant Lockwood would have to accede to their plans or be placed under arrest. With Kislingbury in command, the party could make a safe return to Fort Conger, where there were adequate supplies to pass the winter and fresh meat was abundant. Then in the spring they could easily sledge down the coast on firm ice. Did not such a plan make sense?

As he considered the proposal, Brainard knew that these men were well aware of his close ties to both Greely and Lockwood, yet they came to him. As top sergeant his ascendancy over the enlisted men made him the key to their entire scheme. Just what kind of men were these schemers?

Take George Rice, the bluff, hearty, good fellow whose winning personality made him the most popular man of the expedition. In the barracks he was the life of the party, the keenest wit, friendliest of the lot. Out on the trail he was all man—tough, resourceful, persevering, intelligent, and willing to do the work of two other men. Now, in the boats, he had risen to new heights as an ice pilot.

Yet, as Brainard only partially realized, Rice was not really a soldier. Putting on the U.S. Army uniform had been a pro forma act for Rice back in 1881 when he signed up for the expedition. His ambition was to make photographic history—to be the first man to bring back a set of negatives showing the arctic regions as they really were. He was a civilian at heart, an individualist. Though Brainard was unaware of it at the time, it was in keeping with his character that George Rice considered it a lark, not a breach of discipline, when he and Dr. Pavy in the early days at Fort Conger had discovered and then hidden a can of rum left by the Nares expedition in 1876. ("I suggested to the Doctor that he should cache the rum for our own use and not report it—and this was done," Rice had scribbled in his diary.)

Though he shared a number of Rice's qualities of solid dependability, David Legge Brainard was, in contrast, a soldier from the top of his head to the tip of his boots. Fresh from the farm in Herkimer County, New York, with the light gloss of one year in normal school, Brainard at nineteen had journeyed to Philadelphia for the Centennial Expedition of 1876. In New York City on the way home he found to his dismay that he had lost the ten-dollar bill he thought was tucked safely in his pocket. A diligent search failed to turn up the money and Brainard's pride would not allow him to go home and face his father with such a serious loss. On an impulse he hopped the ferry to Governor's Island in New York harbor and signed up in the Army. As he changed into his first ill-fitting uniform, the new recruit found the missing bill stuffed tightly into the corner of his trousers pocket. But he was now in the Army, and there was nothing he could do about it except try to make good.

During five years' cavalry service in the West, Brainard showed

Sergeant David L. Brainard.

Sea Face of Ice Foot at Distant Cape.

himself the model soldier. As handsome as the all-American boy on the recruiting poster, strong, keen at his work, Brainard believed firmly in obeying orders without quibble. He was soon promoted to sergeant. As ranking non-com of the Lady Franklin Bay Expedition, as well as on the trail with Lockwood to their Farthest North, Brainard had proved himself, as Greely once recorded in his journal, "my mainstay in many things." The commander had told Brainard that on their return to the United States he would push him for an officer's commission. And while the popular, spirited Rice would have been elected president of an enlisted men's club by acclamation, had one been organized, Brainard would have been voted the man most likely to succeed in the Army.

So it was as a soldier that Brainard considered the character of the men who approached him. Lieutenant Kislingbury, he knew, had no legal or moral right to assume the leadership. If Lieutenant Greely were genuinely out of his mind—and Brainard wasn't yet convinced of this—then Lieutenant Lockwood should be the first one consulted, and he should become the commander. Certainly not Kislingbury. There was something disturbing about this man. Brainard doubted that Kislingbury could ever win the enlisted men's full confidence, no matter how much he chummed with them. Kislingbury, he recalled, had got off on the wrong foot at the very start by his peculiar way of inspecting the men on the trip north aboard the *Proteus*. Normally, shipboard inspection was limited to the officer's walking through the quarters to examine bunks and equipment. But Kislingbury had fallen them in line on deck, unbuttoned their coats, vests, and shirts and, most strangely, peered down their trousers. Indignant, resentful, several of the men had muttered that an inspection like this was not customary in any branch of the service. If they were puzzled over what it signified, they had been made to feel most uneasy. Some later looked back on the experience as only the first of many such oddities on Kislingbury's part. Brainard felt sure he would never win the allegiance of the whole party in opposition to Lieutenant Greely.

Now, what about Dr. Pavy? To Brainard there had always
been something a bit mysterious about the doctor. His background had strange gaps, which even Lieutenant Lockwood had
not been able to fill in for him from what he could learn around
the officers' dining table. Brainard had heard that Dr. Pavy was
born in 1844 of Creole parents in New Orleans, and that he had
left the U.S. for France as a child. French had become his tongue,
his English was poor. He had studied medicine in Paris, had become interested in arctic exploration, and was scheduled to go
on the Gustave Lambert polar expedition until this was prevented by the outbreak of the Franco-Prussian War in 1870.

Dr. Pavy spoke often of his part in the war and in the *franc-
tireur* resistance to the Prussians after the French defeat. On the
other hand he never mentioned his liaison with Alice Loiseau,
who bore his daughter in 1869. It was not known among these
men that he had left her penniless three years later when he sailed
for the United States after promising faithfully to send support
for the child. Still pursuing his dream of arctic exploration, the
doctor had gone to San Francisco to promote a venture to reach
the Polar Sea through the Bering Strait; the plan had fallen
through on the death of its principal financial backer. No one on
the Lady Franklin Bay Expedition knew the rest of Pavy's story;
that embittered by the second shattering of his dreams, he had
turned into a misanthrope. For a period he had lived by himself,
friendless and unkempt, on the banks of the Mississippi near
Liberty, Missouri, earning what he could by catching fish, feeding his ego on the conviction that he was superior to other men.
A chance meeting with two clergymen strolling by the river led
to Pavy's being taken in and "saved" by one of them. Before
long, Pavy was wearing new clothes, completing his medical
studies at the minister's expense, and living in his home. The
minister's impressionable, romantic daughter, Lilla Mae Stone,
proved an easy conquest for the Frenchman, whom she worshiped
almost as a demigod with his grand Parisian air and displays of
erudition. But even after their marriage, there remained, still
gnawing within Pavy's breast, the ambition to explore the Arctic.

So it was quite natural that when Captain Henry Howgate was preaching the doctrine of arctic colonization, Pavy should have called attention to his considerable knowledge of the North, promoting himself by writing articles on exploration for the *St. Louis Globe-Democrat*, which Lilla Mae Pavy translated from the French. In 1880 he had left her to sail for Greenland aboard the *Gulnare* with Henry Clay. During his year there he had apparently put his time to good use in studying Eskimo life and collecting natural history specimens.

Brainard recognized that Pavy was skilled in his proper field, medicine, but doubted his ability elsewhere. His overweening ambition to be the leader, or the power behind a nominal leader, were Kislingbury to take over from Greely, had now pushed him to the extreme of mutiny.

For this was what Kislingbury and Pavy were proposing, Brainard realized—open mutiny spawned of discontent and jealousy. Playing cleverly on Rice by exaggerating Greely's ill-tempered outbursts, flattering him with attention, Pavy and Kislingbury had taken Rice in. But it was Brainard's plain soldier's duty to support Lieutenant Greely—and Lieutenant Lockwood after him, should it come to that. No, said Brainard, he would not support their plan, which he could only see as a breakdown in discipline, putting the party in even greater danger than it was now.

From the instant Brainard shook his head, Dr. Pavy and Kislingbury must have realized their plan was doomed. With the first sergeant they were sure they could win over the men and, if necessary, physically overcome Lockwood. Greely and Lockwood both carried revolvers in their belts, but there were four rifles, two shotguns, and ammunition in the boats. Without Brainard, however, an attempt would lead to a gunfight on the ice, with their opponents now forewarned. No man could say what its outcome might be.

The plot fell apart. Though Brainard feared the two dissident officers would not at once give up their idea, he hesitated to speak of it to Greely. That very evening, in fact, Brainard recorded in his diary his doubts of the wisdom of this journey they had undertaken:

> What a fine spring retreat could be made from Ft. Conger with sledges & how much less our sufferings would be compared with what they are now and will be one or two weeks from now.

And a few days later:

> Suppose the ship did not succeed in passing through the Melville Bay pack? What would this party of poor shivering wretches do on our arrival at Littleton Island at the beginning of winter with nothing to subsist on, when by a retreat judiciously conducted we could defy cold, hunger and the specter of death which dogs the footsteps of the unwary traveler in the Arctic?

By August 21, however, the flotilla had passed the halfway mark between Fort Conger and Cape Sabine, which in a straight line lay some 225 miles apart. Now, having skirted Cape Lawrence, they had put about 115 miles behind them, although they had journeyed perhaps twice that many to make this gain. Brainard saw that they could only push on:

> We have crossed the Rubicon and to turn back now is out of the question. We must advance, although I am fearful it will result in another Franklin disaster. . . . We are watching anxiously for a ship, our only salvation.

The fourth week of August found the going a little easier. Fuel and supplies had held up well, and were being augmented by provisions taken from Greely's deposits of 1881 and caches left earlier by the English. On August 26 the English cache at Cape Hawks, halfway down the shore of Kane Basin, yielded 168 pounds of dried potatoes, three gallons of rum, and one keg of onion pickles. The bread casks when opened revealed a mass of green, slimy mold, from which Greely directed that everything edible be selected.

From a hill near the cape Rice returned to report that as far as he could see the water appeared favorable to the south. Greely decided to make an immediate run straight for Cape Sabine, which could be seen distinctly nearly 50 miles away, glimmering in the afternoon sunlight. They had come almost four fifths of the way now; by forsaking the shore Greely hoped they might reach Sabine within two days. At 4 P.M. they set off, with Rice ahead steering the launch. With luck they would soon be at the gateway of Smith Sound.

But luck did not hold. Floating ice grew thicker, slowing their progress. Five hours out from Cape Hawks, as the sun dipped below the northern horizon, the boats were stopped in the pack By morning they were firmly frozen in place. Just one mile ahead, they learned to their chagrin, lay open water.

The men were further disheartened to learn from Israel's calculations that their ice prison was moving northward. As long as they were held fast, there were but two choices: stay on the floe and wait for it to break up, or abandon the launch and try to drag the smaller boats and equipment to water. Greely's decision was to wait.

Brainard suggested a moderate cut in rations, but the commander did not want to take the step—yet. The effect on morale, he told the sergeant, might not be good. On August 30 the two men carefully surveyed the supplies and calculated there was food for fifty days, tea and coffee for forty. In a pinch, they agreed, the stuff might be made to last for sixty. They had 1100 pounds of hardtack, some of it half spoiled, and 1244 pounds of meat, much of it pemmican of various ages.

One day followed another and the men drifted in cold, wet, miserable idleness. Some of them slept in the boats, others in a tepee rigged of oars and sailcloth. Often they spent the full day in their bags, emerging only to answer a call of nature or to get their food. By September 3 Greely thought it wise to call a council of the officers and the two leading enlisted men, Brainard and Rice. Several times he had overheard Kislingbury grumbling aloud concerning his course of action; despite sharp reprimands the disgruntled officer had continued to do so. It would be better, Greely thought, to confine such discussion among the leaders. Because Dr. Pavy had been disputatious in the past over exactly what had been said on occasion, Greely asked Lockwood to take down the discussion in shorthand.

"I have called you together because of the seriousness of our situation," Greely began in his formal manner. Turning to the officers, he continued:

"I have selected Sergeants Brainard and Rice to join in this conference because I consider them the most intelligent of the enlisted men and doubtless they represent their wishes. I might add that I consider Sergeant Rice's opinion and advice especially valuable because he has shown prudence and correct judgment in navigating the ice." The others nodded agreement.

"As you are aware, I myself know nothing about ice navigation, I am disadvantaged by having poor eyesight, and it is my intention in the future to entrust the ice navigation to Sergeant Rice.

"Now, Lieutenant Kislingbury," said Greely, "you are the next in seniority. I would like, if you will, for you to give your views of what we should do."

Kislingbury proposed that they move from one floe to another, and try reaching shore that way. This would mean leaving the heavy launch behind.

"Have you thought this through?" asked Greely. "Have you calculated the weights the men would have to drag on the sledges, what equipment would be taken and what abandoned other than the launch?"

"No," Kislingbury admitted, "I haven't gone into that." A further exchange elicited no plan or an offer to frame one. The commander then consulted Dr. Pavy, who for close to a half-hour roamed over a wide range of topics, finally winding up with the assertion that he favored sending out one boatload over the ice the next day to seek the water's edge and try to reach land. Lockwood in his turn said he had not thought the matter through and had no suggestions. Greely queried him:

"Then, am I to understand that you think it better at present to let things remain as they are and wait for an opening to run with the launch?"

A Serious Nip.

Abandoning Launch *Lady Greely*—September 10, 1883.

After hesitation, Lockwood replied. "Yes."

In turn, Rice counseled against moving yet. They were now gaining gradually by this drift, he pointed out. As long as they had supplies, and there was a chance for an opening, he preferred to wait. If the ice should open and they could get off in the launch and boats, they could go farther in a few hours than they could drag the equipment in days.

Brainard followed up to the same effect, and it was decided not to move. Nor did the decision seem wrong, as the floe soon began moving south and west. On September 7 it passed close to Cape Albert and Israel at noon declared they had drifted 6.3 miles in the last twenty-four hours. On the 8th, the party's thirteenth day on the ice, Greely announced they would seize the chance to make land, abandoning the launch and the *Valorous*. Two days of driving snow delayed the start, forcing the men to keep to their bags, but on September 10 they stripped the *Lady Greely* and the *Valorous* of all portable equipment, loaded the three sledges with the two boats and some 6500 pounds of stores, and set off across the rough pack. Officers leaned to the drag ropes alongside the men. Each load had to be eased past the worst rough spots in turn, with all hands steadying the gunwhales of the loaded boats on the sledges. It was agonizingly slow work, but it at least was progress.

The men's morale at this point was shown by their respect for the expedition's heavy pendulum, which in its carrying case weighed 100 pounds. Greely at the start announced that if any man wished him to do so he would abandon the pendulum because of its weight. The value of the pendulum observations at Lady Franklin Bay, he pointed out, depended on comparative observations to be made with the same instrument after their return home. As one, the men insisted on keeping it.

On the 12th, exhausted from their heavy work and eager to move faster, the party decided to abandon the whaleboat, which was breaking down its sledge. The *Narwhal* was therefore left behind with a signal flag nailed to an upright oar and a record of the expedition's fortunes and misfortunes stowed away under her cleats. After four hard days of travel the men learned once more that they were losing ground. The wind had turned against them. Losing control of himself, Dr. Pavy spilled out his venom against Greely among the despondent men. The commander had chosen a route that would bring them all to destruction, he whined. Furthermore, back in August Greely had ignored his advice to remain at Fort Conger. Now look at them!

Already in a black mood, Greely was infuriated to hear the doctor speak in such a way and for a moment considered taking "the most extreme measures" against him, as he confided in his journal. But on reflection he realized that the men might soon be in serious need of Pavy's medical services. They had been fortunate thus far, since Biederbick's rheumatism was the only physical disability among them. But if they failed to reach a ship soon, it might be quite a different story.

Stoic man of iron that he was, Brainard still found that the situation made a sad chronicle:

> The roar of the moving and grinding pack east of us in the axis of the channel is something so terrible that even the bravest cannot appear unconcerned. To add to this scene of desolation, dark, portentous clouds hang over the horizon to remind us that our floe is not connected with the land, but drifting helplessly in the Kane Sea.

By September 16 the rations were down to a forty-day supply, not counting the 125-pound seal which Jens had proudly dragged in that morning. The men were all feeling hunger now. On occasion the rations had been augmented by seal meat, and Greely found that the extra rum he offered Fred and Jens as an inducement in their hunting proved quite effective. At the kill there was usually spirited competition to catch the blood oozing from the bullet wounds, a fluid which the drinkers agreed tasted something like warm egg whites.

Learning again from Israel's observations that they were losing ground to the current, Greely ordered the astronomer to pass his position data in quietly without notifying the men. After they had toiled all day in the drag ropes it was demoralizing to learn they had nothing to show for their labor. Then Israel and Greely discovered that the floe was rotating in a counterclockwise direction. Nor could they hide this fact when everyone could see one morning that in leaving camp toward the southwest they were following the very tracks by which they had come in from the northeast!

After a raging gale through the night of September 18–19, Greely called his six-man council again. Afterward Brainard, hunched down in his sleeping bag, scrawled across the pages of his pocket diary his concern over what he had heard:

> Lt. Greely favors an attempt to reach the Greenland coast by abandoning everything except 20 days' provisions, records, boat and sledge. Madness!

Now that the storm had driven them right into Smith Sound, Greely believed they must either strive desperately for the shore or be swept south into the broad waters of Baffin Bay. Already Cape Sabine was no longer south but due west, and Cape Isabella, the "Land's End" of the sound, could be plainly seen to the southwest. They must reach one shore or the other. Since they had neither seen a signal nor been signaled to from Sabine, Greely declared, it would be best to head toward Greenland and the Littleton Island cache. During the past two summers, supplies should certainly have been left there.

Dr. Pavy and Kislingbury approached Greely with another suggestion—they should take the one boat remaining, and a group of nine men, and make the Sabine shore, then return. Greely flatly vetoed the idea. Already the wind was driving the floe farther from land, and such a plan, he could see, might result in the malcontents getting ashore while the rest of the party were left on the floe. Still, there was risk in either course, be it action or inaction. On the floe for the moment, at least, no one was in danger of drowning. In a boat, loaded nearly to the gunwhales, one false move might bring disaster.

Though those sleeping in the iceboat under the tarpaulins were uncomfortable enough, at least they had dry wood under them, in contrast to the larger group sheltered by the tepee, who found that their body heat, combined with the warmth given off by the cookstove, turned their ice floor into a ring of puddles which left the underside of their sleeping bags sopping. The little group led by Rice did better; they erected an ice house of frozen snow blocks in which they passed several nights in relative comfort.

Early in the morning of September 22 Private Bender spied what was apparently the mast of one of the abandoned boats, with its flag waving against the sea of ice. Most thought it would have drifted into Baffin Bay by this time. Rice, Brainard, and Jens took out after it in the iceboat, but after coming within 200 yards of the craft, which turned out to be the whaleboat abandoned ten days earlier, they were forced to turn back. Sludge ice, too thick for the boat and too soft to walk on, barred their route. Two days later at Greely's order, Lieutenant Lockwood, Brainard, and Jens made another desperate try to reach the whaleboat floe on foot. They had not gone far before they heard Bender calling to them from behind, and his frantic gestures warned them that something serious had happened. They rushed back toward camp and found that a small crack they had crossed had rapidly widened, threatening to cut them off from their base. The ice broke beneath their feet as the three took a desperate running leap over the lane to safety. This time the boat was gone for good.

September 24 and 25 found the party driven by the wind into the very apex of conflicting currents of Smith Sound, the action of which bit by bit began breaking up their floe. A wild, driving storm came up during the second night, and the dark water foamed about the beleaguered men and broke on the jumbled walls of ice which now weighted down the floe's outer edges. When daylight dawned on the 26th land appeared at least six miles away to the west, separated from them by an expanse of debris ice through which the boat could not possibly be forced. The stretches of open water were seething, white-capped seas which would have swamped her in minutes. Through a day of torment, while they saw their safety point recede steadily to the

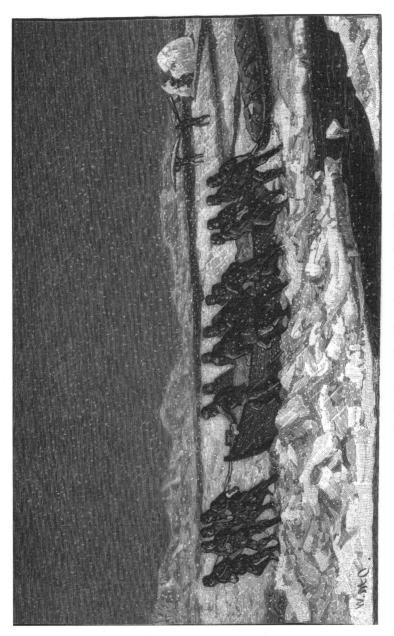

The Crushing of Our Floe—September 26, 1883.

northwest, the men imagined their end in the darkest deeps of Baffin Bay when their floe should break up. Half the party was wretched in the extreme from the cramping pains of a severe diarrhea attack.

Just after 7 P.M. an ominious grinding sound shook the camp. A huge crack began to split the floe, running directly through the snow house. Everyone sprang into action, seizing gear, loading the sledge, and preparing the iceboat for an emergency move. But the boat would never hold them all in this sea.

In the dusk Greely could see that a larger floe had crashed into their own from the north. In a matter of minutes, while the pressure of the wind held the two floes together, men, boat, and sledge were moved across the gap over compressed chunks of rotten debris ice to the larger floe. Hardly had the passage been made than the pressure was relaxed and the broken bits of their old home floated away in the gathering darkness. Time alone could tell how long it would be before their new home would suffer the same fate.

They had been on the ice exactly one month.

5   ABANDONED

A LITTLE AFTER NOON, Washington time, on Thursday, September 13, the first brief news dispatches from St. John's came into the Signal Corps headquarters. The *Proteus* had gone down in the ice, and all her survivors had reached port aboard the *Yantic*. Details would follow.

In charge of the office was Captain S. M. Mills, Acting Chief Signal Officer while General Hazen was inspecting signal posts in far-off Washington Territory. Assisting Mills was Lieutenant Louis V. Caziarc, an old personal friend of the Greelys. Shocked at the news, both men waited anxiously by the incoming wire for the answer to the one question of paramount importance to them. No lives had been lost—thank God for that! But what about Greely? What had been done for him? How long must they wait for a report from Garlington? Within minutes their message crackled out:

> Garlington, St. John's. Received news *Yantic*'s arrival and loss. Did you place any stores for Greely? How much, and where? Can anything more be done this year?—Caziarc, Mills

Three hours elapsed before Garlington's report, which he had had eleven days aboard the *Yantic* to compose, came into the Signal Office. Mills and Caziarc found it little more enlightening than the first dispatch:

> Chief Signal Officer, Washington. It is my painful duty to report total failure of the expedition. The *Proteus* was crushed in pack in latitude 78.52, longitude 74.25 and sunk on the afternoon of the 23d July. My party and crew of ship all saved. Made

my way across Melville Bay to Upernavik, arriving there on 24th Aug. The *Yantic* reached Upernavik 2nd September and left same day, bringing entire party here today. All well.—E. A. Garlington

At about the same time, in another part of the ornate building on Pennsylvania Avenue that housed the War and Navy Departments, a longer report was delivered to the office of the Secretary of the Navy. It was a telegram from Commander Wildes reporting the loss of the *Proteus,* but detailing his own navy duty well done despite great hardship. Like Garlington's message, Wildes' contained no word on what help had been left for the Lady Franklin Bay Expedition.

A few minutes past 2 P.M. in California Henrietta Greely opened the telegram Mills had sent her:

The following has just been received by Associated Press: St. John's, Newfoundland, Sept. 13, 11:15 A.M. The United States Greely relief steamship *Yantic* has just anchored here. Her tidings are lamentable. No word has been received from Greely or any of his party. The steamer *Proteus* was crushed in floe ice at the entrance to Smith Sound on July 23. Capt. Pike, his crew and scientific party are passengers by the *Yantic.* Will send further particulars when received.

Within the next few hours Henrietta learned the worst—that only a small portion of the relief expedition's stores had been left at Cape Sabine for her husband and his men. Inexcusable blundering last season, and on top of it this fiasco! A lesser woman would have been crushed, but last year's failure by Beebe had, in a sense, prepared and strengthened her for this new shock. She sent a demanding message to Mills:

Will not government send out at once another expedition to meet Greely party if on reaching Littleton Island the latter find nothing there and attempt to work south?

In midafternoon of the 14th, Garlington's report on the business he had been sent north to accomplish finally reached Mills and Caziarc:

No stores landed before sinking of ship. About five hundred rations from these saved, cached at Cape Sabine; also large cache of clothing. By the time suitable vessel could be procured, filled, provisioned, &c., it would be too late in season to accomplish anything this year.

Too late? Garlington's failure to send this message immediately upon landing had alone cost a full day. In an ordinary case of army administration, it might be sufficient when the responsible officer on the spot reported that there was no more to be done. But by now this Greely affair was far from ordinary. In 1881 the expedition had stirred few ripples outside the scientific world when it departed from the United States. But the reaction to Beebe's failure last year and the publicity over the relief mission early this past summer had transformed the once little-known Lady Franklin Bay scientific expedition into an intensely personal thing for the reading public. Now millions of Americans were eager to learn what would be done to save "the Greely Expedition," as the newspapers hereafter call the beleaguered party.

On the morning of Friday, September 14, the *Proteus* disaster was splashed across the front page of almost every newspaper in the country. It was the biggest story since the shooting of President Garfield. This affair was beyond the War Department now; it became the concern of the American people.

The *New York Daily Tribune* reported from Washington that the tragic news from St. John's "caused great and general uneasiness among officials of the War and Navy Departments today, and some of them appeared to have lost all hope for the rescue of Lieutenant Greely." Like a busy old gossip, an unsigned Washington dispatch whispered: "Lieut. Greely's friends all describe him as a man whose energy and ambition exceed his powers of physical endurance, and this naturally deepens their solicitude for his safety." In other words, he might play the fool and imperil those under his command. From Newburyport, where Greely's mother, his brother John, and many of his old friends were reading the dispatches, Boston papers reported that news of the disaster had created "the most intense feeling."

Telegrams asking by what means, and how fast, Greely would be saved flooded into the War Department. It was quickly decided that Mills as Acting Chief Signal Officer should sign a form letter to be sent out to allay the clamor. By the night of the 14th the mails were carrying the captain's assurance to the public that their government was not asleep:

I greatly regret the unfortunate termination of the Greely relief expedition of this year. The dispatches from Lt. Garlington and Com. Wildes which have been given to the press are authentic.

The Department fully appreciates the anxiety which must be felt in consequence of this failure. But I beg to assure you that no effort will be spared to set on foot another expedition at the earliest moment possible, and that great diligence is being used to determine the proper course of action.

In the meantime I hope you will not be needlessly alarmed on account of the safety of those of the party in whom you are interested.

—*S. M. Mills*, Acting C.S.O.

Now deeply concerned, Secretaries Lincoln and Chandler were not content with Garlington's first rejection of sending new succor to Greely before winter closed navigation in the northern waters. Another Mills-to-Garlington telegram made it plain to the young West Pointer that he was at the vortex of a problem concerning Washington at the Cabinet level. He must give responsible, specific answers to the questions millions were now asking:

Secretaries War and Navy concur in asking full replies from yourself and Commander Wildes separately or jointly. Why were no stores landed Littleton on your way north? Did *Yantic* leave any stores anywhere after leaving your disaster?

Is the following project feasible: That a steam sealer be chartered to take your party northward provisioned for crew, passengers and twenty additional men for one year, to be purchased at St. John's and elsewhere en route. Outfit completed, all dispatch and steam to Upernavik, thence to northernmost attainable harbor west coast of Greenland, or to Littleton for winter quarters. To pick up dogs, sleds and native drivers in Greenland, and lead small party and as much supplies as possible to Littleton Island, or to meet Greely if Littleton Island is attained?—Mills, Acting C.S.O.

There was an anxious overnight wait in Washington. It had already been determined that four sealers were in St. John's harbor with coal on. The important question was whether the American officers now there would decide to brave the ice once more this season. A confident, favorable reply would tip the scales in favor, Lieutenant Caziarc told himself, but a negative answer, or even a half-hearted one would end the prospect of a new effort. By 11 A.M. on the 15th Garlington had effectively slammed the door on another try to help Greely while at the same time posturing bravely that he was willing to go if others were to decide that he should:

> Stores were not left at Littleton Island because it was not in my programme to do so. . . . The ultimate result of any undertaking to go north at this time extremely problematical; chances against its success, owing to dark nights now begun in those regions making ice navigation extremely critical work. There is no safe anchorage on west shore of Greenland between Disko and Pandora Harbor, except perhaps North Star Bay. . . . However, there is a bare chance of success, and if my recommendations are approved I am ready and anxious to make the effort.
>
> My plan is to buy a suitable sealer, take the crew from volunteers from crews of *Yantic* and *Powhatan,* now in this harbor, paying extra compensation. Lieut. J. C. Colwell to command the ship; two ensigns and one engineer to be taken from those who may volunteer from same ship; also employ competent ice pilot here. The ship must be under U.S. laws and subject to military discipline. I believe nothing can be done with foreign civilian officers and crew. In event of not enough seamen volunteering, remainder to be enlisted here. . . . If anything is to be done it must be done at once.

An officer convinced the venture would probably fail would base it on a pickup crew of navy volunteers, supplemented by Newfoundlanders (foreigners with whom "nothing can be done") to be spurred on by a bounty no one had authority to offer, sailing in a ship he had no authority to buy. On top of it, the man gave no opinion on the practicability of sledging to meet Greely, once the ship had gone as far as possible. If Garlington's message did not alone drive the last nail in the coffin of a further rescue effort, the honor was shared by the accompanying telegram which Wildes dispatched to Secretary Chandler:

St. John's, Sept. 15. To the Sec. of the Navy. To charter another foreign ship with foreign crew for this duty to go north at this late season would simply invite fresh disaster. *Proteus* handled very unskillfully and crew behaved shamefully at wreck. Ship must be American-manned and officered by Navy and thoroughly equipped. Unless winter quarters can be reached north of Cape Athol the attempt would be useless. This cannot be done. Melville Bay will be impassable by October first at latest. Ship cannot winter at Upernavik and cannot sledge north from there.

The subordinates' report from the field dictated the decision in council of their superiors. On Saturday afternoon the 15th, on the strength of these messages, the two Secretaries reached their decision: There would be no further attempt at rescuing Greely. Mills closed down the business of a hectic three days by sending a final wire to Garlington:

Dispatches received. Expedition this year not considered advisable. Will ask for return of your party by naval vessel.

Then, in as thoughtful terms as he could bring himself to phrase, the acting C.S.O. sent Henrietta the message he had been dreading, one he knew would foretell for her a winter of anguished waiting:

The Secretaries of War and Navy have carefully considered with kindly disposition and indifferent to expense the feasibility of sending another vessel this year. Lieut. Garlington and Commander Wildes have made full telegraphic report but the Secretaries concur in the belief that nothing further can be done this year. Every effort will be made in the spring and summer of next year to reach the party at the earliest possible moment.

By Sunday morning the press was striking out in all directions
—blaming, deploring, accusing, demanding—in an orgy of
finger-pointing and name-calling. There was no question, most
editorialists stated, but that Garlington would be ordered home
to face a court-martial. He was condemned on every possible
score as fool, coward, a man too immature for the mission, a
horse soldier ignorant of the ways of the sea.

Greely's chances of survival formed the basis of a grim guess-
ing game. Had he actually moved south from Fort Conger in
August? Could his small boats make the journey safely in view
of the fact that the *Proteus* had succumbed to the ice pack? Were
his men fit for the trip? Should he reach Smith Sound, what would
he do on finding no *Proteus,* no shelter, and insufficient winter
stores? Would he try to cross to Littleton Island, or would he
search out the friendly Etah Eskimos and try to winter with
them? Would he attempt to beat his way back to Fort Conger?
Or stay at Cape Sabine, subsisting on caches in that area?

Every prominent man who had had arctic experience was in-
terviewed. Some counseled a new try at once, others said effort
should be centered on sending a well-planned relief party early
in the spring. While some opined that the expedition could hold
out, more feared that nothing but corpses would be found in
1884. Amid all this, a cruel rumor came in from Britain: unnamed Dundee seamen were said to have learned from Eskimos
that Greely's men had mutinied and killed their leader. Editors
spread the morbid tale in their news columns, then solemnly cast
doubt on it in their editorials.

For Henrietta the weekend brought no relaxation. Before re-
ceiving Mills' wire of Saturday evening, she had telegraphed
Caziarc, a man closer in friendship to her husband than the
Acting C.S.O.:

> Can not a steamer if started immediately with stores reach
> Upernavik or Godhavn and winter, sending sledging parties
> north?

And to General Lockwood, who enjoyed social access to many
important figures in the capital, she sent a similar query:

Can you expedite the sending of a relief vessel to winter at
Upernavik sending sledging parties thence?

Nor did Henrietta rest on Sunday morning, which found her
again at the telegraph office writing out another message to the
Signal Corps head, one in which she took at face value Garlington's offer to try once more:

As Garlington says have chance of success why cannot expedition be sent? If on reaching Melville Bay no chance of helping
party appears, cannot vessel return to Disko? Mr. Greely expressed to me complete faith in the government's care for its own
expedition.

What could Lieutenant Caziarc say to this determined woman,
who would not give up her husband to the arctic winter? The
sting of having a woman remind him of his moral duty to Greely
was doubly painful, no matter how softly put. How could he reply
to her challenge? When, on Sunday afternoon, he learned that
General Lockwood was closeted with Secretary Lincoln in an
earnest plea for reconsideration, Caziarc kindly sent Henrietta a
mild word of encouragement:

General Lockwood now urging an expedition on Secretary of
War but it is thought he will abide by decision telegraphed you
yesterday. Greely probably now at Sabine and he may follow in
boats Garlington's line of retreat on Upernavik reaching there
this autumn. Will telegraph you in any change of programme.

Similarly, on Monday Captain Mills held out a thread of hope
to Henrietta that the Saturday decision might be reversed, thanks
to Lockwood's intervention:

Consultation resumed this morning. Will advise you of decision.

Despite Henrietta's efforts to prevent the ringing down of the
curtain on aid to the expedition before winter, official Washington that day decided that the show, for this season at least, was
over. On Tuesday evening, the 18th, after six days of tenterhook
anxiety, Henrietta received definite word that the government had

abandoned the Greely party. Mills' notification, a pretense at reassurance, was hollow and unconvincing:

> The Secretaries of Navy and War concur after a most laborious and patient consultation by letter personally with Arctic explorers of eminence that nothing can be done this season to reach Mr. Greely, that there is not now the remotest chance of reaching him either by boat or sledge. It is believed that according to the lateness of the season when he reached Cape Sabine he will wisely judge whether to attempt Upernavik or retrace his steps to Lady Franklin Bay with the supplies he must have left . . . and those which are in depots between Sabine and there. His case is viewed hopefully. He will be reached next year as early as possible.

General Lockwood's heart went out to Henrietta Greely as perhaps no other would. Whatever his private sentiments about the decision and about his own son's chances of survival, he tried his best in a long letter to Henrietta to alleviate her anxiety. Written to comfort a young wife, a woman of an age to be his daughter, his letter was at the same time a report to his colleague in their mission to move the government:

> I made every effort to induce the Secretaries of both the War and Navy Departments to fit out a relief expedition at once. The subject was fully discussed and information gathered from every available source as to its feasibility, and I feel sure an honest conviction arrived at, that the relief party sent out would be put in greater peril than those whom they were sent to relieve. Indeed, Mr. Lincoln would not admit that the Greely party were in extreme peril, and gave this among other reasons for declining to risk the lives of others in their present relief. He also said that any future effort in that direction must be under the auspices of the Navy Dept. and this I regard as wise, for Naval men can better accomplish what so particularly belongs to their calling. He was fully willing to meet the cost of an expedition, but insisted on cooperation of the Navy.
>
> After this expression of sentiment I went to the Secretary of the Navy. He had just returned from an interview with the President, who had expressed very great anxiety as to the relief, if

possible. Secretary Chandler accordingly entered upon the consideration of the subject with a strong desire to undertake it. And it was only after experts had pronounced it impracticable that the expedition was deferred till next spring.

I am compelled however reluctantly to acquiesce in this decision, and rely on the promise given to use every effort at the earliest possible day next spring to carry succor to our loved ones.

During the confused week, news reporters had crowded the halls of the State-War-Navy Building next door to the White House, ferreting out the latest developments. Now it was time for official Washington to set the record straight, and again it fell to Captain Mills to sign and distribute a form letter bringing the decision of those far above him in authority to the families of the abandoned expedition members, their friends, and the inquiring public. Nor was anyone left out. The cold, black print of this announcement was dumped in the mail with magnificent equality to utter strangers as well as to John Greely and Mother Greely in Newburyport, and to Henrietta in California. It was both a letter of excuse and an official dose of soothing-syrup, a palliative for the overexcited. After outlining the obstacles to reaching Greely in the fall, Mills' statement dwelt with optimism on his chances of spending the winter in safety and comfort:

> Lieut. Greely's case is regarded as by no means hopeless. He has the advantage of daylight in which to move, if he left his station as ordered no later than Sept. 1.... Arriving at Cape Sabine not far from Sept. 1, perhaps earlier, he will learn of Garlington's disaster and determine on his plans for the winter.
>
> If he attempts to move south upon the Danish settlements, he has 740 rations at Cape Sabine, 240 more on an island in its vicinity ... sufficient without retrenchment for forty-eight days for his command.
>
> But it is said he may choose to regain Lady Franklin Bay, over a distance of about 250 miles. There he had more than a year's supply of the best assorted food, including breadstuffs, canned meats, fruits, vegetables, chocolate, coffee, milk, preserves, sauces also lights, fuel and shelter.

Following this catalogue of comforts, the statement insisted that Greely could handily regain Fort Conger along a coast liberally stocked with food caches. It concluded that Greely himself must be quite confident:

> He cannot fail to know that the most earnest efforts will be made to relieve him next year, and plans will at once be prepared to put on foot an expedition which, it is said, shall meet all the wishes of the most anxious friends of the party. I most fully appreciate the great anxiety which must be felt for those who are of the Arctic party, but I hope this feeling may be relieved by the assurance that a suitable relief party will be put on foot at the earliest practicable date.—*S. M. Mills,* Acting C.S.O., U.S.A.

This was the word—official, final. The book was closed. Yet Henrietta, accepting the decision as fact, was not content that it was the right one. In a calm spirit, without rancor or bitterness, she confided to Lieutenant Caziarc that she was not at all satisfied. As a close personal friend he completely understood her feelings and admired the determined way she expressed them. Yet what could he do, a mere lieutenant, who had pleaded the cause of a fellow lieutenant and lost against the downturned thumbs of two members of the President's Cabinet? Henrietta's letter read like the one clear voice of courage and common sense amid the counsels of fear and despair Caziarc had heard all week in Washington:

> If the *Proteus* could reach Upernavik in eight days from St. John's as she did, another vessel could do the same. Therefore if a steamer had been started from St. John's a week even after the *Yantic* had returned there might have been a chance of its reaching some point above Upernavik so as to render some assistance to the party if they attempted to reach Upernavik as Garlington did.

Surely, no soldier could express more confidence in a leader than this gallant lady did of her husband:

> I have great faith in Mr. Greely's ability to cope with the situation. He has a clear head and great energy and perseverance,

as you probably know, and if any man could escape the dangers
that beset his party I believe that he will, with God's help. All the
same, I feel that the government has not kept faith with the party.
They should not have placed them in this position and then allowed the barest chance of assisting them to pass by. Altho' you
may not think with me, you will understand my feelings, as you
are a friend of my husband's.

All week Caziarc had been torn between conflicting duties. On
the one hand the intertwined braids of military command and
government authority bound him to support his superiors. On the
other, his ties of loyalty to a comrade in peril and to this noble
woman, his wife, impelled him not to give up. Chafing under the
restraints imposed on him by his position, he wrote her in confidence:

> You should know that every word said here has been for the
> sending of a party. Prudence has been laid aside and so long as
> volunteers were ready, counsel has been given to run all the at-
> tendant risks for the sake of getting a few miles nearer this au-
> tumn, or getting to Littleton Island a few days earlier next sum-
> mer. But the prospects of accomplishing anything in a region
> where sun is fast disappearing, and the fact that an expedition
> cannot be started without delays in provisioning, fitting, coaling,
> &c. has led those who must decide to decide unfavorably.

"Those who must decide": the high officials to whom the Greely
party was just twenty-five men on a personnel roster. Not Henrietta Greely's flesh-and-blood husband, not General Lockwood's
son James, not Caziarc's old friend. Hinting to Henrietta of the
dispute behind the scenes in Washington, the lieutenant left
volumes unsaid:

> I feel the restraint of writing fully to you very keenly, I wish it
> were within my power to be near enough to go over the whole
> subject with you.

Meanwhile General Hazen, far from the scene of decision, had
lived a week of frustration in Washington Territory. Had he
only been in Washington, D.C.! Hazen gave vent to his desire to

intervene in the policy discussion by peppering Mills with telegrams of advice, urging action at once on Greely's behalf:

New Tacoma, W.T. Sept. 15. It may be necessary to send men with money and authority to Upernavik to organize and send sledging parties with food north to meet Greely, who is probably at Littleton Island on his way south. See the Secretary about it, and if the President can authorize the money Congress will approve. . . .

Sept. 17. It is very important to get a capable man with money as high up in Greenland as possible and send sledge parties with native food and clothing under pay and bounties to meet Greely. See the Secretary and do it if possible. . . .

Sept. 19. Get orders from Danish legation for men going to Greenland for all Danish authorities to give all possible assistance. . . .

Sept. 20. If it is too early for sledges, parties must start up in boats. . . .

Sept. 22. Do all in your power to prevent delay of preparation. What I want done requires no preparation. Time is more valuable than all else.

Cut off as he was, Hazen did not know that the issue had been settled several days before his last wires were on their way, and when he finally heard the news he was sick at heart. The verdict against one more attempt at rescue this year, he wrote Henrietta, was made after he had first been assured by wire that Secretary Lincoln agreed with him. Reversal of the plan to send out a new party was certainly a mistake, he added. But now that it was done, Hazen resolved that he would make Garlington answer for his miserable failure.

Amid all the spilling of ink and the thousands of words telegraphed back and forth, one letter bespoke the mutual grief of two women, outwardly quite different, separated by the breadth of a continent but closely linked by their concern for their absent loved one. From sixty-four-year-old Mother Greely in Newburyport, a woman of limited education, accustomed to hardship, Henrietta received a message of consolation and affection:

Dear Rettie,

Your letter of the 14 come to hand last evening. I have received two printed letters from the Chief Signal Office, it seams that a relief party will not be sent till spring. I think they should have sent at once as soon as the news of the *Protious* was lost. The suspence is dredful. I am sorry to learn that you are in poor health. My hart goes out to you and the Dear Children. I hope God will support you in this trying time, and we all must hope for the best. I have read all the papers on the subject. Will send you one with this. God onley knows how many harts are aking for the party tonight. Everyone here is feeling bad and is talking abought it. You know how hard I tried to keep him at home. Well, I cant talk abought it my hart is sore. I dont know what to think abought Esquimaux story concerning Adolph. I hope there is no truth in it. I inclose it to you as you may not see it in the papers. . . . I cannot write more.

Your loveing Mother, *F. D. Greely*

ON SEPTEMBER 28 the wild gale that had been driving the Greely party toward a watery doom in the vastness of Baffin Bay finally subsided. When the sky cleared, Brainard and Fred went forward to reconnoiter at the edge of their floe. To their joy they found it had been driven close to shore at the entrance of Baird Inlet, some twenty miles southwest of Cape Sabine, and had become lodged against a grounded iceberg. The pair hurried back to camp to inform Lieutenant Greely that there seemed to be a favorable chance to work toward shore across a lane of open water about half a mile wide.

With spirits soaring, the men sprang into action to move their loads to the floe edge. In seven ticklish crossings of the boat, under the cool command of Rice, all men and equipment were landed on the neighboring icefield inshore. By nightfall they had covered about two miles in all; they now estimated that the nearest land, a high, gray promontory, lay a scant mile ahead. As they settled into their bags for the night they prayed that during the dark hours no ill wind would drive them offshore on the high tide. They were so close now.

This time the gods were kind. Before breakfast the next morning Greely had dispatched Brainard landward to find a sledge route, but the pathfinder discovered that what had appeared one mile in the evening gloom was really more than four miles. Still, through the day the nearness of the shore kept drawing them on. By 6 P.M., after a strenuous day of sledge-hauling over rough ice and repeated ferrying across two more lanes of water, the entire party had made it. For the first time in thirty-four days, their feet could stamp on solid ground. "Shore at last! On land once more!" Brainard wrote in his journal.

On Sunday, September 30, Corporal Salor and Fred Christiansen tried to find a route south toward Cape Isabella, where Greely wanted to check the condition of a cache of meat left by the English in 1875. The two returned in a few hours to report that open water and young ice prevented any effective movement in that direction. Hearing this, George Rice volunteered to go north to Cape Sabine, accompanied by Jens, to search out whatever records might have been left by relief vessels during the past two summers. He would travel light, carrying a large one-man sleeping bag into which both he and Jens could squeeze, and they would take only four days' rations expecting that if they should find supplies at their destination they could, if necessary, dip into them for the return journey. Before leaving, Rice cautioned the commander not to become concerned if he and the Eskimo should not return until October 9, although he expected to be back by the 6th. As the pair moved off the following morning under an ominous sky, two men went ahead to help them with their packs over the first rocky upland. The rest of the party gave the scouting party a hearty cheer. Through the long two months since Conger, Rice had been a pillar of strength to them all—in dogged, hard work, in resourcefulness, and in his cheery humor. And while they rested here, unsure of what the future held, he was once more bearing on his stout shoulders the fortunes of all of them. In his journal that evening Lieutenant Kislingbury could not hide his admiration for the doughty Canadian:

Landing at Eskimo Point—September 29, 1883.

Jens.

He has a long, hard task ahead of him, but he will do it if any man in the party can. Rice is the toughest and best man I ever saw, and the only fault I have to find with him is that he works too hard. . . . I must be pardoned if I praise Rice frequently in my notes, but I can't help it. He is without doubt the best man here.

Later in the day Greely was both encouraged and disappointed when Long shot a walrus in a pool, then lost him. Although the heavy beast sank before the hunter could secure him, this was at least proof to the commander that there was edible wildlife about. The problem now was to stalk game until it was far enough from deep water, then get in shots that would kill clean. A few death spasms often carried the quarry out of reach in the depths. To obtain the meat they must have, Greely named Long, Fred, and Kislingbury the regular hunters, with Jens to join them upon his return.

The rest of the party set immediately to work preparing huts where the lee of a glacier and the bluff offered shelter from winds. Building material was bits of granite strewn about the base of the bluff, ice blocks, and the moss the men discovered by digging down beneath the snow—material painfully gathered with freezing fingers and laboriously put in place. Yet shelters built from such rude stuff could save them from fatal exposure. The sun was already so low at midday that Sergeant Israel could not obtain a reading for latitude. Within a couple of weeks it would disappear for the winter.

The morning after Rice's departure Brainard reported rations on hand for thirty-five days at about the level of issue on the ice floe: 10 ounces of bread a day, 1 pound of meat, and 2 ounces of potatoes per man—about half the normal arctic ration of the American Army. Calling the party into council, Greely bluntly gave them the facts and won their agreement to stretch the rations over fifty days, but only after considerable discussion— in which Dr. Pavy embarrassed Greely by expressing unwilling-

ness to commit himself to any definite reduction. As Brainard
saw it:

> The suffering will be extreme on this greatly reduced diet in
> this low temperature where a man requires from two to three
> times the normal diet. Also we have some very hard labor ahead
> of us incident to the building of winter quarters. Fifty more days
> will bring us to November 15, and at that time we should either
> be on the Greenland side or else in Baffin Bay. Lieut. Greely in-
> sists that when only ten days' provisions remain he will attempt
> to cross the sound to Littleton Island no matter what the conse-
> quences.

The party was divided into three squads headed by Greely,
Kislingbury, and Brainard, each building its own hut by its own
plan. As far as practicable, Greely allowed the men to choose the
companions with whom they might have to share cramped quarters and short rations for some time. As they set to work scouting
for material, they came upon the remains of three ancient Eskimo
igloos, which furnished a certain amount of loose stone, mostly
granite. This discovery also provided a name for the place, which
Greely filled in on his map as "Eskimo Point." His journal described the architecture:

> My own party will first put up an ice house, and then construct
> a stone one inside. The other parties have decided to build stone
> houses first, and then surround them with ice. Our house will be
> eight feet by eighteen.... The boat, with two oars, rudder and
> boathook, was disposed of by lot, and fell to Sergeant Brainard's
> party. I ordered that it should be so used in constructing the
> houses that its future serviceability should not be impaired.
> Everybody worked very hard and cheerfully during the day.

Through this first week ashore, the hard work of constructing
the winter huts was the only thing spurring the men to activity.
Otherwise they might have sunk into complete despair. Lockwood recorded:

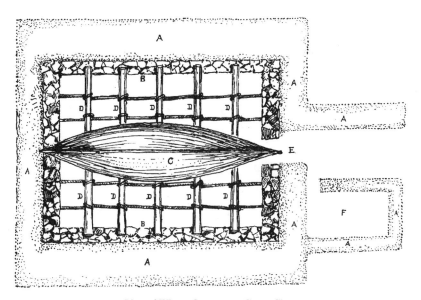

Plan of Winter Quarters at Camp Clay.

A. Exterior wall of snow. B. Interior wall of stone. C. Whaleboat, serving as roof to
hut. D. Oars from which the blade has been sawn connected by cables anchored in
stone wall, serving as rafters to whaleboat roof. E. Door to hut. F. Commissary.

Interior of Our Winter Hut at Camp Clay, During Cooking, 1883.

Our tea is extremely weak. This is a miserable existence, preferable only to death. Get little sleep day or night, on account of hard sleeping bag and cold.

Actually, in conspiracy with Brainard, Greely had been quietly cutting back the daily tea ration from one tablespoon per man to one eighth that amount. Small wonder that Lockwood said his tea tasted like rusty warm water.

On October 6—to Brainard's great surprise—Edward Israel, conspicuously reserved and mild-mannered, suddenly flared up at him. He accused the supply sergeant of being the leader in a "grab game" and "looking out too well" for his own party in distributing the building supplies. Brainard promptly took Israel before the commanding officer, to whom the distraught astronomer repeated his charges, though with somewhat less force. After hearing him out, Greely reprimanded Israel and stated his complete confidence in Brainard. From Israel's troubled appearance, it indeed seemed as if he already regretted his hot words, a fact not lost on the commander, as his journal showed:

It is his first indiscretion since his service with me, and can readily be attributed to his nervous frame of mind, growing out of hard work, insufficient food and severe exposure, which affects him, the youngest and weakest of the party, more than any other.

Brainard, closer to the conversation of the enlisted men, noted that evening that Greely's exoneration of him "has not left some of my comrades altogether certain of my honesty. I understand all the trouble was caused by the fault-finding of Connell."

Brainard's belief in Israel's basic good faith proved justified the next morning when he came to Brainard and apologized for his accusations. He admitted he had been influenced by others to make the remarks, for which he was truly regretful. Greely commented: "Israel today apologized to me in a manly, touching way, and in words which were very affecting, for his injustice to Brainard."

Later Greely called Sergeant Connell to him and announced,

in the presence of the whole group, that as a result of his repeated ill-spirited complaints about the leadership of the party—offenses going back many days during their hardships amid the ice floes— he was reduced to private as of October 1. It was a step Greely had planned for some time.

"There's no love lost between us," Connell retorted truculently. "I didn't ask for the grade, and I don't care that it has been taken away."

As Greely turned aside to avoid any further difficulty, Connell commented in a loud voice:

"I don't care a God damn about it!" To show his continued defiance he added several more remarks reflecting on the commander, the exact turn of which Greely did not catch, nor did he care to. Everyone's nerves were on edge and it was best to leave the matter at that. Linn was advanced to sergeant once more in Connell's place.

At this point Brainard asked Greely to relieve him from the thankless task of issuing the food. He had become heartsick at being the center of ill feeling in a group of men turning selfish and mean as they began to realize they might slowly die on this barren coast. "It is certainly hard," he commented, "to endure these reflections on my fairness, especially when I have tried so hard to satisfy all."

But Greely would not hear of a change in his supply chief:

> I told Sergeant Brainard that I had most implicit faith in his fairness, equity and impartiality in the issue of rations, as well as in other matters; indeed, I think him the model of fairness.

Now the huts were completed and the men dragged in their sleeping bags, stiff with ice that had formed in the buffalo hair. All thoughts turned toward Rice and Jens, still absent on their exploratory mission. In the fading light of October 8, Brainard recorded the concerns of the day:

> Rice has not yet returned. He is probably detained by new ice or a storm. God grant that he comes back to us in safety. We cannot spare such a noble soul from our party. Bender made me

Private Maurice Connell.

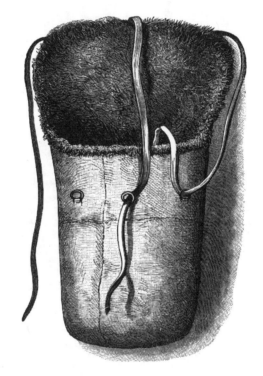
Three-man Buffalo Sleeping Bag.

a pair of scales which, though crude, will greatly assist in weighing out the scanty allowance of food.

A mischievous fox visited the camp last night and succeeded in stealing three-quarters of a pound of meat. Frederik shot two seals, but both sank before he could squeeze himself into his kayak and secure them. It is heart-rending to see this food which is our very life disappear before our eyes.

The ingenious tinsmith Bender was already trying to overcome the lack of a harpoon by fashioning a spearhead from Greely's dress sword—ironic remnant of his trappings brought all the way from Fort Conger, in line with the War Department stricture that a commander should always be prepared to appear in proper uniform.

For Lieutenant Lockwood, October 9 meant his thirty-first birthday. It was also the critical turning point in the party's fortunes. All the men were anxiously awaiting the return of Rice and Jens when at about 3 P.M. the pair was seen approaching camp from the north. Greely hastened from his sleeping bag and without fully dressing himself ran out to meet them. Both men showed in their weariness the strain of a hard journey. Rice's face, beneath his heavy growth of beard, revealed deep concern.

"I bring both good and bad news, sir," he said, pulling out a bundle of papers and handing them to the commander. Greely's eyes devoured Garlington's message, which Rice had found at Brevoort Island off the tip of Cape Sabine, and Beebe's several notes of the year before. The men clustered about, intently listening as he read aloud:

Cape Sabine, July 24, 1883.

The steamer *Proteus* was nipped midway between this point and Cape Albert on the afternoon of the 23d instant, while attempting to reach Lady Franklin Bay. She stood the enormous pressure nobly for a time, but had to finally succumb to this measureless force. The time from her being "beset" to going down was so short that few provisions were saved. A depot was landed from the floe at a point about three miles from the point of Cape Sabine as you turn into Buchanan Strait. There were five hundred rations of bread, sleeping bags, tea and a lot of canned stuff—no time to classify.

The message went on to list various other caches in the Cape Sabine area, which Greely quickly estimated as totaling perhaps 1300 rations. There was the clothing Garlington had left, plus a cache at Littleton Island if they could ever get to it. Garlington's message continued:

> The U.S. steamer *Yantic* is on her way to Littleton Island, with orders not to enter the ice. A Swedish steamer will try to reach Cape York this month. I will endeavor to communicate with these vessels at once, and everything within the power of man will be done to rescue the brave men at Fort Conger from their perilous position. . . . It is not within my power to express one tithe of my sorrow . . .

This was written all of ten weeks ago, Greely told himself. The man's regrets and his brave promises were of little help now. Whether Garlington had got through to the *Yantic,* or whether people in the United States had any idea of the peril Greely and his men were facing, God alone could say. Was there a party at Littleton Island at this moment, waiting to cross Smith Sound to their assistance? Who could tell?

Other intelligence gleaned from Rice, and a copy of the *Army Register* he brought back, told Greely that his family was safe and well during the first year of his absence. Further, Rice and Jens had followed up a narrow ice-covered waterway straight north which led them directly to the edge of Buchanan Strait. Not on any map, this was a new find, which Greely decided they should call "Rice Strait." Its existence meant that Cape Sabine was an island. But the greatest wonder of all turned out to be their abandoned New Bedford whaleboat, which the two travelers had come upon, safe and whole, where the floe bearing it had become wedged between Brevoort Island and the tip of the cape.

The discussion of Rice's tidings was lively, the reaction varied. Sergeant Ralston, one of the meteorological observers, went overboard in his enthusiasm for a rescue which he could envision just around the next headland:

> Glorious news! ... About 1,200 rations at Sabine, which we think will carry us safely through the winter. ... Two vessels outside ice looking for us.

Brainard, however, was coldly realistic:

> The finding of these records has dissipated all the daydreams of rescue which we have been fostering, and brought us face to face with our situation as it really is. It could hardly be much worse. There are little more than 1,000 rations at Cape Sabine and these will not go far toward feeding twenty-five men. Little time remains to hunt and besides game has become noticeably scarce.

Lieutenant Kislingbury engaged in a rapture of optimistic speculation, highly colored by his subjective appraisal of Garlington, who happened to be an old army friend:

> It is my belief that Garlington will have gotten the naval ship to leave all the supplies possible at Littleton I., providing she got there, and providing he got there himself. ...
>
> Of course, we are greatly encouraged by this news, and thankful for the efforts being made by our government for our relief. God bless my friend Garlington for his efforts, and also our government!
>
> Garlington's record telling us of the wreck showed such indifference for their critical condition and misfortune and said he would do everything that man could for us. I was affected nearly to tears and my voice nearly failed me when reading aloud. Poor fellow! His suffering and anguish must have been great indeed ... but I firmly believe he is now at Littleton I. and will be over to meet us as soon as it is possible for him to cross. How willingly we would, if we could, relieve his present anxiety as to our present safety. I fear he will wear himself out, but I have great admiration for him and wonder how he stands it so well.

Compared to their supply of less than fifty days' food here at Eskimo Point, the caches at Sabine loomed a tremendously bountiful store. On that ground the optimism of the moment might have been justified, or at least explainable. But Greely did not close his eyes to the longer view:

> This news makes our future somewhat brighter, and the party are in very high spirits over them, feeling certain we can get through.
>
> I, however, am fully aware of the very dangerous situation we are yet in, and foresee a winter of starvation diet and probably deaths. Our fuel is so scanty that we are in danger of perishing on that score alone. Am determined to make our food last until April 1, and shall so divide it, supplementing it from any game killed.

Stretching the available food until April 1, Greely knew, would not be easy. April 1 was 173 days off. If Garlington's and Rice's estimates were close to the truth, rations must be cut down to a bare fourth of normal. Whether they would get any more by hunting in this barren land was highly to be doubted.

They would have to abandon these huts so laboriously made from the rock and ice and move to Cape Sabine, where the greater part of their supplies lay. There they would once more have to construct a shelter. He would issue wood fuel by the sliver and stearine by the ounce. With the grace of God and the courage of American soldiers they would do their best to come through alive.

6 WINTER

A BLINDING SNOWSTORM on the morning of October 10, 1883, prevented the start for Cape Sabine. While most of the party huddled inside the stone huts in their sleeping bags, Rice proposed a new venture to Greely. Only the day before he had struggled into camp exhausted from his search trip northward. Yet now Rice, the man of iron, asked permission to go scouting again, this time with Fred Christiansen, ten miles south to Cape Isabella. There he would hunt for the cache left by Sir George Nares in 1875, said to contain 144 pounds of preserved meat, and also find the whaleboat Garlington had mentioned in his note as being at the cape. In addition, he would scour the coastline in the hope that the *Yantic* had got through to leave supplies after the *Proteus* disaster. Greely seriously doubted that the *Yantic* had touched this far north, but kept this opinion to himself. Should Rice discover the English cache, that find alone would make his trip worth while. Wondering at the man's apparently limitless endurance, the commander assented.

At an early hour the next morning, well before the main party was ready to start hauling its heavy sledgeload toward Sabine, Rice and Fred set off on their quest. As they disappeared among the ice hummocks, Greely was confident that George Rice would find whatever lay at Cape Isabella.

Four exhausting, bone-chilling days were required to move everything on the big sledge from Eskimo Point over the intervening upland to the ice of Rosse Bay, then across it and through Rice Strait to the north shore of the island of which Cape

Sabine was the eastern tip. The island itself, Greely announced, would be called Garlington Island. Although Kislingbury and Dr. Pavy protested against carrying the heavy scientific instruments and records, Greely was gratified to see all the rest stand behind him when he declared these should be brought onto the island where they would make their permanent camp.

Daylight lasted less than six hours now. The men were compelled to set out when it was barely light and bend their backs with a royal will to drag the loaded sledge some five or six miles in the forenoon. They would then return to the previous night's camp and, the sledge loaded once more, bring forward the second half of their burden before dark. By day the October wind cut through their clothing like a set of knives; at night the snow drifting into their bags laid on the icy ground rendered their hours of rest miserable.

At several points the party passed over dangerously thin new ice which creaked ominously under the sledge, while the men in the drag ropes fanned out as far as possible to minimize the danger. If one spot should be too thin by a half-inch, should one crack give way, a break would surely swallow the loaded sledge and several lives. On October 13, as they passed an immense berg towering twenty-five feet above the waterline and extending an unknown distance into the depths, a huge mass broke from its submerged foot, rose swiftly through the water and burst through the new ice within ten feet of the sledge, shooting up into the air and throwing fragments in every direction. Brainard, inured by now to danger, jested that evening:

> For a moment I felt as if some mighty leviathan of the deep was aiming at our destruction. At any rate, occasional incidents of this kind are a variation from the depressing monotony of our marches.

On the morning of the 15th Greely went ahead of the main party to survey the *Proteus* wreck cache and find the best spot for winter quarters. To his dismay, the supply pile revealed scarcely 100 rations of meat instead of 500, as he had been led to expect from Garlington's message. The man had apparently meant to say "500 rations of bread" plus some meat and other stuff. How much Garlington had exaggerated his estimate there would be no knowing until Greely and Brainard went carefully through the cache. So hungry were the members of the party that when the main body appeared some of the men almost danced for joy at the find. Private Henry, despite his suffering from a frosted foot, wrote a description of the find with his customary flamboyance:

> The commanding officer preceded us to the wreck cache and by the time we arrived they had everything straightened out for inspection. How we gloated over the harvest, and how the tobacco consumers, the majority of whom had been out for a week or more, spit and longed for a chew of the nine or 10 pounds left there. How we gazed upon the box of Durham tobacco and wished it was meat. How we smiled at the idea of leaving two boxes of lemons for hungry men. How disgusted we were at the mere idea of saving three boxes of raisins for us. To rest easy, the tobacco was at once divided among the 18 consumers, and the other seven contented themselves with the division of a box of raisins instead.

The man who penciled these lines was the same one who had startled Brainard the day before by "eating some of the raw seal intestines with evident relish." The biggest man and heaviest eater in the party (he had put on twenty-five pounds at Fort Conger), Henry was not squeamish about his food when hungry. He evidently delighted in recording a few days later the distaste he and others felt for certain canned goods:

> The only objectionable article in the whole cache was the roast mutton, on which the following resolution was adopted by the expeditionary force: "Resolved: that the roast mutton put up by the Castine Packing Co. of Castine, Maine, is a regular fraud upon the public, that it is boiled mutton of the poorest quality instead of roast, that each and every can contains more bones than meat, that the cans contain instead of two pounds scarcely one and a half, and that we all condemn the firm and

will do all in our power to advertize them to the canned-mutton-consuming public through the press, official records and in every way we possibly can, as a fraud and humbug of the first water."

Shortly after the party drew together at the wreck cache, Greely was pleasantly surprised to see Rice and Fred appear. Their news, however, did nothing to cheer him. Rice had found the English meat at Cape Isabella on the summit of a thousand-foot hill, but careful search of the coastline had revealed neither the boat mentioned by Garlington nor any sign of a visit by the *Yantic*. Less than six pounds of meat per man and nothing else at Cape Isabella, the most accessible point to ships on this coast of Smith Sound—and that now forty miles away! Greely decided they would have to forget the Isabella cache and concentrate on gathering in the supplies close at hand. By Israel's calculations the sun would disappear from this latitude on October 25, although on this (the north) side of their island the hills had already cut off its direct rays for the season.

The commander quickly determined that the best campsite was a fairly level neck of land near the wreck cache, close to a small freshwater pond fed in the melting season by a glacier. The body of water immediately ahead and extending west was Buchanan Strait, separating their point from Bache Island. Because its farthest reaches had not been explored, Greely's maps left in doubt whether Hayes Sound completely separated Grinnell Land to the north from Ellesmere Land, where they now were, or whether it was simply a deep fiord. Three miles west down the strait to their left lay Cocked Hat Island; an equivalent distance to the east around the curving shoreline lay the tip of Cape Sabine, with Brevoort and Stalknecht islands standing just off the point in Smith Sound like twin sentinels guarding Payer Harbor.

From a hill behind the campsite one would look over and beyond Sabine to Greenland; when the day was clear Littleton Island could be discerned with the aid of Greely's telescope. Forty miles north, across the edge of Kane Basin, stood Cape Hawks, which the party had left so confidently on August 26. A few miles offshore, they knew, somewhere beneath the drifting ice floes, the hulk of the *Proteus* was locked in her bitter grave, clinging to the many tons of stores that were rightfully theirs.

Two tasks demanded swift completion while light remained: building a winter shelter and bringing in all the supplies scattered on this coast between Rice Strait and Cape Sabine. Greely had chosen a place where sufficient loose stone could be pried and chipped from the earth to build a rectangular house wall measuring twenty-five by eighteen feet on the outside, about two feet thick, and three to four feet high, with a gap left at one end for a doorway. A framework of boat's oars tied with rope was rigged to rest on the wall, and upon this the builders placed the overturned whaleboat, their miracle gift from the sea, which they had laboriously dragged from Brevoort Island. Most of the available sailcloth and tarpaulins were tied down to form a covering above the boat and frame with a piece hung as a windbreak in the doorway. Finally, snowblocks were erected outside the stone walls and laid over the boat-and-canvas roof as protection from the penetrating wind. A vestibule of snow blocks was built outside the door to the hut, with a small commissary room adjacent to it. Rude as it was, this shelter seemed snug and secure to the chilled, weary men when they moved into it on October 19. They had spent seven nights in the open since leaving Eskimo Point, during which the thermometer steadily moved from zero degrees Fahrenheit to 13 below.

The men dug the worst points of rock from the floor, and covered it with gravel and sand. This they had carried in in frozen lumps and crushed underfoot. Sleeping bags were laid in two lines, each man touching his neighbor, heads to the wall and feet extending to the narrow center corridor, the only place a man could stand upright, his head up in the belly of the whaleboat. Anyone sitting erect in his bag would touch the canvas-and-wood ceiling with his head or graze it. While there was not a square foot to spare, the fact that the inmates of the shelter were so close to one another made for life-preserving warmth. Compared to the outdoors, where the wind stung deep into the face and whipped breath away, the hut was an oasis of comfort.

During the first days here Lieutenant Lockwood and Rice directed several sledging crews in gathering all the supplies left by Beebe, the Nares cache of 1875, and the two caches from the *Proteus*. Among the items Rice's party found with the clothing at Sabine was an old brass ship's lantern wrapped in newspaper. The finder was about to tear the frozen sheet away when the heading of an article struck his eye. It was about them—the Lady Franklin Bay Expedition! It had been written by Henry Clay, the same Mr. Clay they had last seen when the *Proteus* sailed away from Fort Conger.

Rice carefully wrapped the treasure in a blanket and carried it into camp, where it was thawed by the cookfire and gently unfolded. The sheet was a page of the *Louisville Courier-Journal* for May 20, 1883, five months old, carrying a three-column letter written by Mr. Clay to the editor. Like most newspapers in America, it confused the spelling of the army lieutenant's name with that of the late editor of the *New York Daily Tribune*, Horace Greeley. This did not matter to the men who listened breathlessly as Rice read this scrap of paper from afar which proved they had a loyal friend at home who had not forgotten them:

> Lieut. Greeley's Safety—Necessity of Sending a Relief Expedition Immediately—The Proper Plan to be Pursued and the Dangers to be Encountered—Henry Clay's Interesting Article.
>
> It seems from a recent article in the *Courier-Journal* that grave fears are entertained in some quarters for the safety of Lieut. Greeley and his party at Fort Conger. . . . Their position is unquestionably a serious one.

Written while the *Proteus* mission was still in the planning stage, Clay's letter attacked as unsound the relief program then proposed, which would have relied on sledging north along the Greenland coast on the casual assumption that a relief party could hire any number of Eskimos and dogs in northern Greenland for the task. Clay criticized the scheme to plant a supply depot and build a winter house at Littleton Island, writing that the party would retreat down the opposite shore and would doubtless not be in condition to cross Smith Sound in the autumn. His letter continued:

> They cannot return to Fort Conger, and there will be no shelter for them at Cape Sabine. The cache of 240 rations, if it can be found, will prolong their misery for a few days. When that is exhausted they will be past all earthly succor. Like poor De Long, they will then lie down on the cold ground, under the quiet stars, to die.

Thus Greely learned of the tragedy that had befallen Lieutenant Commander George Washington De Long in the *Jeannette,* lost since 1879, for traces of whom he had been looking these past two years. So the last American expedition to the Arctic had ended in death for its leader! Clay's letter went on to propose a relief party of two ships, one remaining in Smith Sound while the other would try to push north along the Ellesmere–Grinnell Land side:

> It will be expensive, of course, but the question of expense ought not to be taken into consideration. It is a matter of life and death to a brave band of officers and men, who are acting in the service and under the orders of their government. The companion of their polar voyage, I regard them in a certain sense as comrades. . . . I would be false to the ties of friendship and the instincts of humanity if I remained silent.

This letter must have brought about some change in the relief plans, the men realized, because the *Proteus* had been followed by a second ship, the *Yantic,* and because Garlington had come to this shore. That the *Proteus* had tried and failed was by no means Henry Clay's fault. A lively discussion broke out in the hut, from which arose many declarations of warm affection for the quiet Kentucky gentleman who had performed this service for them. With a shout of acclaim the party accepted Greely's proposal that their winter camp be known henceforth as Camp Clay.

This happily found paper on the lantern suggested the idea of carefully removing every piece of newspaper in which the *Proteus* lemons were wrapped. Greely smoothed these out in his sleeping bag and in the evenings he, Rice, and several others took turns reading them aloud, advertising and all, by the dim light of the seal-blubber lamp. From the scraps they gleaned the facts that Garfield had died from his wounds two years before, that Chester A. Arthur was President, and that the entire Cabinet had changed with the exception of Lincoln. Further reading in the *Army Register* left by Garlington told Greely that several officers junior to him in service had been promoted to captain. Lockwood found, to his delight, that he had been advanced to first lieutenant. It was with this new designation that Lockwood a couple of days later signed a penciled note identifying the cairn he raised above the scientific records of their two years' work at Fort Conger, placed by Greely's order at Cape Sabine:

> October 23, 1883. This cairn contains the original records of the Lady Franklin Bay Expedition, the private journal of Lieutenant Lockwood, and a set of photographic negatives. The party is permanently encamped at a point midway between Cape Sabine and Cocked Hat Island. All well.
>
> *James B. Lockwood,* 1st Lieut., 23d Infantry.

Greely did not announce the reason that prompted him to cache the fruit of their arctic labors several miles from camp, but his journal was explicit:

> In order to insure the safety of the records, I sent them and the pendulum, with orders to cache them in a prominent cairn on the south side of Payer Harbor. I know that point will certainly be visited, and that possibly our present camp might be missed by a relief expedition, and all the records lost if left here. I am determined that our work shall not perish with us.

During these October days of heavy sledge work Greely knew he must permit rations giving the men a high degree of physical energy. By November 1, he resolved, when outdoor work would become minimal, the rations must be so divided as to carry them through to March 1. If Smith Sound were then frozen over they

Our Records and Instruments, Cached October 1883 on Stalknecht Island.

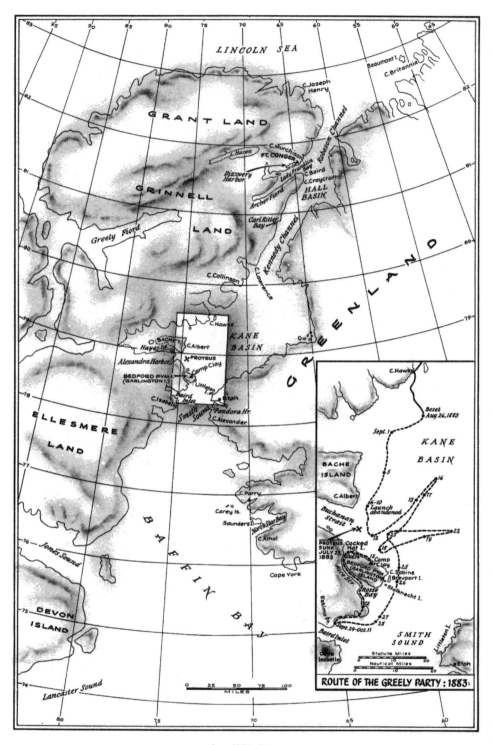

ROUTE OF THE GREELY PARTY: 1883

— from 1961 edition —

could gamble on a crossing to Littleton Island on the ice, carrying their last ten days' rations—provided help did not reach them first.

Using the scales Bender had fashioned from scrap material, Greely and the commissary sergeant weighed out the supplies and made their calculations, carrying the daily ration of each type of food to two decimal places—hundredths of an ounce. In practice this meant that when Brainard cut off a week's meat or butter for each of the two messes into which the party was divided, he must know to a fraction of an inch how to tilt his knife. As it was worked out at the end of October and presented to the assembled party, the daily winter ration per man was four ounces of meat, six ounces of hard bread, and four and a fraction ounces of all other foodstuffs combined. A total of less than fifteen ounces daily, one fifth the normal arctic ration.

Privates Long and Frederick, cooks for the two messes, took turns at the small sheet-iron stove that Bender rigged from the whaleboat sheathing and set up in the center of the passageway. There was no proper material for a chimney. While all others hid their heads in the sleeping bags to avoid the acrid smoke, the cooks bent as low as possible to avoid choking as they blew on the fuel to heat water for beverages and warm the mixed stews that had become the staple diet. Just so many pieces of wood, cut very fine from a barrel stave, were permitted to warm each meal, since the fuel like the food had to last through the winter. Sometimes alcohol, English stearine, seal blubber, and even tarred rope was burned—each experiment provoking a long discussion over the amount of coughing and eye-burning it produced compared to other combustibles.

For lack of fuel, the men were constantly thirsty. Winter had scarcely begun when the little freshwater pond near the hut froze solid, and the men could obtain nothing from it but chopped ice. Greely sometimes put a few pieces in a small rubber bag and warmed it in his sleeping bag, but this was not done often because of its chilling effect on the body. Fuel to melt ice for drinking could not be spared outside the two daily mealtimes.

The nearby caches had not been completely gathered at Camp

Clay when Rice volunteered to lead a party forty miles to Cape Isabella after the English meat. There it lay, unused—nearly six pounds for every man. Bringing it in, Rice argued, would increase the supply by three quarters of an ounce daily for each of them over the 120 days between November 1 and March 1. Once again Greely could not reject Rice's appeal for action. As Rice and the three others chosen to go with him prepared their moccasins, leggings, and mittens for the rigorous journey, each drew a few extra ounces above the normal ration for several days to build up their strength.

Accompanying Rice as they set off on the morning of November 2 under a dark sky covered with snowclouds, with a light wind blowing in from the northwest, were David Linn and Joseph Elison, two of the huskiest men of the expedition, and the earnest Julius Frederick, whose five-foot-two stature had brought him the nickname "Shorty." But his size had no relation to the respect in which the taller men held him. Now considerably emaciated, no longer the roly-poly cook and baker of Fort Conger days, Frederick had emerged as one of the hardiest spirits and most willing workers in the crowd, one who seemed to have the knack of turning his hand to everything.

Brainard rendered the four travelers a salute in his journal:

> They are all brave fellows and the entire party feels that if there is a chance of bringing the meat to Camp Clay they will do it. God grant that they will all come through safely. I have issued them provisions for eight days.

Meanwhile Private Francis Long, the best of the hunters, was camping at Rice Strait with the two Eskimos, hoping to bring in a few seals before it became too dark to identify game at midday. Through two bitter weeks, with only a tent for shelter and no fire, the trio got two seals. When they returned to Camp Clay it was obvious from their report that this area contained far less wildlife than the Lady Franklin Bay region, despite being much farther south.

So hungry were the men becoming that there were always

candidates to grasp for the moldy, rotten hardtack, green with slime, that Greely ordered thrown away when it was discovered in one of the newly opened English casks. Lockwood recorded:

> Occupied some time this morning scratching like a dog in the place where the moldy dog-biscuit were emptied. Found a few crumbs and small pieces and ate mold and all. . . . We now get about one-fourth what we could eat at a meal, and this limited allowance is to be much further reduced as soon as the sledging is done.

A day or two later he developed the hunger theme further:

> Whether we can live on such a driblet of food remains to be seen. We are now constantly hungry, and the constant thought and talk run on food, dishes of all kinds, and what we have eaten and what we hope to eat when we reach civilization. I have a constant longing for food. Anything to fill me up. God, what a life! A few crumbs of hard bread taste delicious. One imagines one thing, and another, another. I spend much time in thinking of bills of fare. . . .
>
> How often my thoughts wander home, and I recall my dear father, mother and the family generally—then come the family dishes of all kinds. Numb fingers and want of light—I can write no more.

Under such conditions it is perhaps surprising that Brainard did not detect any stealing of food until October 27. After visiting the commissary, a structure of snow blocks just outside the hut door, he quietly reported something amiss to Greely, and noted in his journal:

> The commissary was broken into last night and a small quantity of hard bread taken. While one can sympathize with the hunger which drives a member of our party to commit such a despicable act, still the culprit will have to be brought to light and punished.

Two days after the departure of the Cape Isabella mission, Brainard was recording the typical concerns of an early winter day, almost all hinging on the main topic—food:

A huge hard bread pudding for breakfast made us all feel very happy for a few hours. Sunday, the commanding officer has decreed, is always to be a feast day with some rare delicacy to look forward to. We also have an excellent stew made from fox carcasses.

The sense of repletion to the stomach after eating belongs to our pleasures of the dim past. The constant gnawing of hunger almost drives us mad. . . . Long saw the tracks of two bears yesterday while returning to Camp Clay. A good-sized bear is just what this party needs to cheer it up. . . .

Although this is the Sabbath, we began work on the new commissary storehouse. Someone again has been purloining provisions from the storehouse. It is well we are preparing to lock up what food remains.

On November 8 Greely sent Lieutenant Lockwood, Dr. Pavy, Brainard, and five other men to bring in Long's equipment and the two seals from Rice Strait. The thermometer registered —31.5 degrees. When they returned chilled and exhausted after eight hours' sledging, Greely ordered Schneider, his clerk, to serve each man a portion of hot rum. Unable to withstand temptation, Schneider gulped down some of the stimulant without authority, then staggered into the storehouse while no one was watching. His stumbling there in the dark gave his presence away. All hands jumped to the conclusion that Schneider was the thief of several nights past, but the unhappy clerk protested his innocence. Greely doubted that the man had been mentally responsible when he entered the commissary, but took him severely to task for his misconduct.

Who, then, was the thief? Brainard's notes of the following evening show that he was uncertain:

Matters are growing worse. Lieut. Lockwood discovered a can of milk in the commissary storehouse, carefully covered by a block of snow. An attempt had been made to open it with a blunt-pointed knife but the contents fortunately were intact. Marks and scratches made in the hurry of opening corresponded perfectly with the saw-like edge of Schneider's knife. But the knife had been loaned to Henry and was in his possession! We do not know whom to trust in this dire extremity, consequently none in the future will be trusted.

A small supply of extra food came from the occasional hungry foxes that prowled about camp and were shot at point-blank range. Weighing a little less than four pounds each, they provided about an ounce of edible meat per man. The successful hunter was awarded the heart; liver and entrails were dumped into the evening stew. But soon the animals became scarce, as Brainard wrote:

> No foxes have been seen for several days. Our dirty faces and disreputable clothing must have frightened them. No one ever thinks of wasting what energy he has in cleaning his person, or fussing with his ragged garments.

Dinner on the 9th was held off an hour in expectation of Rice and his trail companions, but was finally served around. The meal consisted, according to Lockwood's account, of "tea, a spoonful of English meat and a handful of hard bread." Several of the party later took their turns reading aloud, an evening occupation Greely initiated to combat the loneliness of the hours before sleep, when the men were most likely to sink into moodiness. The scanty store of reading matter included Thomas Hardy's novel *Two on a Tower,* Dickens' *Pickwick Papers,* and *Peck's Bad Boy*—all left by the *Proteus* party—and a Bible that Sergeant Hampden S. Gardiner, a deeply religious man, had brought from Fort Conger in preference to an equal weight of clothing. All finally settled down to sleep, assuming that the Cape Isabella party would come in the next day. About midnight Greely was awakened by the crunching of footsteps in the crisp snow outside the shelter.

"Who is there?" he called out in alarm as the sleepers stirred.

The figure of a broken, exhausted man staggered through the entranceway and fell panting for breath in the center of the hut. As soon as the seal-blubber lamp was lit, the men were horrified to see George Rice stretched out before them, struggling to open his half-frozen lips behind a white muzzle of ice which encrusted his hairy face. He managed at length to gasp out:

"Elison is dying in Rosse Bay!"

For some time he could say no more; then he gathered sufficient strength to give a brief account of his movements during the past eight days and of the serious danger menacing his comrades Elison, Linn, and Frederick. The three had been left in the storm seventeen miles from camp, lying in a sleeping bag protected from the wind only by a small tent-fly. Greely realized that he must send help at once. Almost by instinct he turned to Lockwood and Brainard and gave the necessary orders: Brainard to go with Fred at maximum speed with a light pack containing brandy and food; Lockwood to follow with six others dragging the sledge on which, Rice told them sadly, they would probably bring back Elison's corpse. He did not think the man could last it out.

When he was sufficiently rested to speak at length, Rice told a story of the near-success of his expedition, marred at its end by tragic stupidity. The party had managed the outward trip well and on the third day had obtained the English meat at Cape Isabella. On the return journey across Baird Inlet, Rice noticed that Elison was failing badly. The cause was simple enough to detect. Despite strict instructions to the contrary, he and Linn had been trying to quench their thirst by eating snow, and in so doing Elison had frozen his fingers and his nose. A little later he complained of severe pains in his feet, and for a while he simply staggered along while the other three dragged the loaded sledge. Several times they stopped while Rice and Frederick tried to warm the suffering man's extremities by chafing them to restore circulation, to no avail. They then resorted to double-sledging, first hauling Elison a distance, then returning for the meat. At intervals "Shorty" Frederick even took Elison's arm over his shoulder and half-carried the big man while the latter cried out in his pain. But as the group slowly neared Eskimo Point, Rice saw that they must choose between the load of meat and saving Elison's life.

Ramming a Springfield rifle upright in the snow to mark the spot, the men dropped the four cases of meat off the sledge and put the victim on it in their place. At Eskimo Point, in one of the party's abandoned stone huts, the refugees found shelter from the wind. Without hesitation Rice deliberately cut wood from the English iceboat Greely had cached there, in order to make a fire that would put life back into Elison's limbs. When the poor fellow's face and hands began to thaw out, his sufferings brought the sympathetic Frederick close to tears. But it looked now as if he would be all right.

Refreshed to a degree, the group pushed forward in a gale on the morning of November 10 to mount the divide separating Baird Inlet from Rosse Bay, Linn going ahead with Elison while Rice and Frederick pulled the sledge. In the below-zero temperature and keen wind, Elison's limbs once again became frozen and the ice gathering on his eyelashes froze his lids together. Rice tried fastening a rope to Elison's arm and to the sledge while the three men pulled, but the victim frequently fell and was dragged several yards before they could halt to lift him to his feet. In mid-afternoon, when the sledgers no longer had strength to drag both the sledge and Elison over the hill, they took hasty council and decided that Rice should go ahead to Camp Clay while Linn and Frederick crept into Elison's sleeping bag to keep him alive by chafing and body contact. Taking from his mates only one small chunk of frozen beef to sustain himself, the rugged Canadian set off at once, having had no food but a cup of tea all day. Across Rosse Bay he struggled, through the narrow waterway Greely had given his name, and along the shore of Buchanan Strait toward Camp Clay, fully aware that the lives of all three men depended on his getting through. It took almost all the energy his sturdy body held in reserve, plus that extra degree of determination that makes heroes, but George Rice had what was required.

Now others would set off to save his comrades. At 4:30 A.M. in almost complete darkness Brainard and Fred Christiansen floundered out through the deep, new-fallen snow.

The monotony of the tramp [Brainard wrote later] was sometimes broken by my dusky companion, who uttered half-sup-
pressed English oaths whenever he fell over a projecting point
of ice.

About noon the pair reached the group in the sleeping bag,
where they found Elison's condition somewhat better than Rice
had led them to expect. But Frederick and Linn, exposed as they
were to the full fury of the gale at 30 below zero, were badly
frostbitten about the face and in the feet. Elison, unable to contain his urine, had several times drained in the sleeping bag,
which was now frozen stiff as a board. All three men had therefore been compelled to lie in virtually the same position for many
hours. To add to Frederick's physical difficulties, he had had to
uphold the morale of both companions, as Linn's mind began to
wander under the depressing influence of Elison's moans of pain.
For a time Linn spoke incoherently of wanting to leave the
sleeping bag, from which madness Frederick with difficulty restrained him.

Even now, with help on the spot, Elison's pain had so far
weakened his spirit that he could only shake his head sadly as
Brainard kept up a stream of encouraging talk of their all going
home soon to the safety of their families.

"Kill me—oh, kill me, will you, please?" he pleaded.

A good swig of brandy and the hot meal that Brainard spooned
to them in the bag did wonders for all three. Yet neither Frederick
nor Linn thought he could help the two rescuers drag the sledge
with Elison on it. At best they might make it to Camp Clay on
their own feet. So Brainard and Fred had to take the only other
course possible—turn back to meet Lieutenant Lockwood's party
and hurry them along. As he and Eskimo Fred faced once more
into the howling gale piling down on them from the north, Brainard noticed a bold fox creep deliberately up to the sleeping bag
and try to enter it. The sergeant picked up an ax from the sledge
and aimed a blow at the intruder, but it scurried off into the rocks
above them.

Brainard and Christiansen Succoring Elison, Linn, and Frederick.

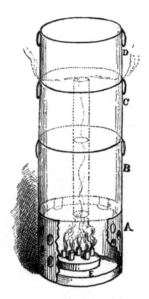

Field Cooking Apparatus.

There the three prisoners remained, unable to move for eighteen hours, through the afternoon and then another long night, until the cheery calls of Brainard and Christiansen again greeted their ears early on the morning of the 11th. They brought word that Lockwood, Dr. Pavy, and four others were only an hour or two behind. The three sufferers took new heart once another hot stew prepared by the first sergeant was warming them, and it was not long before the rescue crew appeared. The stiff buffalo-hide bag was hacked open with the ax, and while the deliverers gently wrapped Elison for his journey on the sledge, Linn and Frederick stretched their cramped limbs in preparation for the seventeen-mile journey they would have to make on their own power. They revived with remarkable speed and before long they had set out for Camp Clay ahead of the main group, who carefully nursed the sledge over the roughest places to spare the groaning Elison as much as possible. It took the sledgers eighteen hours to cover the distance back to Camp Clay. When they finally made it, at 2:30 A.M., they found that Frederick and Linn had pulled in some eight hours before.

Dr. Pavy at first despaired of saving Elison's life. But after the big soldier rallied under the few extra ounces of food Greely allotted him each day, with general approval, the medical man thought he might escape with the loss of some extremities. Both feet and hands were badly discolored from freezing. At just what line they might naturally amputate themselves it was too early for him to say. The doctor did not dare to intervene surgically for lack of proper instruments and clean dressings. Elison could only lie in his bag, helpless as a baby, with Pavy and Private Henry Biederbick, the medical orderly, taking turns tending to his needs. When he had meals, they spooned his food to his lips. When he had to pass water his neighbors held a pan for him, which was dumped in the tub near the doorway used as a urinal by the entire party. Unable to stand on his burning feet, he performed the major function of nature kneeling—a task for which the others went outdoors, once a week on the average.

With the steady diminution of caloric energy from the short rations, the men's bodies became less resistant to the penetrating cold, which Brainard described graphically on November 20:

> Inside the hut the temperature ranges from fourteen to twenty-five degrees; sometimes it rises above freezing when the fire is lighted but falls immediately when it is extinguished. We experience the greatest discomfort from the cold and find it necessary at times to exert ourselves by knocking the feet together in a most frantic manner to prevent them from freezing. Our bags are frozen firmly to the ground, and the hair inside is filled with frost, and the moisture thus produced is absorbed by our garments, which are usually saturated before morning.

Yet in a sense the cold was a blessing, because it could mean their salvation. Only if the surface of Smith Sound were frozen solid could they risk a dash across to Littleton Island. So, while cursing the cold immediately about them, the men were inwardly cheering on Winter to tighten its freezing grip over the route to the island of their hopes. When the sky was clear and the moon afforded some view into the distance, watchers would climb the hill behind the hut to look out toward the east. Water-clouds, vapor hovering over the surface of open water, were a bad sign; their absence was regarded as favorable. One week after another the party hoped for a solid pack to cover the gap between them and the supply pile they were certain awaited them thirty miles to the east. Some, although not Greely, barely hoped that a rescue party might cross over from Littleton Island on the ice.

Amid the suffering from cold, while sporadic signs of midnight theft from the commissary continued to worry the commissary sergeant, while Elison's moans grated on the party's nerves and his survival still hung in the balance, while Greely struggled with all his imagination to find ways to combat the lassitude that overcomes men losing their will to survive—amid all other discomforts, ceaseless hunger dominated the men's thoughts. For Lockwood, food became an obsession to which he devoted page after page in his notebook:

Breakfast this morning of soup and tea, and for dinner corned beef and tea. Oh! this everlasting hunger—it is terrible, and I hope never to repeat it—this feeling of never having enough to eat. Our talk is incessantly about food and dishes, restaurants and hotels, and everything in connection with eating. How we watch the cook and speculate on the chances of getting a good or poor share. This we speculate to ourselves, for we all admit that the cooks are as fair as they can be.

Before long Lockwood's daily entries became dotted with short items headed *Memorandum,* listing various dishes, how cooked and where obtained:

Memorandum: Tripe, eggs, Boston baked beans and brown bread at Godfrey's. . . . *Memorandum: Fromage de Brie,* Magruder's, New York Ave., Washington. . . . *Memorandum:* Vienna Coffee House, Broadway and 14th Street, New York, large assortment of cakes, bread and pastry. . . . Omelettes at the Vienna Cafe. These can be sent for by express from this place; prices moderate.

It was as if the famished lieutenant's mind were wandering, his deft shorthand flicking across the pages of his notebook as rapidly as visions of succulent dishes now denied him by circumstances flashed into his consciousness. The stoic Brainard was less given to flights of fancy over delicacies he once had tasted, and more objective in describing what he actually had in his pan:

Another stew served this evening was thickened with the rotten dog biscuit. I believe that the hungriest cur on the streets would refuse this wretched apology for food. . . .

A bounteous repast was served this morning, with which everyone was well pleased. It consisted of seal-skin and fox intestines, together with moldy dog-biscuit. Nothing approaching food is ever wasted with us, and it is a notorious fact that the cooks are not over careful in cleansing the fox intestines.

Greely looked at food matters as the expedition leader, who felt and thought far beyond his own miseries to his moral responsibility for bringing his men through this ordeal of starvation:

The ravenous, irritable condition in which the entire party are at present cannot but have the effect of making most men morbid and suspicious. Sergeant Gardiner lately said to me that he objected very decidely to passing Rice's ration to him, if it could be avoided. He declared that he realized the fairness of the cooks, but that, in allowing a cup of tea or a plate of stew to pass through his hands, he could not prevent himself from mentally weighing the food as it passed, by comparing it to the portion which came to himself. Such a comparison he knew was small and petty, but his starving condition must explain and excuse it. I readily understood his feelings, as I myself have avoided handling another man's portion for similar reasons.

For the first time in many weeks, the relative bounty of Thanksgiving Day brought the illusion of a feast. There was a delicious rice pudding with raisins following a warm fox stew with seal blubber, bread crumbs, and milk—or "son-of-a-gun," the generic Camp Clay term for an otherwise unidentifiable mixture. A warm punch made with a dozen lemons and twenty-five gills of rum fairly floated the party into a state of luxurious euphoria. Brainard described the day as "one of the most enjoyable of my life."

As December wore on, it became apparent that Elison was going to lose most of his fingers and both feet. By the 19th Brainard was describing the latter as:

> . . . black, shrunken and lifeless; his ankles especially are a horrible sight. The flesh has sloughed away, leaving the bones entirely devoid of covering. He suffers much, but is very patient and bears his troubles with manly and heroic fortitude.

Although he could see what was happening to his fingers as they dried up and broke off, one by one, Elison did not know when his feet came off at the ankles, the left first, during the first days of January, the right five days later, with assistance from Dr. Pavy's surgical scissors and a small scalpel. The wounds were dressed with vaseline at first, but when the supply ran out lard mixed with a little salicylic acid was substituted. For bandages the faithful Biederbick salvaged some pieces of frozen underclothing from the *Proteus* cache and thawed them out against his own chest. So successfully did the other men conceal the truth from Elison that as the weeks passed he continued to complain of the painful itching in his "feet."

To celebrate Christmas, a number of men saved up tiny bits of their rations in order to make a feast. After dinner three cheers were shouted successively for Lieutenant Greely, Rice, Elison, and the industrious cooks, Francis Long and "Shorty" Frederick. Someone recalled the joking ad printed two years earlier in the *Arctic Moon* on behalf of this same pair of kitchenmen: "San Francisco Longman and Frederick Shortman, bakers of fine pies, cakes, rolls, twists, etc." Then the hut resounded to voices singing "O Tannenbaum," led by some of the German boys, "Silent Night" in both German and English, and even the weird, haunting chant of the two Eskimos singing their own native songs and the Danish anthem. Christmas at Camp Clay was a day and evening of defiance of cold, hunger, and gloom. Every man responded to its spirit as if certain of getting through, since they were now for the third time on the downhill side of the long winter night. Lieutenant Lockwood had written of the solstice:

> The top of the hill! The most glorious day of this dreary journey through the valley of cold and hunger has at last come—and now nearly gone. Thank God! Now the glorious sun commences to return and every day gets lighter and brings him nearer. It is an augury that we shall yet pull through all right. Exchanged bags with Jewell during the afternoon and paid Lieut. Greely and his neighbors a visit.

Between Christmas and New Year's Day a craze of food-swapping swept through the party until the hut resembled a cross between an Arab bazaar and the pit of the New York Stock Exchange. My butter for your hard bread! How about trading your biscuit today for mine tomorrow? What am I offered for this piece of seal blubber?

Greely did not approve the market-day atmosphere, since the fraternal attitude of sharing was being lost in the competitive spirit of the trading. When he requested that each man keep his own rations and eat them, the bazaar disappeared almost as quickly as it had materialized. It had been, in fact, more an occupation for idle hours than anything else.

On the morning of January 4, 1884, Brainard entered the commissary, which now had a door with a lock salvaged from the *Proteus* pile, to find a slit cut in the canvas roof. A quarter-pound of bacon had been stolen. The next day he found another slit carefully concealed under snow blocks:

> I think the depradator [he wrote] is one of two men whom I have been watching closely for some days. I gave notice this morning that I had set a spring-gun in the storehouse, and that any man who entered or interfered with the house in any way did so at his peril. I found so much trouble in setting the gun that I finally abandoned the attempt. Of this fact, however, the party, except Lieutenant Greely, remained in ignorance.

The thief shifted his tactics to the inside, for the next day Frederick reported that someone had been tampering with the bacon issued to him for the mess which he served as cook. About four ounces had been cut off. On the 7th Brainard found that someone had hacked into one of the barrels of English hard bread and taken some five pounds. He knew of one man who had been in possession of the ax the day before, but this was not enough to sustain an open accusation. So angry were the entire group that from all sides of the hut came loud calls for the thief to confess his crime. If he would do so, the consensus held, every one would give him a share of his own rations to induce him to stop. But no one stepped forward to admit his guilt.

Late one night Greely was shocked to observe Dr. Pavy steal his hand into Elison's bread can, from which he had been feeding his patient, and take some of it. Turning the matter over in his mind during a sleepless night, the commander decided that he must at all costs prevent an open break with the physician, whose services to all of them might soon become essential. Already the

state of arrest he had decreed for Dr. Pavy had become mean-
ingless. Reluctantly he remained silent. But a few days later
Private Whisler, whose dislike for Pavy went back to the sledging
incident at Fort Conger, told Brainard he had seen the doctor
steal Elison's bread. By this time, however, Elison was no longer
the principal sufferer in camp.

Second only to Private Ellis as the party's oldest man, his constitution undermined by years of intemperance, Sergeant William
Cross had since the weeks on the ice floe suffered from a frosted
foot. At Camp Clay it had turned dark brown, then almost black.
Of a surly disposition under the best conditions, Cross had tended
to nurse his injured feelings alone, to the point where Greely had
ordered him to cut up the fuel wood in the protection of the
vestibule simply as a device to keep the man active.

On January 17 the sounds of labored breathing from Cross'
bag showed that he was in an alarmingly weak condition. Early
in the morning of the 18th Sergeant Jewell, who slept next to
Cross, called out to Greely that the engineer was trying, in a
semiconscious condition, to crawl from his bag. Lighting the
lamp, the commanding officer aroused Dr. Pavy, who examined
the ill man. The invalid then worried down some brandy and
soup, though without gaining his full senses, and lay back with a
moan. He continued to fight for breath until about 2 P.M. Then
he died.

After examining the body, Dr. Pavy confided to Greely in
French that while "dropsical effusion of the heart" might best be
given to the party as the cause of death, it might be more proper
to add "caused by insufficient nutrition" in his official report. In
other words, Cross had died of starvation. He had shown signs
of scurvy about the mouth, the doctor said, but he agreed with
the commander that it would be unwise to mention this dread
disease of the Arctic to the men.

In a few words Greely pointed out to the group, about a third
of whom were aware of the true facts, that the death of Cross
should not weaken the determination of the others, because the

deceased man's endurance had already been sapped by his previous intemperate habits. The duty of everyone, the commander added, was to the living now. Greely's talk that evening seemed to set off animated, even cheerful discussion of their future prospects. The next morning Brainard and Biederbick wrapped Cross' corpse in empty coffee sacks with as much tenderness as they could manage and draped the American flag over the body. At noon, by the flickering light of the smoky oil lamp as the men sat up in their sleeping bags in a circle about the remains, Greely read the Episcopal burial service:

I am the resurrection and the life, saith the Lord: He that believeth in me, though he were dead, yet shall he live; and whosoever liveth and believeth in me, shall never die.

It was a spectral scene, something from the pages of Dante— two dozen shaggy-haired men, Catholic, Protestant, Jew, and unbeliever, the civilized and primitive, the learned and unlettered, deeply affected by the first break in their ranks, attempting to pay a tribute and say a decent farewell. Greely read on:

Man, that is born of woman, hath but a short time to live, and is full of misery. He cometh up and is cut down, like a flower.

With Lieutenant Kislingbury in charge, a six-man detail pulled the body on a sledge just over a ridge some fifty yards from the hut to a grave which the men could hack only fifteen inches deep in the frozen, rocky earth. Biederbick, who had attended Cross at the last, scattered the symbolic dust:

Unto Almighty God we commend the soul of our brother departed, and we commit his body to the ground; earth to earth, ashes to ashes, dust to dust; in sure and certain hope of the Resurrection unto eternal life, through our Lord Jesus Christ.

Brainard recorded the event in his journal:

The body was covered in the stars and stripes, and borne to its last resting place on the small sledge which already has a history in connection with the Elison disaster of last autumn. We ranged a circle of stones carefully about the grave of our lost compan-

Lunar Halo.

Our First Funeral—January 19, 1884.

ion, it being the only attention that we could bestow on him now.

One cannot conceive of anything more unearthly, more weird, than this ghostly procession of emaciated and half-starved men moving slowly and silently away from their wretched ice-prison in the dim and uncertain light of an Arctic night, having in their midst a dead comrade who was about to be laid away in the frozen ground forever. It was a scene that one can never forget.

7 DEBATE

WHEN Lieutenant Ernest A. Garlington stepped from the train in Washington on Monday, October 1, 1883, restraining his huge Newfoundland, Rover, on a leash, he brought the Greely expedition back onto the front pages of the newspapers after a week's lull. It had been settled days ago that Greely was to be left in the Arctic for the winter, and more than enough ink had been spilled over his probable fate. But now the main point of speculation was Garlington. How, it was asked, would he explain himself? And how would the War Department receive his excuses?

The young officer was at first judged severely by the press and by that impatient, critical public opinion with which it was in constant interaction as both its creator and its creature. By the very nature of events, Garlington could only be viewed as a failure who had bungled his assignment in the polar seas. Sensing this from the outset, Garlington discreetly held his tongue except to say that he was preparing an official report of the *Proteus* sinking for Secretary Lincoln. Denied much in the way of firm news, reporters managed to glean from him the fact that his handsome dog had indeed been with the *Proteus* party during the retreat from the wreck, that he had lain in the bottom of the boat and behaved well. No, Garlington said, Rover had not consumed much food and his presence aboard had not denied a scrap of nourishment to the Greely party.

From the mail coming into the department and from the press comment since September 14, Lincoln was acutely aware that the beleaguered scientific expedition, which had left town in 1881 with a minimum of flurry, turned out now to have friends who bobbed up wherever one turned one's head. This fellow Greely's personal acquaintances and his wife's friends and relatives seemed to stretch from Maine to California. Their continual inquiries about "the Greely expedition" were becoming annoying. Therefore by the time that Garlington had turned in his report the Secretary of War was convinced that the public interest demanded a court of inquiry into the *Proteus* fiasco, one which would leave no stone unturned in its search for culpability. Lincoln appointed a court to meet in Washington on November 8, instructed to get to the bottom of the whole sorry business.

In California, where she was living with her two children and caring for her invalid father, Henrietta Greely could find nothing in the newspaper accounts of the plans to investigate Garlington that reassured her. There seemed to be no plan in Washington to rescue her husband and his men—only a scrutiny of the past. However, General Hazen was at least back in Washington, and to him, as to a trusted old friend, she wrote her conviction that action was needed:

> I have not thought the case hopeless from the first, but it was, of course, encouraging to know that you did not take a gloomy view of it. I do not feel that much is to be gained by looking into the failure of the expedition this year. It seems to me the important thing is to bend every energy toward preparing a fitting plan to rescue the party at the earliest moment next year. Still, I do not see how Mr. Garlington as commander of the recent expedition can be completely exonerated from blame for its failure.

Henrietta devoured the scanty news reports, which carried only driblets of information from the department. From these she managed to learn that the court of inquiry was splitting hairs, picking over minutiae, one day after another. Everyone involved seemed to be looking out for himself, excusing his own conduct, blaming others—and hardly giving a thought to those still in peril in the Arctic.

Mother Greely, her mind untrammeled by the considerations

of reputation and career that guided the sophisticated in Washington, matched Henrietta's brave letters of comfort and hope with her own expression of sound common sense. Her "daughter Rettie" was very much closer now than ever before:

> I am glad to know that you are so hopeful abought Adolphus ability to winter in the arctic regions. I hope God will protect them and that they will come home all right. . . . What worrys me most is that Adolphus has left his station and is now suffering with cold and perhaps sickness and hunger. Tis dredful to think of. . . . They ought to have sent out another expedition as soon as the loss of the *Proteus* was known. They dont send the right kind of men. Do you suppose that Adolphus would have acted in the way that Garlington did? I say no. . . .
>
> There is quite a long piece in the paper today about Court of Inquiry. They are going to send for Capt. Pike. But what good does all this talk amount to? It dont help them poor fellows out there. . . .
>
> I am sorry to hear that you are losing your beautiful hair. Tis too bad. I have seen two or three pieces in the papers abought you. They say that you are a Beautiful Woman, and I know that you are as good as you are Beautiful. . . . I am glad to hear that the Babys is so well. I wish I could see them, the Dear Darlings, Adolphs babys. Twas a dredful thing for him to leve you all to go to that dredful place. . . .
>
> I hope you will come East in the spring. I think you could do a grate deal abought getting up the next expidition. But if we should be disapointed again I dare not think of the result. . . . Rettie I want you to know if anything happens to me that every thing here belongs to you and the babys. Please write me soon.
>
> *Mother F. D. Greely*
>
> *P.S.* I have saved all the papers and laid them aside for Adolph, if he ever comes home again to read.

Brigadier General Stephen Vincent Benét, Army Chief of Ordnance, presided over the *Proteus* court of inquiry. Flanking him on either side were Colonels O. M. Poe and R. B. Ayres, with Major Henry Goodfellow acting as judge advocate and recorder of the court. At the very outset Lieutenant Garlington asserted that "grave injustice has already been done me by persons who have reached conclusions unsupported by the facts," and requested in consequence the right to representation by counsel. The court granted him permission to have Linden Kent, a distinguished and skilled capital attorney, to act as his spokesman.

While all witnesses acknowledged the inherent dangers of ice navigation and its almost inscrutable mysteries, they sought at the same time to place all human errors on someone else's shoulders. According to Garlington's testimony, Captain Richard Pike was a half-educated incompetent who repeatedly on the voyage northward had scraped the hull of his ship on submerged rocks and hardly knew how to take his bearings or read a compass. Commander Wildes followed in similar vein, and stressed especially the contrast, as he saw it, between his fine navy crew and the "beach-combers and drifters—a rascally lot" under Pike's command aboard the *Proteus*. To him the deficiencies of the *Proteus* equipment were signs of sloppiness, but the breakdown of his own boilers on the *Yantic* was due to normal use. The separation of their two vessels, both officers maintained, was quite proper under the circumstances and only a series of mischances prevented their joining forces earlier than they did.

General Hazen and his fellow officers who arranged the *Proteus* charter reacted vigorously to criticism of their preparation of the mission. She was a fine ship with officers and men known to be as competent as any in St. John's, they said. Captain Pike journeyed to Washington to testify, and finding himself in potentially hostile territory played his hand cautiously. He and Garlington had got along fine together, Pike said. The nip was just one of those things that happen to the best of ships and skippers in arctic ice. His men and his ship were of the best, he noted, and he had no complaints about the way his owners had supplied her, nor the way the charter party (the War Department of the United States government) had behaved. To the harsh words of Lieutenant Garlington and Commander Wildes he uttered no rejoinder in kind. If he was burning with anger inside, he kept his feelings to himself.

One point that had been repeatedly aired in the newspapers since mid-September was cleared up during the inquiry. This was the mysterious matter of the "additional instructions" alleged to have been given Garlington over and beyond the publicly known plan of relief. The court found out that just before sailing Garlington had been handed an envelope of official orders in which a document termed "Inclosure No. 4" appeared. In it Hazen instructed him without fail to leave a depot at Littleton Island on his way north. But when everyone was interrogated about this document, from the Chief Signal Officer to the clerk who copied it and in so doing committed some errors, Attorney Kent brought out the fact that the item was Hazen's hasty afterthought, not previously discussed with Garlington and in a sense contradictory to other orders which had been discussed in detail. In 1881 Greely himself had made it clear that he expected to meet his relief on the east coast of Ellesmere Land, the west side of the body of water skirting Greenland, and Littleton Island was to be a winter post for the relief party when and if a rendezvous should fail. Hazen finally conceded that Inclosure No. 4 should not have been considered binding on the lieutenant, so no blame should be attached to him for having bypassed the island when the water to the north appeared clear. He was wrong, Hazen admitted, to have suggested otherwise.

But when the fatal nip did occur, the court inquired, how effectively did Garlington labor to secure stores for Greely? Oh, the lieutenant replied, he had been taking precautions well in advance; he had ordered his men to bring some boxes on deck just in case anything should happen. The inquiry slid lightly over the contrast between this testimony and the actual number of rations saved, the lack of any boat drills, the failure to save sledges and dogs. There was no mention of Rover or his appetite. Nor did the inquiry spend much time on Garlington's division of the supplies between those cached for the Greely party and those taken in his flight. The inquiry was, after all, devoted to the loss of a ship, not to the rescue of the Lady Franklin Bay Expedition.

On November 19, with Commander Frank Wildes on the stand, Major Goodfellow nonetheless came close to touching the core of the matter, despite the evasions of the witness.

"Upon your learning of the loss of the *Proteus* did any question occur to you of the propriety of landing stores from your own ship and making a depot of provisions there for the use of the Greely party?"

"Yes, sir," replied Wildes.

"What was your view of the subject at the time?"

"I decline to answer that, sir," said the officer.

Goodfellow was perplexed. "Do you decline on the ground of it tending to criminate you?"

Wildes exploded: "To criminate? No, sir!" Not for him the constitutional defense of silence, which made anyone who used it appear guilty as sin. The major tried again in different words, groping for this man's reason for hesitation.

Had Wildes and Garlington ever discussed his contributing any of the naval vessel's stores for the use either of the *Proteus* party or Greely's men? No, said Wildes, there had been no such discussion.

Well, the judge advocate persisted, when he found that the *Proteus* had failed in her mission, why did he not consider leaving something for Greely? The navy officer hemmed and hawed through a few more exchanges, then declared that his reasons had already been sent to Secretary Chandler, who had asked the same question in his letter of October 16. Under Goodfellow's prodding Wildes finally offered in evidence the relevant parts of the letter:

> On learning of the loss of the *Proteus,* I considered that my first and paramount duty was to pick up the boats, which contained thirty-seven men. Having done that it would be time to consider what next. . . . I had no fears for Lieutenant Greely, who, living in a region reported well stocked with game, had economized his provisions. Should he reach Littleton Island, be-

sides the provisions on the west coast the rocks and waters between that island and the mainland abound in walrus, the stench
from their ordure fouling the air for a long distance.

The court permitted Wildes' bland assumption that Greely
was safe and well supplied to pass without comment.

While this record was unfolding, Secretary Lincoln's annual
report for the fiscal year 1883 was made public. The section
dealing with Greely's prospects stretched every possibility so as
to allay talk that the party had been left in peril. Phrased with
even more ingenuity than the form letter of September 19, it conceded in a few words the need for early provision of another
relief expedition, then continued:

> Their exact situation and condition is only a matter of con-
> jecture. They have had with them at Lady Franklin Bay a supply
> of food, clothing and other necessaries entirely sufficient to last
> them until next summer; and there would be no apprehension
> for their safety if it were known that they had remained and
> were now at Lady Franklin Bay.
>
> It is possible, however, that inasmuch as the relief expedition
> of the year 1882 did not succeed in connecting with Lieutenant
> Greely he, in pursuance of prearranged plans, late in the sum-
> mer of this year left Lady Franklin Bay to come southward to
> the entrance of Smith's Sound, and that, relying upon finding
> there an abundant supply of the necessaries of life, he neglected
> to burden himself in the southward journey with a greater quan-
> tity of provisions and clothing than would be necessary to sup-
> port his party on the journey.
>
> Even in this case his condition would be by no means desper-
> ate, for at this point and further north there are supplies, and if
> they should prove not sufficient to support him and his party until
> a vessel can reach him in 1884, it is thought that it would not be
> impossible for him to retrace his steps and reach the supplies left
> at Lady Franklin Bay.

These were bitter words for Henrietta Greely to read in cold
print over the signature of the Secretary of War. He called it a
"matter of conjecture," but she *knew* that her Dolph was suffering
from cold and hunger. It was not merely "possible" that he had

taken to the boats as planned back in 1881—to Henrietta it was
certain. Lincoln said that Greely may have "neglected to burden
himself"; she was positive that he carried with him all the supplies he safely could. Finally, while the Secretary spoke of the
party's possibly returning to Fort Conger as the winter began,
she was convinced, from what Henry Clay had written, and from
many other sources, that they could never manage such a long
journey at that season.

So low on its list of concerns did the Arthur administration
place the rescue of Greely that in his annual message to Congress
on December 4 the President did not mention an appropriation
for this purpose among the legislative action he considered important. But on December 17 Arthur named General Hazen to
head a four-man board of army and navy officers to consider a
plan for a new relief expedition. It met promptly at the Navy
Department, on December 20, and got down to specifics while
the Garlington court of inquiry was droning into its eighth week.

The final hearing of the *Proteus* inquiry on January 3 found
Attorney Linden Kent winding up a summary speech of several
hours declaiming, in reference to his client Garlington: "From
out the bitter blasts of wrong and detraction, more piercing than
Arctic winds, he comes before this court, bringing in one hand
his orders, and in the other the clean, pure record made there-
under, amid the ice of the Arctic regions."

In its ten weeks of meetings the court compiled a record of
575 printed pages, practically all devoted to the loss of the
Proteus. It examined in minute detail the equipment sunk to the
bottom of Kane Basin—where bought, how ordered, by whom
checked, and so on. After long deliberation the court concluded
that Garlington had merely "erred" in leaving Littleton Island
without waiting for the *Yantic,* but that he had quite properly
taken all the food he could carry from the wreck. His error was
one of judgment, the court held, and no court-martial was indicated. As to Wildes, the court finding noted that:

It is greatly to be regretted that, in his earnest desire to succor
the crew and party of the *Proteus* before they should encounter

the perils of Melville Bay, he should not have risked the delay
of a few hours, or even days, to cache a portion of his surplus
provisions and stores to welcome the arrival of Lieutenant Greely
and party on that inhospitable shore.

After lightly reprimanding Garlington and Wildes, the board
turned all its guns on General Hazen and criticized him vigorously on nine counts of failing to organize the relief expedition
properly and to give its leader the requisite instructions in clear
terms. Yet, the court held, "the foregoing grave errors and omissions . . . are all deemed to have been due to the lack of a wise
prevision and sound judgment . . . and unattended by any willful
neglect or intentional dereliction of duty."

Thus, while slapping Hazen in the face, the inquiry let him off,
as it did Garlington, without a court-martial.

Smarting from the blow delivered by General Benét and his
colleagues, Hazen found himself reporting the recommendations
of his Army-Navy relief board to Secretaries Lincoln and Chandler: that the relief this year should be entirely in the hands of the
U.S. Navy; that the government buy at least two ships and possibly three of the whaler or sealer type, like the *Proteus* and
Neptune, of 500 to 600 tons displacement each; and that the
relief squadron reach Upernavik by May 15 in order to push
through Melville Bay and into Smith Sound at the earliest date
ice conditions would permit.

Here at last was the kind of action for which Henrietta had
been pleading by correspondence. Even as Hazen's board was
preparing its report she had written to him from San Diego: "It
seems to me that no expense or pains should be spared this year
as it is the last that can hope to see the party brought home alive."

On January 20, after the joint board had submitted its pro-
posals, General Lockwood wrote to Henrietta a report of his call
on President Arthur:

I called yesterday on the President and I submitted your views
which, though respectfully received, made but little impression
upon him. He requested me to leave [your] letter that he might

refer it to the Secretaries of War & the Navy for mature consideration. He seemed to think that having referred the subject of relief to them, that he could act only through them. He expressed solicitude as to the condition of the party, but had no apprehensions as to effectual relief next summer.

General Lockwood went on to describe for Henrietta his subsequent interview with Commodore John G. Walker at the Navy Department, during which the chief of the Navy Bureau of Navigation outlined the rescue plans being formulated:

As Walker remarked, no naval commander would dare, after all that has been said on the recent failure, to return without having reached in some way the end of his journey. . . .

My fears are not that the party will not be found and brought back, but that their hardships and suffering will have proved fatal to many of them. I feel sure that they are this day enduring all that mortal man can endure and live.

A week later Henrietta received a small, neatly engraved note marked "Executive Mansion, Washington." It was the typical, noncommittal, bloodless message with which the mighty acknowledge the plea for a boon:

The President has received, and read with much interest, your letter of the 9th instant addressed to General Lockwood. . . . The suggestions it contains will have very careful consideration, and the President wishes me to assure you that nothing which is considered essential to the success of the expedition will be left undone.

Fred J. Phillips, Private Secretary.

At the same time Henrietta and her small group of friends were beginning to stir official Washington by letter and personal intervention, the rescue-Greely movement began to make itself heard in various other forms. One of the advocates was Edward N. Pomeroy, an old army friend of Greely's and an amateur poet reared on Whittier and Longfellow. He did his bit with a sonnet printed in late January in the *New York Independent,* and his effort was followed by many similar ones as the months went on:

Genial companion of my army days
   Here sitting in the soft enchanted light
   Of home, before my glowing anthracite,
I think of wastes of snow, of ice-closed bays,
Of the near North with its auroral glaze,
   Of ghostlike Nature in her gown of white—
   Somnambulist that roameth through the night,
With horror fascinating all that gaze.
But more than all besides, I think, dear friend,
   Of thee and thy heroic band forlorn,
For whose return so many prayers ascend,
   Now waiting for the tardy Arctic morn,
Determined still to battle to the end
   And win "the victory of endurance born."

Lincoln had always found the Greely business a distasteful annoyance, but Secretary of the Navy William E. Chandler had been emotionally involved in it from the outset. Should a navy rescue be carried off successfully, it would be a grand thing for the service, which had been allowed to deteriorate since the Civil War. Chandler was not above a little healthy interservice rivalry. Furthermore, being an intensely political man, Chandler already had eyes on a Senate seat from New Hampshire, where he had served in the legislature for many years. Being in the vanguard of the rescue-Greely movement would dramatically bring his name before the public, not only in the Granite State but also nationally. At least, these considerations lay somewhere near the surface as Chandler took the issue from Lincoln, pressed Hazen's report upon President Arthur, and induced the President to send a message to Congress asking authority to spend the necessary sum to outfit the new rescue mission. Read in the House of Representatives on January 17 and a day later in the Senate, Arthur's brief message briefly outlined the well-known facts and concluded:

The situation of Lieutenant Greely and his party under these circumstances is one of great peril. . . . I urgently recommend prompt action by Congress to enable the recommendations of the

Secretary of War and the Secretary of the Navy to be carried out without delay.

House Joint Resolution 119, Forty-Eighth Congress, First Session, was assigned to the House Committee on Appropriations. Chairman Samuel J. Randall of Philadelphia promptly called on Lincoln and Chandler to testify as to its urgency and pushed the measure through his committee in a day. It gave the President full authority to "prepare and dispatch an expedition" to bring the Greely party home, to spend whatever might be necessary for "not exceeding three vessels" to accomplish this end, and to "submit to Congress on the first Monday of December, 1884, a full detailed account of all expenditures." It provided further that after the expedition the vessels should be sold and "the money arising from such sale covered into the Treasury." In the wake of the financial scandals of the post–Civil War period and the Grant administration, politicians aware of the public temper made it a point to insist on economy and strict bookkeeping. The Howgate scandal, for example, was still fresh, and Howgate himself still at large.

Yet there was something grotesquely ironic in a state of affairs in which the Commander-in-Chief of the United States armed forces was asking Congress for permission to spend money to save the lives of American army men sent beyond the bounds of civilization on an official mission. These men in the Arctic were volunteers, certainly; but they were an army party all the same. In Chairman Randall's view, sending a rescue expedition was the government's plain duty.

As soon as the committee chairman brought the resolution to the floor of the House—on January 21—Representative Nelson Dingley, Jr., of Maine was on his feet. Shipyards in Maine were an important source of revenue, and this bill just might have something good in it for the Congressman's district. Dingley had already caught rumors that the Navy planned to buy British ships, not American ones, for the rescue attempt.

"I desire to ask," Dingley inquired of Randall, "whether the committee has considered the possibility of obtaining a suitable

American vessel or an American-built vessel under this resolution?"

Randall managed to turn aside this pork-barrel feeler, and the gentleman from Lewiston, Maine, did not press the matter. To win the support of the perennial antispending bloc, Randall pointed out all the precautions in the bill—the three-ship limitation, the subsequent sale with return to the Treasury, and the December report to Congress. To convince those who had already forgotten the foreboding headlines of September, now four months past, Randall pleaded: "This appropriation is in obedience to humanity, and to the agreement made with Lieutenant Greely."

To a series of questions from the floor, Randall said that the President could be trusted not to spend money foolishly on the relief expedition, even though the bill carried no ceiling figure on spending; that this legislation was merely for the purpose of bringing Greely's party home, not to continue arctic exploration; and finally that the President could, of course, be counted on to send "weatherbeaten seamen who understand their business" to Greely's aid, not the "drawing-room sailors" about whom one legislator from California complained. There were no adverse speeches and the House passed the bill quickly without dissent.

On the other side of the Capitol, Senator Eugene Hale of Maine showed a zeal for the relief resolution equal to that of Randall. The measure passed by the House was assigned on January 23 to the Senate Committee on Naval Affairs, of which Hale was chairman. His committee approved it at the first meeting on the morning of the 24th, and Hale called the bill up on the Senate floor early that afternoon. This was an appropriations matter, Hale acknowledged at the outset, and ordinarily he would have referred it to the appropriations committee. But since it required swift action he had taken action in his own committee to save time. Chairman William B. Allison of the appropriations committee rose to say he was in full accord with Hale and perfectly willing to let the naval affairs committee action stand.

"This, all Senators must bear in mind, is the last expedition that can be sent," declared Hale in opening the debate. "Unless Lieutenant Greely and his party are found this summer, they will doubtless pass away and we shall never hear more of them."

Senator George G. Vest of Missouri, seated far back on the other side of the chamber from Hale, did not hear very well and asked for clarification. Did Hale mean that this would be "the last expedition that will be sent to the North Pole" or did he mean it would be "the last that will be sent to rescue the Greely expedition"?

Definitely the latter, Hale replied. If Greely were not found this summer, the party "must needs be abandoned. As to the further question suggested by the Senator from Missouri, whether any more expeditions will be sent for adventures and scientific and semiscientific purposes to the northern regions, I believe fully that this will be the last; that we will never have for years to come any more of them. There is no disposition on the part of the War or Navy Department, I think, to send any more expeditions."

Then rose John James Ingalls, a lean, bespectacled, impeccably dressed lawyer, born in Massachusetts and educated at Williams College, now a Kansan. Renowned as an orator who could draw a gallery of admiring listeners, the Senator from Kansas struck out at the futility of a third attempt to rescue the Lady Franklin Bay Expedition.

"Mr. President," he began in his ponderous, rolling delivery, "whatever secrets are secluded in that mysterious region that surrounds the North Pole, they are guarded by nature with the most zealous solicitude. The results of the disposition of man to penetrate every mystery upon the surface of this planet has been one uninterrupted succession of failures and disasters. Expedition after expedition has followed into that dangerous and tempting region with simply one result—and that is an absolute failure to discover any of the mysteries that are alleged there to exist, and with a loss of life that is appalling to contemplate."

Too much public money was wasted on these useless adventures, Ingalls continued. No one could deny that if the Secretary of the Navy under this bill "sees fit to expend ten million dollars,

Congress will be compelled to make the necessary appropriation." Those who held the government purse-strings, who stood
guard at the sacred portals of the federal Treasury, should put a
stop to these fool trips to nowhere, and "if there are any adventurous spirits who desire to tempt the mysteries and dangers of
that region hereafter, they shall do so at their own peril!"

But this was not a case of wasteful spending, Hale protested.
Neither the President nor the Secretary of the Navy should be
restricted by money limits when it came to rescuing Greely and
his men.

"But what guarantee is there," asked Ingalls mockingly, "that
this expedition, disappearing into that profound abyss, not being
heard of for two years, is not to be followed by others upon
which the same vast expenditure is to be entailed?"

Rescuing Greely was the one and only issue before the Senate,
replied Hale. The question was "whether the American Congress
will abandon them now or seek once more to relieve them."
The steam-sealers and whalers of the type required to venture
into the ice, Hale continued, would cost between $75,000 and
$140,000 each. There were only a few such ships in the world,
most of them to be found in British and Canadian ports.

Senator William P. Frye of Maine rose to suggest that in the
State of Maine all three ships could be built in sixty days, to
which Hale rejoined that though this might be so, a fire in the
shipyard or some other mischance could delay the work and seal
Greely's fate.

Up jumped Ingalls again, to send to the President's desk an
amendment fixing a limit of one million dollars to be spent on
the Greely rescue. After a long penny-pinch struggle, during
which several spending limits lower than the Ingalls figure were
barely rejected in close votes, the Senate killed the idea of a
limit.

Hale began to breathe more easily after an upsetting couple
of hours, and felt the resolution would soon be passed. But he
reckoned without the venerable Eli Saulsbury of Delaware, who
moved an amendment providing that the navy relief expedition

"be composed of volunteers." Shaking his white locks, Saulsbury declaimed emphatically:

"I will not grant to the President the power to assign whom he may please to this dreadful service!"

Hale declined to argue the point, and the Saulsbury volunteer amendment was approved by voice vote, after which the amended rescue resolution quickly passed without recorded dissent. The fact that the Senate had added Saulsbury's eight-word volunteer amendment required that the bill be sent to a House-Senate conference committee for resolution of the minor difference, rather than directly to the President for signature and action.

So eager was Hale for the relief work to get under way that he decided the Senate should not insist on its amendment in conference. In reporting back to the House, Representative Randall read a letter from Secretary Chandler stating that none but volunteers would be sought for the relief party. But, Chandler wrote, if the equipment is ready and insufficient volunteers have stepped forward, "are the ships not to move?"

The House approved the conference report quickly, but in the Senate Ingalls and Saulsbury, now joined by John R. McPherson of New Jersey, aimed their oratorical torpedoes directly at the relief squadron. The resolution had been sent to the wrong committee in the first place, exploded Ingalls. The spending of money was the heart of this matter, he said, and therefore it should have been sent to the appropriations committee.

Furthermore, Ingalls cried, the Senate was always receding in its differences with the House. This must stop, or we should frankly declare our Senate committees to be "auxiliaries and annexes" of the House appropriations committee. He made it sound as if American constitutional government were tottering.

Senator George F. Hoar of Massachusetts, evoking the proud seafaring history of his home state, asked the Senate to consider for a moment the intense interest in Greely already manifest across the Atlantic in Great Britain:

"Mr. President, I cannot believe that if this were a British expedition there would be any hesitation on the part of the British

Government in sending a party for relief. I think if the suggestion were made to the British people whether they would allow a party of Englishmen unsearched-for, uncared-for, to perish under the circumstances which the honorable Senator from Maine has described, the expression of the doubt would be received with a burst of indignation from the entire British public."

Despite Hale's valiant effort, a majority of Senators present sided with the obstructionists. Having the last word before the vote, McPherson thundered his conviction that the rescue resolution "for supreme audacity and bold impudence has never been equaled. It confers upon the Secretary of the Navy practically unlimited discretion as to the cost of the expedition, also arbitrary power over the officers of the Navy—and the Senate of the United States supinely submits."

The vote, on January 31, found only twenty-five Senators in favor of the conference report (with the volunteer amendment stricken), twenty-seven opposed, and twenty-seven Senators absent. A full week had passed since Saulsbury had thrown his volunteer monkey wrench into the rescue machinery. It was now at a standstill.

Hale worked desperately behind the scenes to pick up the handful of votes he needed to put the resolution through. On February 8 he told the Senate that Secretary Chandler now promised that the rescue party, in effect, would be made up completely of volunteers, and this should set at rest the fears some Senators had expressed on that score. If no action is taken now, he warned his colleagues, "any further activity for the relief of the Greely party ceases."

Again Ingalls took the floor to upbraid Hale. Might he inquire of the Senator from Maine whether the rumor he had heard were true—that Secretary Chandler, without any authority from Congress, had already begun secret negotiations with British interests to buy a ship to send in search of Greely? If so, then there really was an emergency, and Congress should inquire into it!

No commitments have been made, Hale replied, but the Secretary is looking into the possible purchase of ships from Newfoundland or Scottish sealers and whalers, which are just about the only ships in the world of the type needed to brave arctic ice. If they should leave their home ports for the season before Congress acts, then we can never buy them in time.

Hale had tried too long to control his emotions so that he might not alienate any possible vote in this body of procedure-minded legislators. Now he had reached the bursting point: "If Lieutenant Greely is to be left to perish with his followers, I hope they may die in a parliamentary manner, so that it shall be satisfactory, so that no question may be raised as to their violating any rule!"

"The Senator from Maine," Ingalls replied, "has repeatedly endeavored to enforce upon the Senate the idea that every moment was precious, and that lives might be periled by delay." He repeated all the opposition arguments: unparliamentary handling of the relief bill, only volunteers should go, Americans should be rescued in American-built ships and, again, the cost.

Then Ingalls suddenly held out a new proposition to Hale. If he would agree to a money limit in the resolution, say $500,000 or even $1,000,000 (which the Senate had already voted down) and a volunteer clause (which Chandler had assured Hale was not necessary), then Ingalls would see that the Senate would vote through a relief resolution in fifteen minutes!

Hale listened in amazement, then shook his head. It was really not a genuine offer, but rather one more obstructionist tactic. A money limit voted now would force the House in its turn to take up the bill once more. Or else it would bring about another conference committee wrangle to delay matters.

Somehow, Hale resolved, he would have to persuade enough Senators over the coming week end to appear on the floor next Monday—February 11—and vote with him. Just three or four would do it, provided he could hold those who had stood by him on Thursday of last week. On Monday he would make one more attempt to push the resolution through.

8 PREPARATION

IN LATE JANUARY all attention in the hut at Camp Clay centered on the preparations of Rice and Jens to cross the ice to Littleton Island. Greely and Brainard doubted that the two men would get far, but because so many of the men staked their hopes on the venture, they uttered no word to dispel the party's illusions. Rice and Jens were issued double rations for a week to build up their strength, while Frederick and Schneider worked hard stitching up the best sleeping bag, footgear, and mittens available.

In a thoughtful hour before he set out on February 2 Rice penciled a letter which he entrusted to Lieutenant Kislingbury with instructions to open it only in case he should not return. He wrote:

My dear friend Kislingbury:

In the event of this pending journey ending fatally for me, I desire that yourself and Brainard act as my executors, in conjunction with Moses P. Rice of Washington, D.C. [Listing several items of property for distribution to various members of his family and friends, Rice continued:] Of my trinkets I desire that a diamond ring, which will be found among my effects, to be sent to Miss Maud Dunlop of Baddeck, Cape Breton, as a souvenir of a few sunshiny days. Other articles are to be divided between my mother and Miss Helen Bishop of Washington, D.C., the latter to be allowed the choice of articles she wishes to retain.

[Awarding the same Miss Bishop $1000 from his estate "without condition," Rice concluded with characteristic practicality

164

and good humor:] I am quite aware of the nullity of this hastily written paper as a legal instrument and have paid no attention to testamentary forms, but feel assured that there will be no disregard of my wishes on the part of anyone interested in me, or herein mentioned.

Hoping that we may joke over this in the sunshine of Littleton Island, I remain, your much obliged friend,

George W. Rice

It was the party's first will, though as yet none but its author knew that it had been written. Yet amid the feeling of forced cheerfulness on the morning that Rice and Jens left camp, Brainard found it difficult to restrain his true feelings, which he confided to his journal:

While at breakfast everyone appeared in the best of spirits and each one endeavored to imbue Rice with his own bright view of the future. But to a close observer, this appearance of cheerfulness was all forced and superficial, to give courage and strength to the brave souls who were about to do battle with the elements and face every danger known to the Arctic regions, for us who remain inactive here, powerless to assist. There lurked, deep down in the heart of every man, a feeling of dread of the future—a presentiment of impending evil. . . . A tremulous "God bless you," a hasty pressure of their hands, and we turned away in tears from those brave men who were daring and about to endure so much for our sakes. We waited until their receding forms were lost to view in the bewildering confusion of the ice-fields, and then slowly retraced our steps to the hut. While watching their progress I distinctly heard the hoarse grinding of the moving pack not far away. . . . It is my opinion that Rice will be turned back by open water and his heroic efforts in our behalf thus rendered fruitless.

Brainard recognized far more keenly than most how bad matters had become. Lieutenant Lockwood, technically Greely's second-in-command—a man who during their weeks together had grown as dear to Brainard as a brother, Lockwood of the winning smile and the infectious good spirits, had become a changed person, pitiful now in his physical and mental weakness. His mind wandered frequently. At night he often sat erect in his sleeping bag, talking strangely. There were days when he would perk up, only to relapse later into moody silence, alternating with a manic discussion of good things to eat, tobacco, and drinking water.

Other men were breaking down in different ways. Husky Sergeant Linn had never been the same since his close call in the sleeping bag with Elison in November. Normally a friendly and cheerful sort, he had become sullen, melancholy, and practically useless as far as any work was concerned. Greely observed in his journal that Linn "seems to have given up."

Bender, the ingenious metalsmith, made himself objectionable with his ill-tempered complaints. He whined repeatedly about the discomfort of the dank hut and the shortcomings of his neighbors. It was as though Bender consciously strove for a comforting outlet in words for his self-pity. Private Charles B. Henry of the flamboyant prose, who had been a guffawing practical joker back at Fort Conger, turned with Bender to excessive use of grossly obscene language, trying Greely's patience sorely. Never a ready volunteer for outdoor work even under the best of conditions, as the winter moved on Henry seemed to Brainard to have less work in him per inch of height and pound of weight than any soldier the sergeant had ever known in the United States Army.

Nor did the doctor and Lieutenant Kislingbury now seem to hit it off so well as they had in the old days. Twice they fell into loud, abusive dispute in the presence of the entire party. Greely permitted them to argue their differences out. Indeed, though the commander told himself at times that a vigorous argument was preferable to the boredom that overcomes the thinking part of men when their physical well-being is denied, he was himself frequently lacking in the strength needed to assert control over the disrupters of the peace. And discord was sometimes a welcome relief in the monotony. Of course matters sometimes got out of hand, as when Schneider and Whisler came to blows for a few seconds in the sleeping bag they shared, or when Bender was so abusive to Dr. Pavy that to appease the medical man Greely was forced to punish the offender by ordering him to stand in the cold vestibule until he was willing to apologize.

Throughout the winter Greely labored earnestly to give the men something to talk and think about other than their hunger and misery. He drew deeply from his store of travel reminiscence and lectured on various American states and territories. Others caught his enthusiasm for intellectual exercise and contributed to his work to maintain group morale. Dr. Pavy held forth on France and its history, and on anatomy, medicine, and other branches of science; Israel lectured on astronomy; Jewell told of his winter's experience atop Mount Washington; Brainard told about his battle with the Sioux; Rice described the West Indies; Frederick talked on railroading in Ohio; Schneider dealt with Atlantic coastwise shipping; and several men reminisced about their youth in Germany. Somewhere along the line the idea was conceived of compiling a chronological list of historical events. Brainard kept it in his notebook, beginning with the Egyptian pyramids and proceeding to the Roman conquest of England, the era of Charlemagne, Oliver Cromwell's battles, the American Civil War, inventions, discoveries, American elections.—Its recording was a game with no end.

Turning over more blank leaves in his little leather-covered book than he thought he would ever require, Brainard on page 100 started his food list, to which he added items day after day, with this introductory note:

> N.B. It is quite probable that the reader may (& with good reason) think me insane when he glances over the entries which follow, but on reflection he will be charitable enough to credit me with a sound mind and—an empty stomach. . . . I began this list at the request of a few of my comrades, but mainly as a guide to my future epicurean operations, am I so fortunate as to ever again rest my limbs under a civilized table.

Then followed an indiscriminate list of foods, some with brief directions concerning preparation—a conglomeration expressing unrestrained longing which stretched out page after page, the quality of the handwriting and the smudges on the paper telling a story of frosted fingers and hands encrusted with filth.

Shortly after midday on February 6 the men in the hut were disheartened to see Rice and Jens struggling back from the direction of Cape Sabine. They had traveled some fifty miles, Rice estimated, having gone perhaps ten miles out into Smith Sound on the ice from the cape before being stopped by open water along a wide front. Rice was in better condition than his companion. Jens had on several occasions reverted to his self-deprecation of the first winter at Fort Conger, insisting to his partner mournfully that he was "no good." Nor had his mental state been the only anxiety for Rice. On their last night out the Canadian had saved the Eskimo's hands from freezing by rubbing and by holding them for hours in contact with his body in the sleeping bag. Both men had obviously pushed themselves to the physical limit.

With no bridge of ice to the eastern shore, there was nothing now but to wait. Greely gave orders that preparations should be continued for a possible crossing, though his primary motive was to maintain a spirit of optimism, as far as he could. Even should solid ice close the channel gap, Greely knew they would have to haul Elison and probably Lockwood on the sledges. Furthermore, Ellis, the oldest man in the group, and Linn and Jewell would probably not be able to make the journey on their own feet. Nevertheless, as Greely firmly told Lockwood—when he suggested he be left in the hut with his one twenty-fourth of the rations—no man would be abandoned so long as he was in command. Now it looked as if there would be no crossing at all.

In his more lucid periods Lockwood pulled out his notebook and dashed his shorthand notes across its pages. One entry read:

> Our rations have been counted on to extend to the 10th of March, the ten days of March on a ration of 12 ounces of bread and 10 of meat for crossing the straits. So here is the upshot of affairs. Our bread is now 64 ounces per week every man. The party takes a bold front and are not wanting in spirit. If our fate

is the worst I do not think we shall disgrace the name of Americans and of soldiers.

Going through the motions of preparing the move to Littleton Island, Brainard, with Rice's help, went carefully over the dwindling supplies and calculated the necessary weight of food and equipment to be transported. He reported to the assembled party that it totaled 1600 pounds. That figure alone was enough to chill the hearts of Brainard's listeners, and to it must be added the weight of the disabled. But there was some good news from the inventory—the seal meat ran 17 pounds ahead of Brainard's earlier estimates, and the last box of bacon turned out to be 8 pounds overweight. Greely ordered the excess issued at once, for use during the coming week, but behind this screen he realized he would be forced to announce another cut in the bread ration. It had become a game of figure-juggling and divination of the psychological moment at which to reduce the food without risking revolt.

For a while Brainard was upset to find the contents of the rum cask two gallons short of his estimate. Had there been more thievery? He was relieved when Israel solved the mystery for him. He had been ladling out the spirits in a cup based on the Imperial gallon, larger than the American standard by which Brainard had been calculating, so that everyone had been given a few drops extra.

On the morning of February 11 Brainard climbed to the summit of the hill in the center of Garlington Island and from it heard distinctly the thunderous sound of the moving pack in Buchanan Strait, hidden from his eyes by the dense vapor overhanging the water. As he wrote his fears of the future in his journal that evening, Brainard thought back to the brave words that had inspired them with hope in October: "Everything within the power of man will be done to rescue the brave men at Fort Conger from their perilous position. . . ."

In the dimly lit hut at Eskimo Point, Garlington's message had brought tears to the eyes of strong men. Now four months had passed without bringing the promised assistance. They had seen

no signal flashes, no column of smoke from Littleton Island.
Today they were no longer a party of strong men.

SINCE NOON the United States Senate had been running
through a call of the calendar of petty bills. The hands of the
clock over the President's desk were pointing to four and the
gaslights had been turned on when the Clerk of the House pushed
his way through the swinging doors from the other wing of the
Capitol. He bobbed his head in salute to the presiding officer and
announced that the House of Representatives insisted on its ver-
sion of H.R. 119, "making an appropriation for the relief of
Lieutenant A. W. Greely and his party, . . ." Senator Eugene
Hale, at his front-row desk, asked that the bill be considered at
once.

All barriers of parliamentary irregularity had been removed,
the Senator from Maine declared. There was no danger of any
unwilling man or officer being ordered to go on the relief expedition, and surely the President, "after all this discussion and all
this delay will be moved by a feeling of closely scrutinizing and
inspecting" every item of cost. Now, Hale said, he hoped the
Senate would vote to recede from its amendment and pass the
original resolution.

"I do not know how I should feel," he pleaded earnestly, "if
the expedition should go up there and it should be found that
those unfortunate men had perished within a fortnight of the
time when the relief reached them, and that delay had been
caused by our delay here. I hope that will not occur; I do not
prophesy anything of the kind; but it seems to me now that the
Senate will see the importance of not further delaying this matter
by insisting on its amendment."

Senator Francis M. Cockrell, a Missouri Democrat, taunted
Hale for "yielding to the wishes of the House." He would be
delighted later in the session, Cockrell said, when differences
between House and Senate always arose "to see that distinguished
Senator yielding with that childlike blandness and sympathy
which he exhibits in this case."

Once more Delaware's Saulsbury took the floor to declaim the danger of the resolution without the safeguard of his volunteer amendment: "I do not believe there has been any more vicious legislation than this whole bill. I am in favor of relieving the Greely party if it can be done. . . . But a bill has come to us without a single limitation upon the power of the Secretary of the Navy to enter the vaults of the Treasury of the United States and take *ad libitum* any amount of money that he may see proper. . . . I hope that this bill will fail and that no such bill, vicious in its character, dangerous as precedent, will pass! The bill proposes not only to grant the Secretary of the Navy the absolute right to dispose of the treasure of the United States as he pleases, but to give him the absolute control of every officer in the naval service, so that if he has an enemy whom he wishes to punish he is given the opportunity to do it!"

Over the week end, Hale had worked diligently to persuade busy, indifferent Senators to respond to the quorum call on a dull day of routine legislation. The fate of the bill today, as on January 31, lay with the absentees because the known pros and cons were about equally divided. Just before the clerk began to call the roll, Hale was delighted to hear Senator Garland of Arkansas announce that his colleague, Senator Walker, and Mr. Lamar of Mississippi had been detained in their rooms by sickness. These had been two opposition votes last time.

Halfway through the tally Hale realized that he had won. The final count gave him a margin of twenty-nine votes for his motion to twenty-two against, with twenty-five Senators absent. Yet, despite all the argument over the urgency of Greely's situation, he had brought over to his side only two Senators who had voted against him before.

Now, thank God, the suspense was over. The Congress of the United States had given approval for the Executive to spend money—not necessarily to rescue Greely and his men, but only to prepare to try to rescue them. The bill was on its way to the White House in the exact form approved by the House twenty days ago, twenty-six days after the President had called on Congress to grant him authority to act.

Through it all, not one member of Congress in either chamber during the entire month spoke of any of the beleaguered party or of their loved ones at home as constituents. It was as if the men had no spokesmen in Congress, no home states or home towns. They were an impersonal lot, an isolated army band— rather than American citizens with homes and the dignity of free-born voters.

Secretary Chandler had not waited for Congress. As early as December he had put out informal, secret inquiries of shipowners in Dundee, Scotland, and St. John's with an eye to purchasing the best available vessels as soon as Congress gave formal authorization. He learned that the steamer *Bear,* owned by Grieve & Co. of Greenock, was already at sea on her way to St. John's following a thorough overhauling. A sister ship of the *Proteus,* the *Bear* had been fitted the year before with a new steel boiler; she was rated about the best vessel in the St. John's fishing trade. Chandler at once opened negotiations through the U.S. consul in St. John's under a blanket of secrecy, and by January 23, while the relief resolution was still bogged down in the Senate, he won consent of the owners to sell her at once for $100,000, delivered in New York. The *Bear* arrived in the U.S. port on February 15, four days after Hale had won his battle on the Senate floor. Chandler jokingly remarked to a newspaperman who questioned what might have happened if the Senate vote had gone the other way: "Well, I would have become the part owner of a good ship!"

Meanwhile, another sealer of the Dundee fleet, the *Thetis,* was offered for sale by her owners, Stephen & Son; purchased by gentleman's agreement before the final Senate action, she passed her final inspection and was taken over by a United States Navy crew in Dundee on February 25.

On the 18th, Chandler had announced the name of the relief expedition leader. He was Commander Winfield Scott Schley, a courageous, experienced officer of forty-five who was known as a rigorous and thorough executive. Nearly three years before, in July 1881, Schley (then stationed in Boston as district inspector of lighthouses) had seen an item in the newspaper announcing the sailing of Greely's arctic expedition from St. John's. He had commented sarcastically to fellow officers at the Charlestown Navy Yard: "This means that some Navy officer will have to go up there and bring them back."

For a year he had forgotten about Greely, until the news of Beebe's failure to reach him in 1882 and then the fiasco of Garlington's mission had led Schley to think further about the problems of navigating in the arctic seas. Excessive caution, he now felt, was the greatest drawback of the experienced voyager in the Arctic. The man in command of a rescue must not only be thoroughly prepared but also bold. He had made his views known in conversations among navy officers in Washington, so that when Secretary Chandler called him to his office to ask if he were prepared to volunteer to lead the mission, Schley told his chief he stood ready.

Under Schley there would be no slip-up in instructions as in the Garlington-Hazen imbroglio, because Schley would both plan the expedition down to the last boathook and lead it himself from the bridge of the *Thetis*. Mature well beyond the callow Garlington, a seaman by profession, from the moment he took charge Schley radiated confidence in the success of his mission, both in his manner of speaking to those who met him personally and to the many who saw only his picture. A high forehead, deep eyes, straight nose, and bearded face with the chin whiskers coming to a point, gave this Marylander something of the appearance of Stonewall Jackson. Newspaper readers throughout America became familiar with the etching of his sober, bushy face.

GREELY, *February 12*

Dr. Pavy was accused openly, by Jewell, of selecting the heaviest dish of those issued out, and in consequence of the fact being established by other testimony, I directed that in Lieutenant Kislingbury's mess hereafter the name of the man for whom any dish was intended should be designated as it was handed out by the cook. Our own mess have escaped any such condition of affairs, and have trusted implicitly in the honor of the cook. . . . Both Long and Frederick, in addition to their self-sacrificing duties as cooks, have repeatedly asked that a second man should divide the food and that they might be allowed to take the dish rejected.

GREELY, *February 13*

I thought it best today to turn over to Lieutenant Lockwood a favorite pistol of his, which I brought down on my person at his personal request, and which he spoke of yesterday. His mention of it gave me an unpleasant feeling, for it looked as if he was putting his house in order.

GREELY, *February 17*

We have used the last of our seal-meat in a fine stew, and also the last of onion-powder, peas, beans, carrots, corned beef, and on Wednesday used the last of our English beef. In consequence, we have for future use the strongest and best food in the shape of boiled bacon and pemmican.

The sun was above the horizon today for the first time in one hundred and fifteen days.

BRAINARD, *February 18*

I think that we no longer need delude ourselves into believing that we will escape alive; but however horrible the end, all are prepared to face it like men. One, however, (Bender) would rather devour all the provisions now and die at once than to prolong them as far as possible with the hope of ultimate rescue. This person has done very little this winter towards the regular routine of duty, and has made many unreasonable complaints which have gained him the contempt of his companions. Today he complained bitterly that his bread was not up to the standard weight, and although he admitted that no partiality had been shown, and that he had the same quantity as the others, and that no injustice had been done, still for the sake of grumbling he felt that he must do something. Assuming that this attack was directed towards me, I at once requested to be relieved from the duty of issuing provisions, but the commanding officer would not listen to my appeal.

GREELY, *February 22*

Received this evening from Lieutenant Kislingbury a communication recommending that as soon as Smith Sound freezes over, he, with a party of the strongest men, be allowed to cross to Littleton Island for game or assistance. He based his recommendation on the ground that we cannot cross as a party. This proposal strikes me in no other light than an abandonment to their fate of the weak of the party.

GREELY, *February 23*

This morning I brought to the attention of the party Lieutenant Kislingbury's recommendation.... I told them that the party cannot be divided with my consent; that whether we can cross as a party or not could be determined only by trial; and, until we had exhausted all efforts no man, as long as my authority remained, should be deserted or abandoned. If any messenger for a forlorn hope was needed, it should be the strongest and fittest man at that time.

Nobody seemed to indorse Lieutenant Kislingbury's plan. Dr. Pavy spoke to me most strongly against it in French, although he refrained from expressing his opinion publicly. Lieutenant Lockwood was very much affected by the proposition and called our prospects exceedingly dismal, but gave no opinion regarding it. Indeed, we have not been able to obtain one from him for several weeks; and, in view of his willingness to sacrifice himself, as shown by his proposition of a month since, it cannot be expected that he would urge the strongest of the party to pursue any course which would show consideration for him.

BRAINARD, *March 1*

Long tells me the following little episode, which he considers a very good joke. On the evening of Henry's birthday, Jan. 27, he (Long) neglected to add the allowance of tea while preparing dinner, and did not discover his mistake until after he had issued a cup of hot water to each person. As no one detected the absence of the tea, Long of course did not care to acknowledge this omission, and has said nothing about the matter until today, when he related it to me in confidence.

RICE, *March 1*

My breakfast at Godfrey's today would be scrambled eggs, boiled smoked herrings, baked Irish potatoes and butter, Parker House rolls, soft boiled eggs and a cup of chocolate.—My breakfast WAS a half can of tomatoes, a few grains of rice and desicated potatoes, and some crumbs of dog biscuit, made up to a few ounces of stew.

My dinner would be a half dozen raw oysters, bean soup, roast goose, and applesauce, fowl, cabbage, bread pudding, sweet potato pie, apples, oranges, raisins, nuts, cheese and crackers.—However, four ounces of tallow and bacon and six oz. of bread for dinner is what we DID have.

I fear this wind will break up the new ice in the channel. Five months ago this day I left Eskimo Point for this place and five months will place us beyond the Arctic Circle or, more likely: "Beyond that bourne, etc."

BRAINARD, *March 3*

Temperature at 7 A.M., —27.5°. A high westerly wind which amounted at times to a moderate gale. The commanding officer has made calculations for the future, and says that on the present ration we can live until the first week in April. If no opportunity occurs for crossing the sound to Littleton Island before the 16th instant, all hope of leaving this place must be abandoned; and if we do not succeed in securing game, our end will not be far distant on April 15.

On my recommendations, the commanding officer appointed Frederick a sergeant in the general service, vice Cross, deceased. This is a fitting recognition, at this time, for his excellent services this winter. Biederbick has been very ill with cramps, but he has now improved to such an extent that he is again enabled to perform his duties as nurse and hospital steward. . . . Bender's inventive genius appears to be limitless; he has designed and constructed several candlesticks of an entirely new and original pattern, which may be used for a double purpose. Schneider is making stearine candles, and Frederick is still working on the sleeping-stockings intended for our journey.

BRAINARD, *March 5*

Cloudy and stormy weather; temperature at 7 A.M. —22.0°. The wind is blowing with persistent and relentless fury. . . . I issued the last of the corn, soup, tomatoes and English evaporated potatoes. . . . Bacon stews, with a large proportion of rancid tallow added, are generally liked. The strong rancid flavor is something that a delicate stomach would at once rebel against, but to us it is agreeable and palatable; it affords a welcome change from the ordinary routine by having a peculiar flavor which is both distinct and pronounced in its nature.

BRAINARD, *March 7*

Bender has been very aggressive in his conduct today; he flatly contradicted Lieutenant Greely and in addition made a very extravagant and reckless use of profanity.

GREELY, *March 7*

Bender in a fit of passion again. I cannot endure this state of affairs much longer, I am afraid.

RICE, *March 7*

Unpleasant discussion occurred during the evening, in which the true nature of some of the party was pitifully exhibited. Lt. Lockwood appears to be much demoralized, while such men as Bender, Ellis and Schneider of course act only as men of such dispositions and calibre can be expected to.

I much fear the horrors of our last days here, as no doubt many, or at least some of the party will become completely demoralized.

BRAINARD, *March 8*

For the first time this winter, hair-cutting was extensively indulged in. The style of the cut was comfortable but scarcely artistic. Those wishing to reduce the length of their hair crawled on their hands and knees to the foot of their respective sleeping bags and held their heads in the passage, while the tonsorial artist passed along the line armed with a huge pair of shears, and about ten seconds were devoted to the removal of the superfluous burden of matted hair on each head. Mine was over six inches in length.

GREELY, *March 9*

Heavy gale again today. . . . Such violent storms must break up all the ice in the channel, and I think our chances of crossing are about gone. Unless the mercury freezes, I shall send Long and Christiansen to Alexandra Harbor on Tuesday, and have given orders to prepare their outfit for the trip. Brainard is anxious to go but I cannot spare him.

Rice and Frederick offered their services as volunteers to attempt recovering the hundred pounds of English meat abandoned in Baird Inlet last November, which I declined, thinking it too hazardous a journey for so little food.

RICE, *March 9*

Weather still execrable. Had son-of-a-gun today, but this dish is but a ghost of its former self. It consisted only of lard, blubber, bread and water boiled together, but we think it delicious. The minute quantities of our different delicacies have all run out. The lemons, butter, vegetables, raisins, blubber, etc. are all gone, and there remain only a few grains of potatoes and a can of extract of beef. We have lard enough to grease another son-of-a-gun, which must be our last.

Lt. G. has decided to send Long and Fred the Eskimo to Alexandra Harbor to look for game, and Frederick (Shorty) and I have volunteered to go to Eskimo Point and try to find the meat we abandoned in Baird Inlet last fall.

GREELY, *March 11*

I gave Long and Christiansen an extra ounce of bread and two ounces of bacon at breakfast. Rice and Ellis who went out to give them a lift got off with the sledge at eight o'clock, followed at 9 A.M. by Long and Christiansen. Our hopes and good wishes are so much bound up in this important trip that we can scarcely wait the week to know what will come of it. . . . I am sanguine of success, owing to the many signs of game seen in Alexandra Harbor by Nares and Feilden in 1875. . . .

The variability of spirits is shown by a little incident today. Jewell has such faith in Long's success that he already imagines us supplied with game, and in consequence requested that I would permit him to go into Hayes Sound with the party that I have talked of sending for geographical purposes in May. This visionary trip I have talked of more to encourage the men than anything else.

RICE, *March 11*

Sun shone on our house for the first time and raised our thermometer six degrees. Ellis tells me of being intimidated by the other occupants of his sleeping bag and talks of cannibalism. I am much afraid of a demoralization of many of the party. The conversations and hints show a state of warped imagination, which may result in things too bad to contemplate. I hope that if the worst comes, I may retain my mental powers even after my physical have failed.

GREELY, *March 13*

Long returned unexpectedly, at 7:15 P.M., from Alexandra Harbor. Both he and Christiansen very much exhausted. They saw no game and no tracks, except of a single fox. . . . The party traveled nearly seventy miles during their absence, and their sleeping bags having been frozen up, they were unable to get into them farther than the hips, and were compelled to get what rest they could alternately, one resting while the other walked. . . .

The fates seem to be against us—an open channel, no game, no food, and apparently no hopes from Littleton Island. We have been lured here to our destruction.

If we were now the strong, active men of last autumn, we could cross Smith Sound where there is much open water; but we are a party of twenty-four starved men, of whom two cannot walk and a half dozen cannot haul a pound. We have done all we can to help ourselves, and shall ever struggle on, but it drives me almost insane to face the future. It is not the end that affrights anyone, but the road to be traveled to reach that goal. To die is easy, very easy; it is only hard to strive, to endure, to live.

IN ENGLAND, cradle of great seafarers and explorers since the days of Cabot and Drake, intense public interest had been mounting in the drama of the lost Greely expedition. An entire generation throughout the British Isles had followed avidly every bit of news concerning the search for Sir John Franklin; now Sir George Nares and his lieutenants Markham, Beaumont, and others were on hand to interpret for the public the story of the Americans who were suffering at the very point on the top of the globe where they had nearly succumbed only a few years before. While the rescue resolution was still deadlocked in Congress, First Lord of the Admiralty Northbrook privately offered the *Alert,* one of the veteran ships of the Nares expedition, to the United States as a gift to fill out the proposed relief squadron. The offer, in the name of Queen Victoria's government, was accepted with enthusiasm. By the time America had, by Congressional action, definitely determined to act, Secretary of State Frederick T. Frelinghuysen had written to the British Foreign Secretary:

> The spirit which prompts this act of generosity, and this evidence of sympathy with the object in view, receives the highest appreciation of the President, as it will that of the people of the United States.

As work of inspection, refitting, and delivery of the three rescue ships was pursued in haste, Commander Schley was choosing his officers and men from among a host of eager navy volunteers. The physical standards were rigorous, and the commander was anxious that every man who stepped forward should realize he might be compelled to spend a winter under great hardship in the Arctic if the vessels should be caught in the ice. He considered it imperative to have aboard each ship at least one officer with experience in arctic waters. Accordingly he named Chief Engineer George W. Melville to the roster of his flagship *Thetis,* a man whose heroic part in the tragic De Long expedition aboard the *Jeannette* marked him as a candidate of unusual stature. Lieutenant William H. Emory, Jr., commanded the *Bear*, with the respected Lieutenant John C. Colwell as one of his officers. Commander George W. Coffin was assigned to the *Alert*.

Although all three ships had been originally built for work in the North, it was thought wise to strengthen them further. At the Brooklyn Navy Yard the whale-oil tanks were pulled from inside the fishing vessels and additional beams laid between those already supporting the lower decks. Watertight bulkheads were put up at the forward and after ends. The ships' bottoms were strengthened with sponsons to resist the crushing force of the ice. Schley, Emory, and Melville supervised the work in relays from early morning until late at night.

While the Navy was carrying on preparations for the rescue effort in the East, Henrietta Greely, in San Diego, was convinced by a number of her correspondents, especially civilians with arctic experience, that something more was needed in the search than a three-ship squadron. To be covered were thousands of miles of coast, indented with hundreds of bays and fiords. They lay in a latitude where tight fog might hide the lost party from rescue ships, or the other way around, at any time—just as Garlington had been twice hidden from the searchers aboard the *Yantic*. Since the civilian fishing fleet cruised the Greenland coast every summer north of Upernavik, it seemed only common sense to induce them to a little extra effort to skirt the coast while on their normal summer cruise. The British government traditionally offered bounties in all manner of searches, such as that for Sir John Franklin, and had thus through the years enlisted many civilian allies for whatever official parties were sent out.

General Lockwood, to whom Henrietta wrote urging the introduction of a bounty bill in Congress, was enthusiastic. He proposed it to Senator Conger of Michigan, the legislator who had originally taken a keen interest in the expedition. When Conger failed to introduce the measure, Lockwood turned instead to Senator Joseph R. Hawley of Connecticut, who complied at once. But it was already growing very late, as the grieving father of her husband's comrade told Henrietta, reporting on one of his trips to Capitol Hill to lobby personally for the bounty plan:

> So much time has been wasted that unless the reward can be proclaimed within 12 or 15 days, the opportunity for doing good will be lost. . . . I feel very sure that the Greely party will be rescued by the efforts already put forth by govt. My fears, as you know, have ever been as to the condition in which the party will be found. Still, while thus thinking, I fully recognize among the possibilities that of another failure, and this failure due to the search being made chiefly at and beyond the straits, to the neglect of Cape York and below there.
>
> We can all see that with the heavy foot-ice along these shores and constant fogs, vessels may pass and repass many times and no one be seen tho' only a few miles away. How important then that this shore should be viewed by many—that thus no stone may be left unturned. I must say that the opposers of this reasonable precautionary measure assume a very grave responsibility, and will be the subjects of just censure, should the future disclose that the turning of this little stone would have averted the direst catastrophe.

In the first year, after the failure of Beebe in the *Neptune,* Henrietta had hesitated to thrust herself forward in the campaign to save her husband and his party. Now she threw all restraint to the wind. Her pen was busy daily as she urged every person among her large, scattered family and her many women friends, some those of her schooldays, to help in the labor that to her meant the life of her dear one.

Henrietta's brother Otto called on the editors of every daily paper in Boston urging them to write editorials backing the Hawley bill, which offered a $25,000 reward to "such ship or ships, person or persons, not in the military or naval service of the United States, as shall discover and rescue or satisfactorily ascertain the fate of the Greely expedition." One of Henrietta's cousins in Atlanta interested Colonel Henry W. Grady of the *Atlanta Constitution* in the campaign. A second called on Joseph Medill of the *Chicago Tribune,* and others did their bit in Denver, New Orleans, Philadelphia, and elsewhere. Standing like a rock beside Henrietta all the way was her old friend and neighbor Douglas Gunn, who had danced with her in the carefree days of their youth before she had met Dolph Greely. Now editor-proprietor of the *San Diego Union,* Gunn knew the power of the press on public opinion and, in turn, on government, and he encouraged Henrietta with his advice.

The bounty bill worried Secretary Chandler, who did not want to see others than the Navy involved in the rescue effort. And though General Hazen shared Henrietta's and General Lockwood's view—that inducing the sealers and whalers to make detours from their normal route to the northern fishing grounds in order to look for signs of the lost party would only add to, not hamper, the hunting force—Lincoln and Chandler on March 17 reported to President Arthur their opposition to the scheme. It would be unwise, they stated formally, to induce civilian captains from other countries to take risks in dangerous seas for a reward offered by the United States, for this government would then feel a moral obligation to come to their aid should any of them get into trouble. Such action would divert the Navy from its mission of rescuing Greely. But the press campaign was making itself felt in the capital, and Lincoln and Chandler could feel its power. They concluded their report to Arthur:

> Recognizing, however, the importance of the question we have stated, and the difference of opinion on the subject among persons whose judgment should be given great weight, we submit the subject to you to receive your decision thereon, or in order that you may place it before Congress.

The potato the two Secretaries tossed to him was too hot for President Arthur to handle. Within a day he dumped it into the lap of Congress, by forwarding to the legislative branch the detailed negative report from the heads of the War and Navy departments, with his own covering letter of one sentence making no recommendation for action. It was up to Congress and to public opinion now.

Already John B. Benton, assistant editor of the *New York*

Journal of Commerce, had come out strongly in an editorial favoring the Hawley bill. His wife wrote to Henrietta urging no let-up in the campaign:

> Mr. Benton says that the thing for you to do now is to write yourself to the President a strong letter, with your heart in it, appealing to him as a woman to his manhood & trying to arouse his sympathies. Never mind whether it is dignified or not! You want to *wake* him to the full sense of the situation as it is with regard to yourself and the other wives &c connected with the expedition. The thing is, Mr. Benton says, to throw yourself on his generosity. The President has full power & control over any amount of money. All the responsibility rests with him, and to appeal to him is to do more good than anything else.

ON MARCH 14, the day after Long and Fred had returned without game from Alexandra Harbor, Brainard brightened the spirits of the entire party by coming into camp with three ptarmigan he had shot—the first game since a scrawny fox killed in early February. The catch had a symbolic value well beyond the two ounces per man that the birds yielded, as the diarists noted:

LOCKWOOD

This looks like a good omen. . . . Lieutenant Greely announced today that we could live here for four weeks more on substantially our present rations. This of course would leave nothing for crossing. Our only hope lies in getting a seal.

GREELY

Elison, who is in wonderfully good spirits, says that Brainard has broken our evil spell. It certainly encourages us to get a little additional food at this critical season.

BRAINARD

No portion of these birds except the feathers was wasted. Everything else—feet, heads, legs and intestines—was thrown into our stews and devoured without the slightest feeling of repugnance.

Two days later Long and Eskimo Fred returned from a hunting trip to the open water with the kayak, bringing in four dovekies in winter plumage; they weighed exactly four pounds after being plucked. Indeed, luck had turned, for the birds were apparently coming back to this area from their winter haunts. Three owls were seen flying north, then a raven. Ideas for increasing the food supply began to spring from the men's minds. Brainard, acting on a suggestion Lieutenant Greely had advanced long ago, proposed rigging a kind of cloth net to trap the tiny crustaceans, about the size of a wheat grain, which some of the party called "shrimps." Rice tried the net in the tidal crack a mile west of camp and caught a couple of ounces of the creatures. There was not much to eat in the first haul, since the crustaceans were largely indigestible shell, but it was a start. Then Gardiner was inspired to fashion a rake from barrel hoops with which they might dredge for seaweed and perhaps mollusks, if any could be found along the shore. Bender tried to fashion a fishhook which Connell said he would use.

On the strength of Long's success with the dovekies, Rice noted in his journal:

> I think now that although there are months of great hardship and privation before us, we shall pull through. I have long since given up the idea of the straits allowing us to cross. A ship shall furnish us with the only transportation we shall get from this point.
>
> There's a hard trip before Shorty and myself to look up that meat, unless a large seal is soon secured. I talked with Brainard today and cautioned him to look out for the commissary, as it is greatly to be feared that certain of the party cannot be trusted in case we come to extremes. I have my eye on a gun and will not hesitate to use it if occasion requires it.

One week later Rice's confidence was even stronger:

> Lt. G. says we can live on our present rations until about the 6th of April, as he has reason to believe the tallow on the English

bacon is extra, that is, it is not counted in the weight in cans. He says we can then probably exist a short time longer by using a few ounces daily and also by trying to use the stearine, our boots, the kayak, etc.

Then I hope that Shorty and I can find the meat at Baird Inlet. I am quite confident we will pull through in spite of all. The only thing I fear is that if we do not secure a seal or bear before any further reduction, we will all be too weak to take advantage of any game, no matter how abundant it may become.

On March 21 a severe storm blowing in from the west and —20-degree temperature prevented anyone from leaving the hut to hunt or dredge for seafood. Dr. Pavy lanced an ugly carbuncle on Kislingbury's finger. During the operation the officer fell into a faint, after which he vomited. Both Eskimos were suffering from swelling about the face, wrists, and feet, rendering them almost helpless. Thus, on the spring equinox, when winter and summer touched for a brief moment, the men were seemingly at the crossroads between life and death. Greely summed up the state of mind of his command:

It is surprising with what calmness we view death, which, strongly as we hope, now seems inevitable. Only game can save us. We have talked over the matter very calmly and quietly, and I have always exhorted the men to die as men and not as dogs. There is little danger of these men failing in the dire extremity, for the manly fortitude and strength of the many compel respect and imitation from the few. Other than Henry's blasphemous remarks, I have heard none speak of our coming fate other than with decency and respect.

I have instanced, as a fine example of the spirit with which men should meet death, the English troop-ship Birkenhead, when the men, drawn up at parade-rest, went to the bottom of the sea without a murmur, while their wives and daughters filled the boats. One supreme effort is easier far than this long-drawn-out agony, when, too, it is easier to think of death than to dare to live.

9 SPRING

THE MORNING of March 24 dawned clear. A light wind was blowing over the hut from the west and the outside thermometer stood at —23 degrees. Inside the hut Biederbick was heating tea for breakfast over an alcohol lamp. The last bit of wood fuel had been used and the cooks had for some days been warming the rations with alcohol and English stearine. All at once the hungry watchers saw Biederbick sway to one side and heard him complain feebly of feeling nauseated. Then he fell over in a faint.

About the same time Sergeant Israel collapsed at the other side of the hut. Greely and Dr. Pavy went to the assistance of the two men. Just then several others started to speak of feeling weak. A cry rang out from Sergeant Gardiner, who had discerned what was wrong.

As the men quickly realized that the insidious alcohol fumes had poisoned their air supply, they made a concerted rush for the outside. Frederick snatched away the rags that had been stuffed the night before into the ventilation hole above the cooking place.

By the time Greely managed to stagger outside he came upon Brainard lying on his back in the snow, his face white. To all appearances he was dead. Everything seemed to happen in whirling confusion. Whisler fell to the ground near Greely; just as the commander went over to aid him, he in turn fainted. When he awoke others were stretched out around him, some were sitting, others staggered about as they breathed in deep gasps of the fresh morning air. The sudden change brought a stabbing shock

187

to their lungs and to their bodies, which were not protected by outer garments. They had tumbled outdoors into twenty-below weather from an interior temperature some fifty degrees higher.

Greely discovered that Gardiner had pulled him to his feet and was trying to force a pair of mittens on his hands, which had been freezing from direct contact with the snow while he had been lying prostrate. Whisler recovered quickly enough to help Gardiner, but shortly afterward Greely and Whisler had to lend their shoulders to Gardiner, who was affected by the same cold shock that had knocked them from their legs a little earlier.

Brainard, revived by fresh air and by his stinging snow bath, pulled himself to a sitting posture and stared down at his half-frozen fingers. Half to himself, half-aloud, he recalled later, he was moaning:

"My fingers—I am going to lose them! They are too far gone to save now. My poor fingers!"

Then the tough sergeant staggered to his feet, only to fall again from dizziness. He rose and fell more times than he could later remember, as he sought to regain the shelter of the hut, back to which most of the men had crept for warmth. They were now so chilled and weak that Greely ordered a quick special round of rum and two and a half extra ounces of bread per man. It had been a terrible experience—an accident that might have wiped out most of the party in a few minutes. The men discussed it in quiet tones for most of the day and as they reconstructed the scene their recollections of what had actually occurred were woven into a tissue of suspicion. One man after another added strands of evidence. Finally, the whole affair erupted in a violent denunciation when it was found that someone, during the confusion of the morning rout, had stolen a half-pound of bacon which Biederbick, as cook for Greely's mess, had stored on the boat thwart overhead. Henry, several men recalled, had been one of the few not affected seriously by the fumes. Unlike Dr. Pavy, Frederick, and the Eskimos, who had aided the victims, Henry had not come to the help of the others, either indoors or out. He had stood aloof, watching the rest of them drop like poisoned animals, showing no sign that he cared. Or perhaps he was anxious for some of them to die? The conclusion, horrible in its implications, seemed inescapable.

Shortly before the evening meal Brainard, Rice, and a few others who were watching Henry closely were not disappointed when he complained of being nauseated. Before he could reach the outdoors the suspected man vomited into a pan. Frederick quickly examined the stomach refuse and declared to the men that it was half-chewed raw bacon, and others to whom he passed it confirmed his words. At once the other men began shouting threats against Henry, and Greely controlled the situation only with difficulty.

During the afternoon Brainard found that his hands, though extremely painful, were returning to normal in response to rubbing and body contact. In his diary several lines about "the contemptible thief":

> He will never be acknowledged by the remaining of us if we succeed in getting out of this scrape and will be at once ostracized when we reach a place of safety. . . . I will never forget this horrible day. Death so near to visiting us all, and when he did not know but his comrades were dying this fiend thought only of feeding his inordinate appetite.

Neither Brainard nor Greely nor any other person at Camp Clay knew the full truth about Private Charles B. Henry. His real name was Charles Henry Buck, and it was his face and inverted name, printed in *Harper's Weekly* in 1881, that had arrested the attention of the cavalry officer who had known him.

German-born but with a ready command of English, Henry had worked in the printshop of the *Daily Monitor* in Moberly, Missouri, under the name of Charlie Buck. In 1876 he had sought adventure in the West by joining the 7th Cavalry. A big, strong man and a crack shot, Henry was the average company officer's idea of splendid soldier material. He was quick, spoke the military language smoothly, knew how and when to defer to rank, and had clear handwriting. He soon became a company headquarters clerk, close to the supplies. In the fall of 1877 while his regiment was stationed at Fort Buford, Montana Territory, following its campaign against the Nez Perces, Henry turned his hand to victimizing post traders with forged checks. Caught and convicted, he was sentenced to a dishonorable discharge, forfeiture of all pay, and a year at hard labor. After his release Henry roamed the West, killed a Chinese in a barroom brawl at Deadwood, Dakota Territory, then enlisted in the 5th Cavalry Regiment, Greely's old outfit, as Charles B. Henry.

From Fort Sidney, Nebraska Territory, Greely had received in early April 1881 a letter which in its bold, sweeping hand and respectful military language indicated the writer to be a man several cuts above the ordinary. The strong recommendation of the applicant's company commander, Captain George T. Price, meant more to Greely than an ordinary endorsement because he and Price had been friends since their San Diego days in 1877, when they had engaged for a few weeks in friendly rivalry for the interest of Henrietta Nesmith. Greely had therefore been naturally inclined toward Price's man, whose application looked most promising:

> My object, in addressing this letter to you, is to request you to intercede in my behalf and use your influence to procure the detail for me. I have always been accustomed to cold climate, and am desirous of distinguishing myself by extraordinary service.
>
> Hoping for a favorable consideration of the much coveted detail,
>
> I am, very respectfully, your obt. servant,
>
> *Charles B. Henry*
> Private, Co. E, 5th Cavalry
> Fort Sidney, Neb.

The volunteer practically telegraphed his way into the expedition by repeatedly reminding Greely that he was available. One wire read:

> If any of detail backs out or fails to pass, consider my application.

When Greely finally determined that he had a place for Henry, the soldier got permission to stop off in Chicago to visit relatives, and managed to make an arrangement with the *Chicago Times* to act as that paper's special correspondent with the Lady Franklin Bay Expedition. Never one to hide his light, Henry mailed his friends printed cards bearing this title, and later he actually sent one lengthy story, splashed with journalistic color, by the *Proteus*. It described the Eskimo belles in Greenland, and the rugged arctic country soon to be tamed by the *Chicago Times'* intrepid correspondent.

During the two years at Conger, Henry had often importuned Greely for the post of chief clerk, but early in the game the commander had learned not to trust him. Not merely had he seen Henry pilfer canned goods, he had caught him in numerous lies. By now even the less shrewd members of the party had caught up with Henry.

When the complaints against him were formally examined, the day following the near-fatal accident, Henry opened his own defense by pleading that the bacon he had thrown up was that issued to him for supper. But Frederick, Biederbick, and even Greely testified that he had eaten none of his rations before being overcome by nausea. Jens, in pantomime and in his broken English, demonstrated how he had observed Henry steal his hand up to the food shelf during the confusion of the day before.

Henry objected to the testimony of an Eskimo being used against him, but the rest showed absolute confidence in the integrity of the "little man," as they termed Jens. Even Henry's own particular friends among the malcontents of the party turned against him. Then Long recalled that he had noticed something strange the day before when the rum was issued, and said he realized now that in the confusion Henry had got in line twice! Angry shouts broke out, and within a few minutes all of Henry's old offenses, about which others had remained silent, were presented. Ellis had seen him steal canned food back at Conger, as had Greely. Connell had noticed a can of beef in his possession under suspicious circumstances last fall when the supply piles were gathered in. Schneider testified that it was Henry who had stolen the canned milk when the knife marks had pointed to himself. Greely questioned the men around the circle; without exception, everyone judged Henry guilty of the bacon theft. As to his punishment, Rice suggested that the party should take extreme measures.

Greely had to admit that if anyone had the right to ask that Henry be put to death, it was George Rice. This brave man, not a soldier at all, had many times risked his own life for the party's welfare. In recent days he had struggled through the subfreezing weather to net shrimp when others did not bestir themselves, and he had been begging the commander to permit him to go back to Baird Inlet to recover the English meat abandoned in November. But because Greely had not made an issue of Dr. Pavy's stealing Elison's food, he felt he could not bring himself to put the private to death for a similar offense. He settled the matter by placing Henry under close arrest, which meant that he was to perform no expedition duties. Further, he was not to leave his sleeping bag without permission, or leave the hut unaccompanied.

A few hours after Henry's trial, Long and Fred Christiansen returned from an unsuccessful hunting trip as far as the tip of Cape Sabine with the indefatigable hunter practically carrying the exhausted Eskimo most of the way home. Fred fell into his sleeping-place as though his end were near. Long, ever the optimist, assured Greely that he would yet bring in some game with which to celebrate the commander's birthday, two days off.

Rice, meanwhile, was having better luck at shrimping. His rig, perfected with the help of Brainard and Schneider, consisted of a burlap bag attached to a barrel hoop, at the bottom of which were fixed weighted baits—fox feet, bird feet, and skin sewn around stones. The trap was lowered to the bottom of the water in the tidal crack between a grounded berg and the rocks, about a mile from camp. After several minutes the net was raised and the sea lice were brushed off the bait into a pail. The process was repeated until the shrimper was so cold that he had to return to the hut. It was hard, lonely work, but Rice kept bringing the pail back with ten, fifteen, or twenty pounds of crutaceans a day, which made the difference of a few vital ounces each morning in the stew. The methodical Israel, so weak that he now spent most of his time on his pallet but mentally as keen as ever, counted a batch of the shrimp and found that about 1300 were needed to fill a gill measure. Greely estimated the shrimp were two thirds shell and only one third digestible matter. Lockwood compared them in size to canned corn. Noting that they loosened his bowels, he said that he could see the shells in his stools.

Another food was seaweed. The shrimper dredged the strands from the water with a kind of spear-hook, fashioned by Bender, as he waited for the sea lice to gather on his bait. Cooked with whatever else went into the stew, the seaweed was considered quite palatable by Camp Clay standards.

After a day of cloud and high wind with driving snow, the morning of March 27 dawned clear and calm, with a temperature at 7 A.M. of −12 degrees. It was to be an eventful day.

Long and Jens went out to the open water this morning accompanied by Salor, who carried the kayak [Brainard wrote]. The latter returned in about two hours with fifteen dovekies which Long had shot, and which Jens secured with the aid of his kayak. Lieutenant Kislingbury and Connell at once went out with more ammunition, and soon returned with eighteen more birds. Long was the hero of the hour, and probably the proudest moment of his life was when he threw these birds at the feet of Lieutenant Greely as a birthday offering. Cheer after cheer was given the hunters, and general good feeling prevailed. In value, each dovekie is equal to about a pound of meat. This appears to be the turning point in our fortunes. . . .

Henry asked Lieutenant Greely to be allowed to perform some share of the daily routine in the hut, and on being refused said: "You will kill me with injustice if you do not." Crocodile tears to create sympathy came at his bidding, and flowed freely from the eyes which, a few days ago, looked on the wretched condition of his companions without remorse or pity. He has been socially ostracized. . . .

Ellis was again detected in the act of eating stearine, and to prevent a repetition of this violation of orders he was placed under guard. His entreaties and promises were made with so much earnestness and sincerity that he was finally released. . . . Israel tells me that he detected the Doctor in the act of stealing bread from Elison's store.

Long had another good day with the shotgun, and Rice did very well with the net, so much so that on March 29 Brainard was writing of the improved fare:

> Our breakfast consisted of 4½ ounces of bread, 1 ounce of bacon and 6 ounces of shrimps to each man. . . . For dinner we had each 1⅓ ounces of dovekie, an ounce of bacon, 2½ ounces of bread and 11 ounces of shrimps. This made a most delightful stew, and its solid contents were rather more than we had been accustomed to eat for both meals. . . . We are already beginning to note a favorable change in our condition.

Elison, whose ration had been raised by degrees to twice that of the other men, complained to Dr. Pavy that morning: "Doctor, my toes are burning something dreadful! The soles of my feet are itching. They are terribly uncomfortable. Can't you do something to relieve them?"

Through all the weeks that Biederbick and Dr. Pavy had been dressing his stumps with lard, Elison had not learned that he no longer had feet.

By April 2, despite further good kills of dovekie and hauls of shrimp, Brainard was writing in quite a different tone:

> Notwithstanding the fact that 3 ounces of dovekie, 2 ounces of bacon, 2½ ounces of bread and about 12 to 15 ounces of shrimps are being consumed daily by each member of the expedition everybody is ravenously hungry, and all are growing daily weaker. The shrimps are of very little benefit; they possess little or no nutriment, and in fact they serve only to fill the stomach. In no case have they ever alleviated the pangs of hunger.
>
> We are all longing for a thick, rich stew of the flesh and blood of a seal, to strengthen and restore our reduced and emaciated bodies to their former vigorous condition.

Food! Food!—is the constant cry of the hungry, the continual topic of conversation among us! This gnawing hunger has driven from our minds all other thoughts and feelings; and, like animals, we have little left except the instinct for eating. Even the passions peculiar to men in vigorous health are dormant and forgotten in our weakness and craving for food.

For several days Eskimo Fred had been extremely weak. At times he complained loudly that he was not getting enough to eat, then he would mumble his despair of ever seeing his home in Proven again. Greely recognized that his difficulty dated back to the exhausting journey with Long to Alexandra Harbor in early March. The more recent trip to Sabine had further weakened him. Late in the evening of the 4th Fred became delirious. During the night he wandered from the hut, but returned unassisted to his sleeping-place. He ate his breakfast the next morning, his condition apparently not such as to alarm his neighbors. Then, the meal finished, he sank back, as if in relief, and soon was dead.

The suddenness of Fred Christiansen's passing shocked the men. They had long ago recovered from the first break in their ranks. Cross had died eleven weeks previously; it seemed even longer. But Cross had never been a strong man. Now that the sturdy Eskimo halfbreed had succumbed, would not others quickly follow? Brainard, Lockwood, and Greely all noted in their diaries that Linn, Jewell, and Lockwood appeared the next most likely to go.

"Action of water on the heart induced by insufficient nutrition" —the medical circumlocution by which Greely explained Fred's death after Dr. Pavy had carefully examined his body fooled no one. It was simply that the commander, like everyone else, dreaded using the plain, blunt word *starvation*.

Fred's body was committed to Cemetery Ridge beside that of Cross, and Jens was observed to be greatly depressed by the loss of his countryman.

The death made Greely realize that the time had come for Rice's desperate gamble to reach the English meat at Baird Inlet. At first he had refused permission for the venture, then decided to allow it, then again reversed himself when Long had his day of triumph with the dovekies. Now, despite the luck with birds and shrimp, it was obvious that the party must have more substantial food.

Greely and Rice held a conference in the commander's bag, during which Greely pointed out that Brainard had offered to go with Frederick, in view of Rice's having drained his energy for days on end going for the shrimp. The Canadian convinced him, however, that he was the logical man to hunt for the abandoned meat, since he and Frederick had both seen where it was dropped in November and were the best team to search for it. Still, Rice did not deceive himself about his reserves of energy, as his diary that evening showed:

> Spent the morning fishing. Have caught in all 180 lbs. of shrimps and have initiated Salor, who caught 15 lbs. yesterday and is after more today.
>
> I start with Shorty to Baird Inlet after the meat tomorrow, although I am pretty well used up, weakened and hungry, with face and hands freshly frozen. . . .
>
> I hope Long gets a seal today. It will be our salvation.

On April 6 Kislingbury, Brainard, Ellis, and Whisler dragged the sledge and equipment to the crest of the island so that Rice and Frederick might start with a downhill haul to Rosse Bay. The load consisted, besides the sledge, of a two-man buffalo sleeping bag, a rifle, ax, alcohol lamp, and cooking pot. Their rations were six ounces each of bread and pemmican daily for six days, with a cooking-alcohol ration of five ounces a day, some rum, and spirits of ammonia. There was no tent to spare; even had there been one it would have been too heavy for the weakened pair to drag with them.

Shortly after noon, while the sledge party was still out, Linn became unconscious. In the evening, after asking in vain for a drink of water which no one could furnish, he closed his eyes and quietly slept into a painless death. So quickly after the passing of Eskimo Fred, the loss of this once-husky, friendly, loyal soldier was a blow to all present. Everyone liked and respected him, and all recognized that the enfeebled man who had lain among them since November, a wreck of his old self, was not the real David Linn they had known. The incident long ago at Fort Conger when he had been insubordinate toward Greely about the hunting rifle was the one exception in his excellent record. Wistfully, he had repeated over and over during the dark winter: "United we stand, divided we fall," the motto of the state of Kentucky. Observer Ralston, a particular friend, wrote in his diary on Linn's final day:

> Linn desired me today if he died to take charge of his final statements, pocketknife, notebook and gold pen that are in his bag and to send them to his eldest brother, Charles C. Linn, 1904 Lombard St., Phila.
>
> If we don't get a seal soon, we will all go by the board. I have not yet lost courage and our commander is very cheerful and hopeful. All the men are cheerful, no repinings heard among them. . . .
>
> Later—Linn quietly passed away at 7 P.M. without a struggle and gone to his eternal rest. He done his duty manfully in the Arctic. Peace be with him.

Since there was no other free place, his own bag being on the ridge with the sledge, Rice that evening crawled into the three-man sleeping bag beside the corpse of Linn, with Ralston on the other side of their dead comrade, and slept soundly for a few hours until it was time to leave. To Brainard this was a sign of the change that had overcome them all:

> How indifferently we regard anything of this nature now; what stoicism is shown when the skeleton hand of Death removes from our midst one of our intimate companions. But could it be otherwise? Our own condition is so wretched, so palpably miserable, that death would be welcomed rather than feared. . . .

As contemplated, Rice and Frederick departed on their hazardous mission at 9:15 P.M. Farewells were uttered in husky voices and tremulous lips; the silent prayers of those who remained went with them, and eyes to which tears were strangers now became dimmed from emotion.

Emaciated, weak and despondent, they take their lives in their hands and go out alone in the bleak, dreary wastes of an Arctic desert to suffer mental tortures indescribable, and to endure famine and to face the frosts of winter to save or prolong the lives of their comrades.

Snow fell all day on Monday, the 7th, impeding the task of burying Linn. Kislingbury scratched a grave six inches deep on Cemetery Ridge, which was as far as he could penetrate the frozen gravel. As eight men with great difficulty pulled the emaciated body uphill on the large sledge, they thought of Rice and Frederick, who must now be struggling wearily through the heavy drifts somewhere to the southwest.

The wind picked up and snow continued to billow down upon the hut during the following two days. Anxiety for the absent men continued to mount. To counteract the depressing effect of the storm, which curtailed Long's hunting, Greely directed Biederbick to make a warm drink with diluted alcohol and a slight touch of ammonia flavoring. The men were delighted with this excellent moonshine, as they termed it. It proved such an effective morale booster that the commander had the medical orderly brew a batch daily as long as they were confined by the storm. Only Brainard ventured out to the shrimp grounds, Salor having complained of being too weak to endure the one-mile trip and return, and by the end of the week Brainard had assumed the daily task on top of his commissary duty, in default of other able volunteers.

On the evening of the 8th Lockwood fell fainting in the passageway while attempting to go outdoors. With great difficulty he was revived and returned to his bed. He passed a quiet night, but early in the morning lost consciousness. His decline was painless, without struggle, and by 4:20 P.M. his fitful breathing had ceased. Of Lockwood Brainard wrote:

We had been companions during long and eventful excursions toward the north and west, and my feelings toward him were akin to that of a brother. Biederbick and myself straightened his limbs and prepared his remains for burial. It was the saddest duty that I have ever been called upon to perform, and I trust I may never experience the like again.

With the death of Lieutenant Lockwood, Greely took a step he had long been contemplating—restoring Kislingbury to duty with the expedition. Never once since August 26, 1881, had Kislingbury asked for restoration to duty as an officer. For nearly thirty-two months Greely had hoped that the stubborn Kislingbury would swallow his pride and request this step, which Greely would have been happy to take in order to resolve an embarrassing and inconvenient situation. But as a commander and as a man Greely could not bring himself to importune his subordinate, so Kislingbury had remained in his strange limbo status throughout the winter ordeal. He had been an annoyance during their days adrift last summer and fall. But after they had reached land at Eskimo Point, Kislingbury had begun to work harder than most of the men, especially in gathering the supplies at Camp Clay, and in Greely's eyes he had quite redeemed himself. Greely had been unwilling to restore him to authority ahead of Lockwood, who had been faithful throughout; but now the third officer's passing had removed this obstacle. Greely congratulated Kislingbury on his past work and, giving him his hand, said that he trusted they would work harmoniously together in the days ahead.

How many days would there be? Brainard's inventory showed 156 pounds of meat of all kinds, and 70 pounds of bread. May 10 was the earliest date at which they could hope that a ship might come through to them. Could they hold out that long? It all depended on Long and Jens, the hunters; on Brainard, the shrimper; and on Rice and Frederick, who had now been gone the better part of a week. Would they ever return? After the past four days of storm none could be sure.

On April 10 Private Whisler told Greely and Brainard in confidence of the incident at Fort Conger when Dr. Pavy had proposed stealing the best of the dogs so that he could better the northern latitude record set by Lieutenant Lockwood. Greely was greatly disturbed by the doctor's behavior, but felt helpless to take any action. Repeatedly in recent weeks Dr. Pavy had urged an increase in Elison's ration. Although Greely was well aware of Pavy's trick of appropriating bits of his patient's food, he felt that he could not refuse without a public explanation and this might precipitate a crisis. At all costs he must retain Pavy's cooperation. And just now Dr. Pavy had volunteered to chop ice for their cooking from the pond that lay in the direction of Cemetery Ridge, where Cross, Eskimo Fred, Linn, and Lockwood lay—half-buried beneath the gravel and half exposed to the wind, sun, stars, and to the view of starving men.

On Friday, April 11, with the storm past and the sun bright, Long chased a young walrus out on the floes. The ice broke free and began drifting toward Kane Basin. Jens paddled out in his kayak to join Long, whom he had taken to greatly since the death of Fred. Long cried to the Eskimo to go back and save himself, but Jens insisted on remaining.

The two called back and forth to each other for some time, until a turn in the current brought Long's floe into contact with shore ice once more, and he could spring to safety.

After dinner that same evening, while Brainard's shrimp net was on the bottom and the sergeant was pacing up and down swinging his arms to keep warm, he chanced to look up toward the point of Cape Sabine. To his amazement he saw a medium-sized white bear. It was about 200 yards off, and moving toward him. For days the hunters had been coming across bear tracks on the island without sighting the animal. Now here it was—and Brainard was without a rifle, and too far from the hut to attract attention.

The sergeant's first instinct was to reach for his hatchet and the kelphook and wait behind an ice hummock for the beast to come close enough for an attack. But he then realized how futile and dangerous such a move would be. Seizing his bucket

Our Hunter, Sergeant Francis Long.

Long and Jens Killing the Bear—April 11, 1884.

of shrimp, Brainard ducked his way among the blocks of shore ice and gained the path to the hut without being detected. How long it took him to stumble his way to camp Brainard did not know, but he disencumbered himself of his bucket and heavy mittens as he passed over Cemetery Ridge approaching the snow-covered house. Crawling through the entryway on his hands and knees, he pushed the canvas door open with his head and fell into the passage completely exhausted. He could scarcely pant out his message.

Instantly the party came alive. Long and Jens pulled on their outer garments and seized their rifles while Brainard, revived with a swig of brandy, gave directions on how best to approach the animal without frightening it. The two hunters were followed by Lieutenant Kislingbury, carrying his Remington. But the officer fell in a faint after running a few dozen yards uphill to the ridge, and soon he returned to the hut in a state of near-collapse.

Long and Jens separated so as to approach the bear from both flanks. The animal caught sight of them and headed for the open water some three miles away, but the hunters, with dusk in their favor, took advantage of ice hummocks for concealment and closed the gap as it neared the safety of the sea. Fearing that the quarry would escape, Jens fired when the bear was some fifty yards from the water, striking it in the forepaw. The animal paused, shocked, then limped on toward the dark water's edge. Long, recognizing that the critical point had come, threw off his hat and mittens for an unimpeded shot, dropped to one knee, took careful aim, and drilled his bullet into the bear's head. The animal fell. Before it could stir both hunters fired a second shot. They rushed forward to make certain of their prize; this was salvation for an indefinite period.

It seemed an eternity to the anxious men in the hut from the time they heard the approaching hunters' footsteps in the crusted snow until Long and the Eskimo burst into the passageway to report their great success. Eager volunteers, including some of those who had done nothing for the party in days, hustled out with the sledge to retrieve the game, which lay about three miles off. Brainard did not find time until evening of the following day to record the events of both days:

April 11 . . . The open water was reached at midnight, and with considerable difficulty the animal was loaded on the sledge and securely fastened. The blood which had flowed over the ice from the bullet wounds was chopped out with a hatchet and saved. This is Good Friday, so I am told, and it is also the last "fasting" day that we are likely to experience in these regions. . . .

Saturday, April 12. Clear, calm; temperature −24°. We reached the hut at 2:20 A.M. . . . With feeble cheers our still more feeble men hauled this glorious prize, the bear, through the passage to the middle of the room, where he was turned over to Bender and Biederbick to be skinned and dressed. Everything connected with this animal will be utilized—intestines, lungs, heart, head, &c. will each be used in time. The liver, wind-pipe, feet and the stomach (which is nearly empty) will be used by me for shrimp bait. The blood will be used for thickening stews.

We look on this fellow as the means of our salvation; without him, in two weeks Ellis, Connell, Bender, Biederbick, Israel, Gardiner, Salor and Kislingbury would be in their graves; as it is, they are just snatched from its brink. What words are adequate to express the rejoicing manifested in our little party tonight? There are none. . . . For days and weeks we have been expecting death at any time and its approach has been robbed of all its terrors by our sufferings. Life has seemed to us a vague something in the misty distance, which was beyond our power to retain or control. The knowledge that it is now restored to us, and that ere many months we will have returned safely to our homes, is sufficient cause for tears among the weaker of our party. Life now seems ten times sweeter.

But amid its rejoicing over the capture of the bear, the party, Brainard noted, had another member to mourn:

Jewell died at 10 A.M. today without a struggle. Biederbick and myself closed his eyes and straightened his thin, emaciated limbs. At 2 P.M. he was placed beside the others on Cemetery Ridge.

Poor fellow! He might have been saved had the bear been killed 24 hours earlier.

While Brainard turned exultant and optimistic, Biederbick in his irregular diary became clinical. The word *weak* ran through his journal as a sort of leitmotif as he observed his patients in the early days of spring. On April 12, for example:

> The bear is our salvation because we are all very weak and do not know who will follow next. I noticed the C.O. today after having a hard stool outside. He came in very much exhausted. He shook all over, though. I hardly think he knows how weak he was. I feel a great deal better myself today, though very weak and tired. But I see diverse others very weak and low, for instance Ellis, Kislingbury, Israel, Gardiner and Connell.
>
> The latter (Connell) is not so bad off, but seems to save himself. My only fears are for Rice and Frederick, who so nobly toil for us, which causes my present restlessness, knowing our weak condition. Rice had worked very hard before leaving us, and I think was looking weak.

THE HAWLEY BILL providing a $25,000 bounty for the private seafarers who might first find the Greely expedition, or their remains, was reported out on the Senate floor on March 27 and was voted through the following day after minimal debate with a tap of the President's gavel. But to General Lockwood's dismay, it got stalled in the House. On the afternoon of Saturday, April 5, armed with a strong letter that Henrietta had addressed to President Arthur and confided to him for delivery, the worried old gentleman found himself pacing up and down outside the White House, debating whether he should try to push his way through the crowd of congressmen surrounding the Chief Executive at his regular Saturday open house, in order to speak to Arthur. At length General Lockwood decided it was a hopeless effort; he left the message with the President's secretary, who promised to put it into his chief's hands.

The following week Lockwood haunted the corridors of the

House wing of the Capitol. To his great joy on Good Friday, immediately after the opening prayer Representative Ellis of Louisiana reported the bounty bill from the Committee on Appropriations. Ellis showed good heart, but an abysmal ignorance of what the Lady Franklin Bay Expedition was all about. His emotional appeal drew on "The Charge of the Light Brigade," as he called on the House to pass the bill that would help rescue the brave men who had been sent north by their government "to do and die," as if they had no chance to reason why. He asked unanimous consent that the bill be passed at once.

Up jumped Luman H. Weller of Iowa, a congenital "I object!" Congressman. Weller considered it more important in politics to be seen and heard than to speak with wisdom. Ellis, he cried out, should be ashamed. There had been a perfectly good bounty bill introduced in the House, but here he was moving a bill that had originated over in the Senate! This giving in to the Senate simply had to stop, he declared. Then old Irish-born William E. Robinson of Brooklyn, New York, rose to sound his patriot's dismay that America had to go "begging" to England for the *Alert,* when the rescue ships could well have been built in American yards to the profit of American industry and American craftsmen.

Fortunately for Ellis and the bounty bill, Weller and Robinson represented just splutters, not a concerted drive to defeat the measure. When the Speaker put the question after an hour's rambling discussion, not a voice was raised to vote Nay. After all these weeks the determined efforts of Henrietta Greely, one woman three thousand miles from the Capitol, and General Lockwood, one aged father of an expedition member, had with the help of the American press pushed through Congress a bill that had been frowned on by the two department chiefs most affected by it, and if not opposed, certainly not favored by the President himself. Not a single vote was on record against it in either house. Truly, its adoption proved that the cause of Lieutenant Greely and his gallant band had captured the sympathetic interest of the entire nation.

EASTER SUNDAY dawned clear and calm at Camp Clay, with the thermometer up to a moderate −9. The cheerful chirping of a snow bunting on the roof of the hut hushed every voice until the bird flew off. Then excited voices broke into discussion of the good omen, which followed so soon after the killing of the bear. The mood of optimism was reinforced when Long came into camp soon after noon with news that he had shot a large seal. To resounding cheers Greely ordered that the daily meat ration should be immediately increased to a full pound.

Early in the afternoon Brainard was near the entrance of the commissary when he was startled to see the weary figure of Frederick almost at his side. He was alone. Sorrowfully he told Brainard that his companion had died of exhaustion on the ice of Baird Inlet on Wednesday evening.

Brainard turned into the passageway ahead of Frederick and relayed the crushing news to the party within the hut. It was as if a light had suddenly gone out. George Rice, their sturdy oak, the one on whom they had all learned to lean during the months of their travail, had gone. No one could ever take his place. Tears came to every man's eyes, as Frederick, after being invigorated with a drink of rum which Biederbick issued him, recounted his adventures of the past seven days.

It had been a moderate −8 degrees when they started out on Sunday evening, April 6, but shortly after they reached their loaded sledge on the crest of the island and started down the far side the wind mounted to a gale. They floundered through drifts to Rosse Bay and out over the ice, but after ten hours' labor the driving snow was so heavy that they were compelled to pitch camp. Lighting the alcohol lamp in the wind was out of the question, so without a warm drink they unrolled the icy sleeping bag and forced their way into it, each man taking a few mouthfuls of cold pemmican to restore his strength. The snowstorm held them prisoners for twenty-two hours, and they did not push their way up and out through the heavy blanket of white that covered them until the morning of the 8th.

Frederick and Rice then found they were too cold to cook. They therefore "picked up their traps," as Frederick said in his teamster's vernacular, and got moving at once to permit the hard work of sledge-hauling to restore circulation. Later, refreshed by a hot meal cooked in midmorning, they worked their way forward, covering perhaps a mile each hour. Nightfall found them not far from the old campsite at Eskimo Point, where they spent another night partially sheltered from wind behind a grounded berg and a glacier. The morning was calm and the sky clear on the 9th, enabling the pair to reach Eskimo Point within an hour. Here they decided to leave the heavy sleeping bag so that they could travel faster the last six or seven miles to the spot where they had cached the English meat.

The break in the weather did not last. By noon the wind had whipped into a fury from the northwest, driving more snow before it, and the two weary men could hardly see forty feet ahead. Search as they might, they could find no signs familiar to them from the previous fall: The places Frederick had remembered as smooth ice were rough, and vice versa. Carefully crisscrossing the icy area, they could find no trace of the rifle left as a marker, no old sledge tracks, no meat. Frederick proposed to Rice that they upend their sledge as a guide mark, return to the sleeping bag at Eskimo Point for the night, where the old stone-and-ice huts offered a windbreak, and return to search again the next day, or as soon as the weather cleared. But Rice insisted on continuing the search, since they had come this far.

About four o'clock Shorty noticed that his companion was staggering from weakness. This was most unusual for the sturdy Rice. Alarmed, Frederick insisted that they take shelter under the lee of a nearby iceberg and with great effort they managed to reach it. Here, as he lit the lamp and prepared tea and warm pemmican, Frederick realized that Rice was not merely a bit tired, as he kept protesting in his jocular way; he was close to complete exhaustion. The warm food and drink, with some brandy and spirits of ammonia, seemed to revive Rice, but

Sergeant Julius R. Frederick.

Sergeant George W. Rice, Our Photographer.

The Death of Rice—Baird Inlet, April 1884.

Frederick decided that they could not remain seated on the sledge, unprotected from the storm, for fear of freezing. He pulled Rice to his feet and tried to start him back toward Eskimo Point, but in vain. Shorty kept up a joking banter about Rice's being too drunk to walk straight, to which the Canadian feebly jested in reply, his chest heaving with the effort of drawing breath.

> He was too weak to stand up [Frederick wrote later, in an official report], and his mind seemed to be taken up with recollections of his relatives and friends at home, of whom he spoke, and he also kept talking of the different meals he would eat when he should have reached home. He seemed to realize his critical condition, for he asked me, in case he should die here and I were to survive, to send his manuscripts to the New York Herald, and his personal effects to his relatives.
>
> We remained here on this desolate piece of ice with the wind blowing a hurricane for two hours or more, after which time my poor heroic companion lost consciousness. I did everything for him that my limited means permitted. I wrapped him up in my *temiak* in order to keep him as warm as possible, and remained on the sledge amidst the drifting snow with my unconscious friend in my arms until 7:45 P.M., when poor Rice passed away.
>
> My situation can be easier imagined than described. Here I was, left alone with the body of my friend in an ice-bound region, out of reach of assistance. . . . As I stood there completely exhausted by the remains of poor Rice, shivering with the cold, unable to bury the remains, hardly able to move, I knew that my chances to reach Eskimo Point were small indeed. . . . I felt more like remaining here and perishing by the side of my companion than to make another effort, but the sense of duty which I owed to my country and companions and to my dead comrade to bear back the sad tidings of the disaster, sustained me in this trial. I stooped and kissed the cheek of my dead companion, and left him there for the wild winds of the Arctic to sweep over.

Now Frederick began a lonely ordeal. He required seven hours to reach Eskimo Point, and when he did, he found the sleeping bag frozen too hard for him to open in his weakened condition. A few drops of spirits of ammonia pumped just enough strength into his limbs for him to undo the bag with a supreme effort, and he managed to crawl into it for a few hours' sleep. The next morning after a warm meal he retraced his steps to the spot where Rice's remains lay, stiff and dark against the white of the ice and snow which were to be his tomb. For several hours the devoted Frederick chipped away at the ice with his hatchet to dig a scant grave for his comrade, and covered him as best he could against possible desecration by wild animals. Then he turned away, hoping that the spring tides would bear the body of George Rice out to sea for a final clean union with the arctic elements.

So weary was Frederick on the return journey from Eskimo Point to Camp Clay that on the upgrade before Rosse Bay, which had caused so much grief with Elison in November, he found he could not draw both the sledge and the heavy sleeping bag. He therefore fastened a rope to the sleeping bag and hauled it first, then returned to drag the sledge. In this tiresome manner "Shorty" Frederick took three days to make his solitary way back to camp. Reporting to Greely, he turned in the uneaten portion of Rice's rations, as if the act were a matter of course.

The Easter Sunday that had begun so well ended as the saddest day the party had yet known. One man, unable to control himself, broke down into loud lamentations, and the others roundly rebuked him for giving vent to such feelings—which they all shared. In their grief they realized how deeply they had relied on George Rice, how much they had taken his many patient acts of self-sacrifice for granted. In his diary that evening Brainard termed the fallen Canadian: "one who was as brave and noble as any that the world has ever known."

Biederbick likewise paid his respects to: ". . . our so dearly beloved and esteemed friend and comrade, G. W. Rice. . . . My heart bleeds, and I need not write any praise of the departed, for never can I for a moment forget his nobleness in every respect."

10 DEATH

THE SUN SHONE warmly down on Camp Clay on Monday, April 14. Except for mealtimes, Frederick slept soundly through the day, and by evening he appeared largely to have recovered from his remarkable journey. Out on the ice near the open water, hunters Long and Jens, in 15 degree weather, unprotected from the biting wind, spent a fruitless day. Brainard remained a long time at the fishing ground by the berg and returned to the hut bearing twenty-two pounds of his tiny shrimps. With more than 500 pounds of the bear and seal meat on hand, plus a few remaining army rations, it looked as if the nineteen men now left alive had a chance of pulling through.

Greely, however, was beginning to have doubts about his own chances. His heart action bothered him so much that he ventured from the hut as little as possible. Decisions about the party's consumption of fuel and food, detailing camp labor, recording of barometer and temperature readings three times daily, and concern with the men's morale and discipline were about all that he could manage. Simply thinking and speaking now clearly took great effort from a depleted system.

Restoring Kislingbury to duty had been an obvious step with Lockwood dead, but since his collapse during the excitement over the bear on Friday night, the second officer had been showing signs of losing his grip. There were hours when he was perfectly lucid, yet the periods between seemed to be getting longer. By the evening of April 14 Greely had written a brief order naming Brainard as his successor to command, but he held it between the pages of his journal rather than issue it yet. He secured Pavy's word of honor that he would be informed if his survival seemed doubtful.

Henry Biederbick, medical assistant and faithful chronicler of the physical condition of the party, was writing more in his journal than he had in the many months before. He summarized the situation on the 15th:

> Lt. G. told me confidentially today that after hearing from Dr. Pavy the weak condition of Lt. Kislingbury, and after a great deal of mental worry, he had allowed himself an extra allowance of a small quantity of pemmican and hard bread as he saw the necessity of keeping himself up for the well-being of the party, to which I surely agree, knowing what Lt. G. has done for us during these dreadful past days, and should he die, Lt. K. would be in command. But he being in a poor state of health at present might also die, leaving us in a very unsettled state of affairs. The Doctor being a civilian could not command, although he might like to do so.
>
> Sgt. Brainard should be the next, but there might be some division of thought about this in the party. It is in any case better to keep Lt. G's health up. I for my part have tried all along to do my best for him, and everybody else here. I will further try to do my duty. Lt. G. has shown himself to be a man of more force of character and in every way greater than I had believed him to be. I think it better that he and our records be saved than all of us together. I am very sorry not to have found out sooner his full worth, and have often done him injustice in my thoughts in Conger and while on the retreat coming down. Lt. G. has during the winter done everything for us that one man could do to keep us up and alive.

On Friday, Dr. Pavy reported that Kislingbury, Israel, Salor, Biederbick, Gardiner, and Connell were the weakest of the party, with Whisler not quite so poor. The physician examined Greely and assured him he was slowly gaining, with the result that the commander discontinued his own extra allowance of food, which he had been taking along with the other sick men.

Observer Ralston was still dreaming of food:

Hospital Steward Biederbick.

> Lunch to be given by me to Lt. G., Israel, Brainard and myself in Washington, as follows: one doz. chicken croquettes, charlotte russe, one piece of sponge cake with fancy ice cream, biscuit glace, one doz. chocolate cream puffs, one doz. cocoanut kisses, one doz. macaroons, lemon pie.—My big toe is getting worse. Lost the nail today. Doctor forbids me walking. Says I'm getting weaker, thinner.

Dr. Pavy, fearing that Rice's notebooks might contain references to the mutiny plan of the previous August, urgently requested that they be sealed and put in the charge of Brainard, the dead photographer's one remaining executor in good health. Without understanding the purpose, Greely did so. The doctor figured almost daily as a disturbing influence as Greely struggled to hold to his sanity. One day Long informed Greely that he had seen Pavy drinking part of Schneider's rum. Then Pavy complained to Greely that Elison had not shown him the proper gratitude for his patient care. Despite the fact that they still had more meat on hand than in the preceding two weeks, the outlook became bleaker as six days followed Easter Sunday with no new game killed. On the 19th Brainard wrote:

> Ellis is worse, much worse. He could not eat his breakfast of shrimps owing to the nausea which their appearance produced in him. His days of life are doubtless very few. Biederbick, the faithful hospital steward, is better. Whisler broke down utterly today. He says he can do nothing more. The fact is that we are all very weak, and it is difficult to find men enough to carry out the necessary routine of daily work. I hauled eighteen pounds of shrimps. . . .
>
> The issuing of the fresh meat is the greatest difficulty that I have to contend with; it is firmly frozen and has to be cut with a handsaw. My weak state renders this duty both irksome and trying, and I often feel like giving up in despair; but thoughts of the future, which may yet have something bright in store for us, nerves me to the task, and by sheer force of will alone I continue the work.
>
> The frost and ice which during the winter formed in the boat and all other portions of the roof is now thawing rapidly, and

almost everything is saturated with the dripping moisture. We are removing this ice as fast as possible. We now have a sufficient quantity of shrimps on hand to admit of everybody having all they may desire. These shrimps have very little nutriment, and if taken in large quantities they have a tendency to nauseate.

Brainard wrote of Sunday dinner on the 20th as if it were a feast:

The stew for this meal was composed of the trimmings of the bear and the seal heads, their heart, lungs, kidneys, &c., and a large quantity of the blood which had flowed from the bear when he fell dying on the floe. Every ounce of this blood had been chopped from the ice and saved for this purpose. It enriched the stew beyond the conception of anyone unacquainted with its use; it supplied it with a thick, delicious gravy and imparted a delicacy of flavor which proclaimed it superior to anything that we have eaten for months.

A full week now having passed with the hunters utterly luckless, Greely decided that the party could no longer afford to consume nineteen pounds of meat daily. At this rate, he calculated, their supply would be gone on May 7. Just sixteen days—far too short a time. They must cut the daily ration by one third to make it last until May 15. When Greely announced that on Monday morning the ration would be reduced from a pound per man to ten ounces, Dr. Pavy protested loudly. Finding the commander adamant, he turned to his old confederate, Kislingbury, for support. The next day the second officer, prompted by Pavy, handed Greely a formal letter urging that the meat ration be restored to a full sixteen ounces, and hinting that Greely was not quite all right:

You are, I know, doing everything for the best, and I have but *one desire, to help you* all I possibly can in this trying ordeal. . . . Your sufferings this morning and weakened condition alarm me. Our stronger men are gradually weakening.

Greely held to his decision for two days, then in compromise raised the issue to twelve ounces. The bread issue was now down to two ounces. These fourteen ounces per man, plus the shrimp and weak tea, were the party's total daily nourishment. The reduction in rations, the failure of the hunters, and the depressing loss of George Rice, whose resounding voice used to buoy them with hope—all this led to increased bickering among the men. Whisler and Connell accused Schneider at one point of eating food belonging to the mess for which he was supposed to cook. Taking a hand in the dispute at once, Greely told Schneider that he would continue cooking, and that if anyone saw him misappropriate any food he would be summarily shot. Connell, the inveterate complainer, jumped on Schneider and called him "the worst thief in camp" and threatened to "let daylight through him." Schneider turned sulky, complained of being sick, and in the afternoon appealed to Greely to relieve him from cooking. When the commander ordered him to stick to his duties, the miserable ex-clerk threw himself down on his sleeping-place and sobbed like a baby. Greely sought to shame Schneider by preparing the afternoon meal himself, but when the men joined in a chorus of indignant protest against the commander's feeling forced to this extreme, Jens stepped into the breach and insisted on helping his leader by heating the evening tea. Before going to sleep that night Greely appealed to Schneider as a man and a soldier to pull himself together. Finally he gave an ultimatum: If Schneider did not cook, he would not eat with the party.

The next morning Schneider obeyed, and later he made genuine attempts to redeem himself.

On the ground that Brainard was among the strongest, Dr. Pavy urged that his extra ration as shrimp-gatherer be discontinued. After a lengthy discussion Greely reluctantly consented, but only after getting Pavy to agree to take a turn at shrimping himself. Later Brainard went to the tidal crack to draw up the nets which the physican had put in position. He found them so carelessly fixed that nothing had been caught. When charged with his error, Pavy shrugged it off, telling Brainard that at the moment he had been "thinking of something else."

That evening he agreed, when Greely insisted, that the shrimping ration should be restored so that Brainard would keep up his strength. Brainard had been making two and three trips a day to the tidal crack, and frequently returned to the hut dizzy and staggering.

On April 22, Greely's journal entry included testamentary data:

> Dr. Pavy says that Sgts. Israel and Gardiner are doing the poorest and that I am at a standstill. My heart gives me trouble. I had a terrible passage this A.M., weakening me terribly.
>
> I gave Sgt. Brainard instructions about my effects &c. if anything should happen to me. I want Brainard commissioned, my daughters raised as analytical chemists and that all that can be done be done pecuniarily for Mrs. Greely by Genls. Hazen & Ruggles in the way of a special pension.

A day later the commander infiltrated into the text of his journal a message for General Hazen:

> Sgt. Elison reported to me this A.M. that Dr. Pavy while feeding him last evening stole part of his bacon, taking and dropping pieces into the sleeping bag. He requested me to make a note of it. This A.M. Dr. Pavy requested on the *ground of smoke* that Ralston feed Elison, and I have so agreed. I presume now that Sgt. Elison can handle his own bread and can watch his own stew, that Dr. Pavy no longer finds it profitable to do the work. No food has reached Elison for all these months which has not in some way paid toll to Dr. Pavy.

Elison's old hostility toward the commander, once expressed in the bitter, carping diary he had maintained during the frustrating days of the retreat from Conger, had long since been replaced by a deep gratitude for the care tendered him. Two years earlier Greely had been injudicious enough to dictate a personal evaluation of Elison for Schneider to write in his official journal, instead of writing it himself. Elison, he had noted, was "one of the best of my men, though not as *bright* as some." Greely had recognized his error and not used Schneider again for such confidential clerical work.

Many times during his slow recovery Elison had told Greely
how much he appreciated his extra rations, the mattress from
the *Proteus* cache which had been awarded him by common consent, and the steady day-by-day attention paid him. He knew
now that while the doctor had taken advantage of him, the commander was his true friend. Frequently he had urged his comrades
to keep up their spirits and that he would willingly, if he could,
accept their chance for survival as his lot, if he could but have
their whole hands and feet.

In a long session with his journal on April 23, Lieutenant
Kislingbury poured his heart into his writing as though he were
no longer the dissident officer at loggerheads with his chief, but
had reverted instead to the emotion-torn widower of three years
earlier who had passionately thanked Greely for the chance to
brave the Arctic, and to leave behind "a world that has been
so cruel to me":

> We are all very weak and a breath will almost brush any of us
> away. What a study our poor wasted frames would be for the
> physicians. We are nothing but skin and bones, the latter pro-
> truding almost through the former. Yet our spirits are good,
> away up, in fact. How we shall think of this life in the future!
> It is a dream now. Everything we do is done in a mechanical sort
> of way, but we float along and know that every day brings us
> nearer relief.
>
> Poor Lockwood, Jewell, Eskimo Frederick and Linn died of
> starvation. Cross partly from that but more from scurvy and a
> broken constitution caused by former intemperate habits. Rice
> from exhaustion, exposure, hard work and starvation. Frederick,
> his companion at the time of his death, has made my heart bleed
> by his recital of the self-sacrificing sufferings and nobleness of his
> death. When the world hears the story as told us by our noble
> Frederick, I venture few will learn of it who will not wonder, or
> whose hearts will not swell with deep emotion.
>
> But there are many things for them, the world, to learn, and
> wonder about. Oh, the heroes! Rice, who actually died, sacrificed
> his life for us and in the performance of his duty trying to do
> what he did for the slightest increase of our very limited allow-

ance of food. I desire so very much to be able to give the details of these two noble men to the world.

Then of our noble Brainard, and our noble Long, our cook and hunter, our Eskimo Jens. The self-sacrificing, silent suffering unremunerated works done for duty and us by them, will endure them in the hearts and affection of all humankind. We could not have survived to this day had it not been that we were blessed by such men.

Great God help that the tale of their noble deeds can be told that they may shine forth in all their lustre that others may profit by their noble example.

As the date for the departure of the relief squadron approached, Henrietta Greely received a letter from Maryville, Missouri, along with a card announcing the opening there of "Mme. Lilla Pavy's Select School for Young Ladies." The letter was from the romantic, impressionable clergyman's daughter, Lilla Mae, whom the doctor had swept off her feet five years before. Just when the two wives had every right to allow hope to mount, now that the rescue effort was about to be made, this handwringing woman saw fit to moralize to the determined, effective Henrietta, who had for all this time taken seriously the old injunction that God helps those who help themselves. It must have given Henrietta a wrench to read Mrs. Pavy's commiserative sentiments:

Trusting in the God of all destinies we have passed through days of gloom with their accompaniments of sighs and tears until this hour's arrival, which finds us on the eve of that longed-for month in which the departing vessels sail toward the North, where our loved ones have long been imprisoned by barriers of ice. . . .

There was a wise purpose in the mind of the Designer of events. . . . Through final submission adversity has brought to me its "sweet uses," for which, until my days are numbered, I will have cause for expressions of thankfulness. I trust that your heart has already become submissive and that you heard, and knew, the voice of the Comforter speaking even as the blow fell upon you. . . .

If sorrow must visit either or both of us, let us pray and trust God in full and unshaken belief that "He will be sufficient for the hour"; and that while we bow to the earth with wounded and crushed hearts, that God will point us to usefulness, and make true the saying in our lives: "You can glorify God in the fires of affliction."

In New York, someone pointed out to Commander Schley that April 25, the day on which Lieutenant Emory had been scheduled to sail for St. John's in the *Bear,* fell on a Friday. Giving in to the old sailor's superstition against Friday sailings, Schley ordered that the date be moved up to the 24th, since a postponement on such grounds would be unthinkable. On the 23d hundreds of visitors boarded the *Bear* lying at her pier in the Brooklyn Navy Yard, and by sailing time at noon of the 24th the foredeck was covered with floral displays given by friends and well-wishers. In return the ship gave to many a new spring glove and gay parasol a smudge of the *Bear's* wet paint, a souvenir of the refurbished sealer about to head off into the unknown.

At noon on April 24 the ship's whistle blew, the decks were cleared, and the ship, her shiny white figurehead of a polar bear gleaming beneath her bowsprit, was pulled by a tug out into the East River. As she passed beneath the new engineering wonder, the Brooklyn Bridge, thousands of people lined it to wave down at the blue-jacketed seamen and cry Godspeed. Out into New York harbor the *Bear* glided as a light April drizzle began to fall, past more thousands waving from the Battery and the Brooklyn side, as every boat and ship within sight blew its whistle in salute—past Governor's Island, down through the Narrows to Sandy Hook, where she paused to swing ship for compass deviation, then out into the North Atlantic. Schley and his flagship *Thetis* were to follow on May 1.

While Schley and Emory were proud that they had not lost a single day from their departure schedule, the editors of the *New York Daily Tribune* gravely counseled caution ahead of speed:

We trust that Commander Schley will prove himself a prudent as well as an energetic officer, and not be tempted to expose his fleet to useless hazard. We are not sure but that it would be wise to resist the temptation to make an exceptionally early passage of Melville Bay. If the Greely party have survived the winter and are alive on the 1st of June, a delay of a few weeks in effecting their rescue will not be of serious moment. If alive in June, they are likely to be alive in July and August, and the risks of the rescue will be materially diminished.

The next day, as the *Bear* plowed her way northward past Nantucket Island, Schley wrote Henrietta Greely a cheering letter in his cabin aboard the *Thetis* at the Brooklyn Navy Yard:

> You may rely on the expedition to get some news to your husband and I don't think I overstate its purpose when I say it will remain as near to him as practicable until substantial mental and bodily relief has been afforded him and his noble party.
>
> Yes, my dear Madam, I leave the dearest home ties in the earnest hope & with the sincerest purpose to return to you the noblest of husbands. May God bless our efforts and help you to be patient in the long hours between our sailing and return.

Though written in a tiny hand that was agonizingly difficult to decipher, Schley's words bore a message of tremendous cheer and hope. This was a man of action—no incompetent like Beebe or young Garlington, but a man in whom Henrietta could have confidence. For the rescue task, Secretary Chandler had picked the ideal executive and sailor in Winfield Scott Schley.

PRIVATE CHARLES B. HENRY had been paroled and given permission to move about the hut, but on April 27 he returned to his old ways. Ralston's account:

> Another horrible, disgraceful affair occurred at 11 A.M. The "another" is the black sheep Henry, who volunteered without orders to assist in the issue of diluted alcohol. A short time after its issue he went to his bag and was soon observed vomiting.

Lt. K. noticed him, and upon looking at it observed him in a stupor and smelling strong of alcohol. During the evening he acknowledged doubling up on Biederbick who issued it. The man has no principle and is evidently a born thief. Whisler and Gardiner wanted to beat him. Henry also insulted Lt. K. by telling him to go to hell, and that he was able to take care of himself and the crowd too.

With the exception of Henry, whom he characterized as "a man without conscience, principle or heart, in short, a perfect fiend," Brainard this day looked on the bright side of his comrades' characters:

> Jens, who is a faithful and indefatigable worker, and who is greatly reduced in strength, said in his honest pathetic way: "Eskimo no good." We are struggling bravely for life—how bravely the world will probably never know, as none are likely to live to tell the tale of our trials and sufferings. Words written in these journals are inadequate to express or describe the horrors of our situation, and I doubt if any intellect is equal to a full comprehension of our circumstances unless having passed through a similar experience. At the present time, with the exception of the one who is branded with the title of thief, all are doing their best to prolong life and to live harmoniously together.

Greely passed a more stern judgment on his subordinates than did the first sergeant. The failure of some to hold up in the crisis tortured him, for he felt solely responsible for maintaining discipline:

> A sharp and bitter discussion ensued between Dr. P. and myself, regrettable, but the man is so double-faced and unreliable. Pvt. Connell made remark that somebody would be held responsible before God for the graves on the hill. I told him that such language would be followed if repeated by summary punishment. Any such attempts to incite mutiny must meet death in our trying circumstances—there can be nothing but death for all in division.
>
> Pvt. Henry took advantage of my illness & others being in the bag to arrange for the "moonshine" & took extra alcohol & so

got himself drunk. The disgust of everyone over such baseness is excessive. I suppose I should be justified in killing the man for certainly his thefts imperil our safety.

Two days later Long returned to the hut in midafternoon with a dispirited air, and shocked the party with his abrupt message that Jens was dead.

The two hunters had been near the open water, and while Long waited on the ice, Jens went ahead with the kayak to stalk a large oosuk seal resting on a pan across several open leads. In launching the sealskin craft, Jens must have scraped the hull on a sharp projection and ripped it. Suddenly Long saw his comrade paddling furiously as the bow of the kayak tilted downward and its stern rose in the air. Without uttering a single cry for assistance, Jens stood upright for a few moments, then fell forward into the icy water. The body and the half-submerged kayak floated for two hours, while Long desperately tried to reach them from the slippery edge of the ice at the risk of his own life. At one point he came within a few feet of the drifting body, but it finally sank just beyond his grasp.

To the weeping men who listened to Long's story, more had been lost than a good hunter and a loyal companion. With Jens was also lost the kayak, their one means of recovering game shot over water, as well as the Springfield rifle, the most reliable hunting piece in camp. Fate, as Greely told the men in reminiscing about his long conversations with the Eskimo back at Fort Conger, had brought to Jens the same end it had decreed for his father, who had likewise drowned in his own kayak near Proven while hunting.

Now they were eighteen men. Henceforth Frederick would hunt by night, there being twenty-four-hour sunlight, and Long would hunt by day. But now they must shoot only when game would fall on land, or on ice which they could reach on foot. The return of the sun had brought the temperature above zero, "above the nothing," as one of the German boys put it. On May Day Brainard again recorded his iron determination to stick it out:

The Death of Jens.

An Etah Native.

Will this sad blow, the death of Jens, which has robbed us of the means of securing game, prove fatal to us? Something tells me it will not. . . . After three years of incessant toil and arduous experiences in these regions, how can we die this horrible death by starvation without first telling the world of the results of our really magnificent work, and enjoy for a brief period the fruits of our dearly-bought success? . . .

Lieutenant Kislingbury's mind is almost completely gone. Poor fellow! It is only a few days ago that he spoke so hopefully of the future, and the happiness he anticipated in meeting his young sons on his return. Yesterday I saw him lying on the small sledge outside weeping like a child. Turning to me he said with a half-smothered groan: "It is hopeless. I cannot fight this starvation longer; I am doomed to die here!"

Lieutenant Greely asked the individual opinion of every man with reference to the extension of our provisions beyond the date already agreed upon. The majority were in favor of reducing them to the minimum.

On May 3 the last of the bread was handed out and nine days' meat remained. With Greely lying helpless in his bag and Brainard at the shrimping ground, Bender and Henry broke open the commissary door. Whisler came up and, finding himself unable to resist temptation, seized a piece of bacon and ate it ravenously. Bender and Henry covered their guilt by raising a hue and cry against Whisler when others saw the situation, and Whisler, thoroughly penitent, said he was ready to pay the penalty for his impulsive act. Greely was impressed by the man's genuine sorrow and took no severe action. But Brainard, usually generous in his comments on weaker men, that evening wrote harshly: "Whisler is the most abject coward and craven that ever disgraced mankind by his presence."

During the day the first sergeant had shot a brace of ptarmigan on Cemetery Ridge and brought twenty-five pounds of shrimp and six pounds of kelp into camp. Little wonder that he was bitter over men like Whisler, Bender, and especially Henry—who, he noted, was much stronger than any other person in the party:

With thieving men totally devoid of honor among us, can we endure this life much longer? It seems impossible, for their dastardly acts not only take nourishment from our bodies but add trouble to our minds.

The final note to a distressing day was Long's report, after a painful trek for game all the way to Rice Strait, that he had shot a seal—only to see it sink out of reach ten feet from him.

During the first week in May, as Greely seemed to be sinking, Brainard awoke to the full realization of what the loss of the commander might mean. He had been told of his succession, in view of Kislingbury's deterioration, and that he would be followed in order by Sergeants Ralston, Gardiner, Frederick, and Long. In a contemplative moment on May 5 he penciled his estimate of his leader:

> Everything looks dark for us. If the C.O. does not pull through the expedition will have lost its best friend & the full benefit of our three years' work lost. As for me, I had rather be laid by his side on Cemetery Ridge than go back without him, so great is the respect, admiration & affection that I have formed towards him this winter. He has indeed proved himself the man under the most trying circumstances.

Greely was decidedly ill when, on May 6, the smoldering hostility between him and Pavy exploded into a furious discussion over increasing the daily rations or stretching them out, each charging the other with making false statements. Finally Greely could stand the doctor's impertinence no longer, and ordered him to hold his tongue. But Pavy insisted on pushing his views upon the ill commander in abusive language.

"If you were not the surgeon on this expedition, I would shoot you!" Greely burst out.

At this point Private Bender tried to interfere on behalf of Pavy, whereupon Greely turned on him with a command to hold his tongue. Emboldened rather than checked, Bender continued to assert his opinions in support of Pavy. The distraught Greely thought he saw a mutiny brewing and reached for Long's hunting rifle. Bender cowered behind Lieutenant Kislingbury and begged for his life.

Connell cried out to Brainard that he should stop the aroused commander; and before Greely could aim the weapon Brainard had taken it from his feeble grasp and helped him back to his pallet. Bender, at Brainard's order, retired to his sleeping bag. Soon Greely, Pavy, Bender, and the witnesses to the dispute had sunk back into the lassitude that now followed any excitement, the reaction of overtaxed nervous systems. In a short while the men were talking imaginary bills of fare in the never-never land of their rescue, as if nothing had happened.

While a hard spring storm confined the party for several days, a number of the men wrote their wills. Whisler named his seven brothers and sisters in Lafayette, Indiana, as beneficiaries; Salor named his father at Steinfort, Luxembourg. Brainard consigned his notebooks and other relics to his father in Freetown, Cortland County, New York—and, as if in contradiction to preparing for his own death, consented to act as executor to several of his companions. It was all done with calm deliberation and no excessive solemnity.

Henry wrote a postcard to Captain Price, his old commander, which hinted at matters left unsaid:

> Captain: Only six more days provisions are left us. Starvation looks us in the face. Seven of our party are dead already and the rest of us are resigned to follow. The expedition has been a success but I have unfortunately not been. Give my respects to Col. Compton and remember me to my old comrades in your company. Thanking you for past favors, I am yours, living in feeble hopes of succor, C. B. Henry.

Ralston noted:

> My feet getting worse and worse. All toenails coming off. Have not been outside for several days. . . . No game. Spirits all good, though, with bright hopes for the future, in either this or the other world.

On Monday the 12th Greely decided, after consulting Brainard, to divide up the remaining rations, which would last until noon on the 15th. It would be better to give the men the remnants now, he decided, than to run the risk that one or two of the worst men of the party might break into the storehouse and steal them. After the 15th, unless Long and Frederick could bring in game, the diet would be shrimp and kelp. Brainard recorded the end of the provisions:

> The issue consisted of twelve and one-half ounces of tallow and bacon to each man. . . . Six ounces of tallow for each man have been reserved for use in our shrimp stews during the next six meals. The extra rations for the hunters and shrimper extend only to tomorrow. Heaven only knows what we will do now. The present circumstances indicate that we can do nothing but die. . . .
>
> We speak freely of death, but it is more in a spirit of a business matter than with dread of its approach. I think that all feel resigned to the inevitable, and I am sure that none fear death, even in its worst forms.

On a narrow strip of paper torn from his journal, Greely began on the 10th what he thought might be his last letter to Henrietta. On the 12th, finding himself still capable of writing, he added to it:

May 10, 1884.

Mrs. Greely
Darling Ritta:

> I could wish that one of the girls or perhaps both be educated as an analytical chemist. Such would enable them to support themselves if they showed aptitude. I would neglect music & singing but cultivate painting if either has the talent. Instruct them in useful branches only—including german even if french is neglected. I would like a set of plants to go to the Newburyport Public Library, where also I would wish my private journal to go when *you* or *daughters* have no further interest in keeping them as family records. Our chances are going fast—no game now in 27 days, & only 3 days food remaining. I have cut off some hair

for you. I send you a complete set of unmounted photographs—
They are precious and cannot be duplicated. Lt. Lockwood
brought you a stone from his island—the farthest north & it will
come to you with your napkin ring, fork &c. I have directed that
photographs be buried with me. Necessarily many things were
abandoned by me at Conger. At least $1000 of property were
there abandoned which I hope Congress will reimburse you but
am doubtful.

May 12, 1884.

Issued last rations today—They cover two days—the 13th
& 14th—with two ounces of tallow for two stews of *sea kelp* &
shrimps on the 15th. Our hunters are indefatigable but there are
few chances of seal on ice owing to the very backward stage of
the season. Of course I think very much of you all these times.
The whole party are prepared to die, and I feel certain that
they will face death quietly and decently when it comes as have
those who have passed. My will is as strong as ever and my
health is wonderfully good. I have suffered very little in the way
of physical pain. I froze my hands badly Mch 24 when the whole
party nearly perished from asphyxiation from alcohol fumes in
cooking caused by ventilator being closed but lost no joints &
they are now quite well.

On the 16th Greely added a few more lines:

Our last regular rations—4 oz. bacon, 4 oz. tallow—given out
today. We have 1½ oz. bacon & 2 oz. tallow for tomorrow, with
a small supply of wretched *kelp* (seaweed) and shrimps. Our
chance of seaweed & shrimps decreases daily. I think but one or
two have any confidence in surviving. My heart troubles me &
grows worse so my chances are very slim. As regards your future
residence I trust to your own good judgment. I have no wish to
constrain you but Newburyport has many advantages—cheap,
good society, excellent schools, *widows House* not taxed &c &c.
Eventually in case of Mother's death you could hardly do better
I think but I trust to you. Maj. Appleby has a Hunt Atlas for
you. I would like some book from my library to go to Lucius, one
to Riss & one to Meade Emory as keepsakes. As to my watch I
should like to have one of the *twins* wear it with the understand-

ing that it goes on his 21st birthday in perfect condition to the
first male-born of either daughter. There is a man in N.Y. who
for about $4.00 make a carbon picture about 2′ × 1′ on canvass
on a stretcher. It seems to me that a dozen such negatives of the
most striking of our photographs would be a good investment.
You can finish them up and sell for from $50 to $100 or more
according to your talent. Try it. Gen. H. will undoubtedly allow
you the use of the negatives. There are 48 in all. The *musk ox*
head would be very effective as would others as you can see.

A.W.G.

Greely tucked this message in his pocket, along with a brief
will, which began:

I give and bequeath to my beloved wife, Henrietta Nesmith
Greely (whom may God bless & keep in the hollow of his hand),
all my property, real and personal. . . .

Private Roderick Schneider in his will remembered his old
battery-mate in the 1st Artillery, Sergeant Albert Perrin, and
bequeathed him fifty dollars "for his kindness in keeping my
property" during the arctic expedition, and willed the rest to
his father in Dorfschellenberg, near Chemnitz, Saxony. Francis
Long wrote his final testament in his native German, comment-
ing with ironic humor on his unsoundness of body:

I, Franz Joseph Lang of Boemenkirch, Wurtemberg, being of
sound *mind,* do hereby. . . .

As the last of the rations were distributed, there occurred the
first of several discussions of life after death, a topic which apparently had not come up at Camp Clay before. In these talks
about "a future state," as Ralston put it in his diary, the party was
about equally divided. Greely had continued his Sunday reading
of scripture through the winter, but none of the men had made
obvious professions of faith as they felt death drawing near. Yet,
Ralston noted, discussion of the hereafter slipped naturally into
the here and now:

In the meantime we still hope and discuss imaginary meals and
by turns we invite each other out to dine. A slight fisticuff be-

tween Whisler and Biederbick. Spirits are all good, though the flesh is very weak.

Elison continued to be the medical marvel of the party, and Dr. Pavy declared that he might outlive them all. The doctor now frequently busied himself at the lake near Cemetery Ridge chopping ice for fresh water, which was more activity than he had displayed before. The days were getting warmer and when the sun was bright the men tried to absorb warmth and energy by basking outdoors. On the 18th, after five weeks without game, Long shot a scrawny raven, of which he was awarded the liver. The rest was set aside for shrimp bait.

Frederick excited the hut early on the 19th by rushing in with word of a bear within a few yards of the hut. He and Long seized rifles and went cautiously out, followed by Brainard, who had picked up ball cartridges to use, as a desperate expedient, in the shotgun. Frightened by the disturbance, the bear lumbered off and distanced the feeble hunters over a chase of several miles. One after another they turned back. Even as Long, last of the three to return, fell exhausted on his sleeping-place, Private Ellis, the oldest man in the party at forty-four, quietly breathed his last. There had been no deaths for a five-week interval. Now there were seventeen men left.

On the 20th, with Ellis barely covered with a thin layer of gravel on the ridge, the most active men were outdoors picking saxifrage, which was now pushing forth in sheltered spots bare of snow. The dry stalks were twisted into bunches for fuel, and the green shoots were added to the stew by some of the men.

Fully nineteen-twentieths of it [Greely noted] is dead plant, but with the faintest tinge of green at the ends. My appetite and health continue good. It is evident that I shall die, as have the others, of lack of food, which induces dropsy of the heart. Lieutenant Kislingbury and Ralston are very weak. Dr. Pavy is working wonderfully hard getting ice for water and, strange to say, is making a collection of stones covered with lichens. His strength and energy lately are quite surprising. I am glad to write something good of him.

Greely's motive for emphasizing this apparent improvement in Pavy was prompted by his having in recent days slipped messages in various places for General Hazen regarding the medical man's past misconduct, in the belief that Pavy would survive him. On a strip of journal paper Greely now penciled another such note. It was written in a plain, deliberate hand that betokened clear thought and physical control:

May 21, 1884.

Gen. Hazen: I send through this way a triplicate of the account of Dr. Pavy. He is our strongest man and will probably survive. Every man is at point of death by starvation and the greater part utterly helpless. In this condition while treating medically every man & having all at his mercy he has written out and had *copied* by Sgt. Israel a certificate as to his medical skill &c during the winter. No one can refuse to sign such a document as you can well understand. A similar certificate was extracted from me May 13th—given in the interests of the party. I have had five sworn statements of Dr. Pavy's stealing bread from Sgt. Elison, his crippled patient, & other evidence of his stealing the extract of beef from the medical stores, meat from Sgt. Elison & whiskey from Schneider. I myself detected him stealing bread from Sgt. Elison. I have taken every precaution to have this statement reach you. A similar statement will be found in Sgt. Israel's diary on a page by itself near the middle of the journal. A second account is to be found in a little book containing many notes to you and entrusted to Sgt. Brainard to be sent to you. This for fear that the records will be tampered with. Dr. Pavy's record, *except as to medical skill,* has been thoroughly bad. I say all this as a matter of duty to you, as I feel myself on the edge of the grave & above all private animosity or hard feeling.

A. W. Greely
1st Lt., 5 Cav. A.S.O. & Asst.
Comdg. L.F.B. Exped.

The certificate of which Greely wrote so bitterly was a testimonial to "the devoted zeal and professional skill displayed by Dr. Octave Pavy in discharge of his medical duty during the full length of the expedition." It had been signed by every living member of the party other than Pavy himself, Greely, Elison (who could neither hold a pencil nor excuse the doctor's thefts), and Whisler, in whose memory the sledging incident still cast a shadow.

GREELY, *May 22*

It is now eight days since the last regular food was issued. It is astonishing to me how the party holds out. I have been obliged to feed Ralston for a couple of days past. About 2 P.M. he succeeded in eating a part of his dinner, but the rest he could not force down. When tea came, about 3:30 P.M., I asked him if he wanted it and he said yes. I raised him up but he became unconscious in my arms, and was unable to drink it.

The strength of the party has been devoted today to pitching the wall-tent some three hundred yards southeast of the present hut, on a level, gravelly spot in the sun's rays. The Doctor says that the party will all die in a few days without we succeed in moving from this wretched hut. The melting snow rains down such a quantity of water upon us that we are saturated to the skin and are in a wretched condition.

May 23d. Ralston died about 1 A.M. Israel left the bag before his death, but I remained until driven out about 5 A.M., chilled through by contact with the dead. I read the burial service over him, and ordered him to be buried in the ice-foot northwest of the camp, if the party were unable to haul him to the hill. The weakest of the party moved to the tent upon the hill this afternoon. Whisler managed to get up the hill alone; he became weaker, however, in the afternoon and is unconscious this evening. Israel was able to walk half way, but the strongest had to haul him the rest of the distance. I succeeded in getting to the tent with great difficulty, carrying the afghan in which I have been sleeping, using it as an inner bag.

On the morning of the 24th Ralston's remains were dragged to Cemetery Ridge. They had barely been covered when Whisler gave up the struggle. His body was pulled from the crowded tent after Greely had read the burial service over it, and left in the open for the time being. Dinner was a handful of saxifrage

boiled with several spoonfuls of shrimp, and a little weak tea.
Brainard:

> The Doctor works like a Trojan in assisting the sick, and in
> doing various little offices to improve the condition of those about
> him. Caterpillars are now quite numerous on the bare spots in
> the vicinity of Cemetery Ridge. Yesterday Bender saw one of
> these animals crawling over a rock near the tent, and after watch-
> ing it intently for a moment he hastily transferred it to his mouth,
> remarking as he did so: "This is too much meat to lose."

On May 25 Brainard recorded that sealskin thongs were cut
into small pieces and introduced into the shrimp stew. A small
amount of this skin was also burned to a cinder on the fire and
then ravenously devoured by the hungry party. On the 26th
Brainard catalogued the food resources in stark terms:

> The few inferior shrimp baits now in use I will endeavor to
> extend until June 1, but after that date, unless we get game, our
> only resource will be kelp, saxifrage, and the small rock lichen
> (tripe-de-roche) which grows here in abundance on the rocks.
> A few garments of seal-skin, boots of the same material, to-
> gether with our oil-tanned sleeping bag covers, will have to be
> used by us as a substitute for meat. Today the soles from an old
> pair of seal-skin boots, with a few shrimps, provided us with a
> breakfast and dinner.

11 SUMMER

The *Alert's* Mission

The Stars and Stripes are at the peak
    The south winds softly blow;
Determined men sail forth to seek
    Brave men 'mid frost and snow.
Now clear the deck; make all things trim!
    The pack with deadly grip,
Awaits the prey with terrors grim—
    God guide thy course, good ship!

The frame is firm as rock, and long
    In England's forests grew;
Beneath, thine own proud heart beats strong;
    And pants for conquests new.
Now double-sheathe thine oaken beams;
    Off every weakness strip;
Wake like a giant from thy dreams—
    God gird thy strength, good ship!

Hailed thus in poetry by *Harper's Weekly* and by a twenty-one-gun salute from the Navy Yard as the British ensign fluttered from her foremast, the *Alert* steamed from New York on May 10. Thousands waved and cried their farewells to her as they had to the *Bear* and the *Thetis*. From this point on, America could only wait and hope.

In Newburyport, self-possessed as always but with her anxious heart riding with the relief squadron, sixty-five-year-old Mother

231

Greely allowed herself no illusions. She had prepared for her son's homecoming, she wrote to Henrietta, and had sent him a greeting in Schley's care:

> I only sent one letter and two papers to Adolph. I felt that if he comes home he would know all that has transpired. I wrote him how many letters I sent in the first box—eight I think, and seven in the last box, besides two large loves of cake in each box. I have saved all the papers for him if he lives to get home, and God grant that he may.
>
> I think now the government has done everything that they could in fitting out the last expedition. How nice it was in the Queen to give the *Alert*. I shall always love her. She is a noble woman. . . .
>
> I have taken the best care of Adolphus clothes. I hung them out the other day, gave them a good airing and packed them away for the summer. . . . What a hero Adolph will be if he ever gets home. But I dare not think of it. Everybody is talking about him and wanting to know what I think. I tell them I dont no no more about it than enny one, but live in hopes that he will come home all right.

When Lieutenant Emory reached St. John's aboard the *Bear* on May 2, he found the old port alive with talk of the $25,000 bounty for the rescue of Greely. By the time he sailed for Godhavn on the 4th, Emory had sent word to Secretary Chandler that at least ten vessels of the whaling fleet would skirt the Greenland coast as far north as Littleton Island, if they could, for a try at the prize before crossing the so-called North Water above the ice pack to fish the west side of Baffin Bay.

The prevailing currents in Baffin Bay churn its mighty ice pack in a counterclockwise direction. The primary force is the warm current that sweeps around Cape Farewell at the southern tip of Greenland and moves northward up the coast. When it strikes the northwestern bulge of Greenland it is pushed to the west, where it makes contact with the moving polar ice annually forced down into the bay through Smith Sound, and from Jones and Lancaster Sounds to the west. North of the moving wheel of floes is an ice-free zone known as the North Water, the goal of the Dundee and St. John's fishing fleets in July. The traditional northward cruise route in Baffin Bay, almost since the time of the Vikings, has therefore been along the Greenland shore, as early summer warmth opens leads toward the north and west.

While in an open season this coast could be sailed with relative safety in midsummer, as far as Emory could determine from the Danish governor at Godhavn, the past winter had been far from a mild one and the ice would probably be thicker than usual. Moving up this treacherous, indented coast was slow work, with gales, snowstorms, fog, and pack ice retarding progress. The *Bear* was ahead, the *Thetis* in her wake by a margin of several days, accompanied by the collier *Loch Garry*, which the U.S. government had chartered to deliver coal to Littleton Island. The *Alert* was farther in the rear. Unfamiliar with these waters, at times finding their charts plainly inaccurate, the navy skippers worked their way northward past the Arctic Circle and into the zone of twenty-four-hour daylight. The *Thetis* finally caught up with the *Bear* early on the morning of May 29 at Upernavik, the northernmost Danish settlement in Greenland. Emory had found further progress blocked by solid ice a few miles north of the tiny outpost.

Schley called a council of officers aboard the *Thetis*, at which it was decided he would leave a message here for Commander Coffin in the *Alert*, ordering him to wait in the shelter of Upernavik until the ice had broken sufficiently to permit a safe trip across Melville Bay and into the North Water. The *Alert*, veteran of the Nares expedition to Lady Franklin Bay, was a tough ship; the *Loch Garry*, her five hundred tons of Welsh coal in sacks for possible use in a winter base at Littleton Island, was an ordinary iron-hull vessel with no special protection for ice pressure. The *Alert's* task would be to break path for the *Loch Garry* and stand by her in case of trouble; the *Thetis* and the *Bear* would push on. Already eight whalers were lying just north of Upernavik at Brown Island, prepared to move. They were commanded by Newfoundland and Scots whaling captains who had sailed these waters for years. The bounty offer had brought them into the ice zone several weeks earlier than they normally ventured. Though he looked forward to friendly competition in the cause of finding Greely, Commander Schley hoped that he could make this rescue an American Navy triumph. Ever since the Civil War, the service he loved had been allowed to deteriorate, and Secretary Chandler was counting on him to help restore its prestige.

Late on May 29, as *Thetis* and *Bear* crept north from Upernavik to dare the Melville Bay pack, both skippers knew they were attempting a feat so far never accomplished this early in the season. Sometimes strung out in a line, at others clustered amid the floes, the two navy ships and their eight accompanying whalers progressed only fifty miles in sixteen days. Occasionally, when the pack prevented any motion for hours, the captains walked across the ice to one of the ships for a "mollie"—a session of seafaring talk—helped along by a pitcher of hot lemon juice and rum. On June 14 a big lead opened ahead, and by the 18th the two American ships finally reached Cape York, having distanced all but two of the commercial whalers, the *Wolf* and the *Aurora*. Here the churning pack had thinned out, and ahead lay almost clear water, stretching around the cape and up through the North Water into Smith Sound.

Because Lieutenant Colwell was familiar with the lay of the land through his misadventures with Garlington the previous autumn, Schley ordered Emory to land him from the *Bear* with a sledge and dory to work his way across the ice to shore and communicate with the Eskimos known to summer at the cape. Colwell was crossing the ice toward the coast when the *Wolf* turned her prow southwest and steamed out into Baffin Bay toward the fishing grounds of Lancaster Sound. The *Aurora* followed.

Still somewhat anxious lest the whalers steam out of sight and then turn north to race for Littleton Island and the bounty, Schley ordered Emory to follow them southwest in the *Bear,*

then after a day to move north, checking for messages at a number of capes and at the southeast island of the Carey group on
the way to Littleton Island. The three ships were still in sight,
their smoke pluming black against the gray evening sky, when
Colwell was back aboard the *Thetis* to report that the natives
had seen no white men all year and had heard of none. Greely
had obviously not come this far south.

During the next two days the *Thetis* moved up the Greenland
coast, through more ice which belied the first impression that
they had cleared the pack, checking at each prominent land-
mark for messages, and twice more parlaying with Eskimos
through the interpreter brought from the Danish settlement for
that purpose. Nowhere did they find any news or sign of the
Greely party. Early on the morning of June 21 the *Thetis* came
alongside Littleton Island, a familiar site to Colwell and to the
civilian ice pilot of the *Thetis,* James Norman of St. John's,
who had been Captain Pike's first mate aboard the *Proteus* in
1881 and had again come here with Captain Sopp aboard the
Neptune in 1882. Norman, Colwell, Schley, Chief Engineer
Melville, and several others went ashore at once. At first they
found nothing but an abandoned sock. Then they uncovered
the coal pile Greely had established in 1881.

Despite gale-driven snow, the searchers formed a line to sweep
the rocky island from one end to the other. At length one of the
men prodding the snow in a gully with a boat-hook struck a barrel—part of Beebe's cache. Each box and barrel was neatly let-
tered: *Lieutenant A. W. Greely, Fort Conger, Grinnell Land,
via St. John's and Greenland.*

Other evidence was found, including the cairn erected by
Sir George Nares in 1875, and Commander Wildes' letter to
Garlington dated the previous August and left in a bottle. It
was clear that Greely had not touched here.

This was Midsummer's Eve, the 21st of June turning into the
22nd, with the sun at its farthest point north of the Equator, and
a storm blowing full blast. Schley considered his course. Should

he wait longer for Emory? Or should he cross Smith Sound, lying before him completely free of ice, to see whether there might be some sign of Greely at Cape Sabine?

The commander was on the point of ordering his officers to stand by to sail without the *Bear* when the masts of his companion vessel slowly crept from behind the height of the island. By 3 P.M. on Sunday, June 22, with sledges, dogs, and equipment ready on the decks, the *Thetis* and the *Bear* were steaming north of west through the storm toward Sabine.

Every man of the expedition liked Edward Israel. Soft-spoken, personable, well-educated, Israel had never been anything but considerate of his comrades, no matter how trying the circumstances. All the other men had been volunteers; Israel had joined the Lady Franklin Bay Expedition as its astronomer at Greely's request, after the commander had a strong recommendation from Israel's professor at Ann Arbor. Although his departure for the Arctic had saddened his parents, who ran a prosperous house furnishings business in Kalamazoo, Michigan, they bowed to their son's desire to follow his professional bent even when it meant putting his life in danger.

As he felt himself slowly sinking toward death, Israel frequently remarked to Greely, whose sleeping bag he shared, that he was satisfied in knowing that he had not an enemy in the world. The commander, without Israel's knowledge, had been feeding the young astronomer a few extra ounces daily, hoping to save him, in part because he felt a personal responsibility for his presence in the party, but during the night of May 26 it became obvious that Israel was in his last hours. His mind wandered. He spoke of home, of persons he had known in Michigan, of his mother's fine cooking. Then he lapsed into unconsciousness and shortly after midnight he died.

At eight the following morning without leaving the tent, where most of the party was now living, Greely read the burial service, considerately taking his text from Old Testament sources only. Brainard wrote a farewell tribute:

Everyone was his friend. He had no enemies. His frankness, his honesty, and his noble generosity of nature had won the hearts of all his companions. His unswerving integrity during these months of agony has been a shining example; and although his sacrifices were lost to a few, still the effect has produced good fruit. For lack of strength we could not bury him today.

During the week that followed it seemed that the fourteen men left alive had nothing for which to wait but death. All edible sealskin in camp was declared common property and gathered together to be locked in the commissary. Long, sometimes spelled by Frederick, faithfully went forth with his rifle to hunt and managed to bring in an occasional dovekie. Brainard dragged himself down the rocky trail to his shrimping grounds when the weather permitted, and returned each time with about ten pounds of kelp and crustaceans. Frederick did the cooking, cutting wood from the boat that had been the roof of the hut, in which a few of the men were still quartered under a makeshift canvas cover, and gathering saxifrage to add to the fuel supply. Biederbick tended Elison's stumps with the little remaining lard and fed the sick ones, barely able to rise from his bag himself because of painful swelling of the joints.

Dr. Pavy, more irritable now than ever, had a violent dispute with Greely on the night of Israel's death over disposition of the medicine in his keeping. Two evenings later he and Salor, who shared a sleeping bag with Brainard, refused to let him into its shelter when he returned in a snowstorm from shrimp-gathering. The sergeant, too exhausted to quarrel with them, forced his way into an abandoned bag outside the tent and spent a wretched night, chilled and soaked, smarting over the wrong done him. When he had a chance to write in his journal a day or two later, the sergeant wondered at the mystery of their endurance:

I cannot understand how we manage to survive on six to ten pounds of shrimps per day, but I suppose the vegetables and seal-skin possess more nutriment than we imagine. Those who are too weak to work seem to retain wonderfully well the little vitality they have left. Doctor Pavy, Long, Frederick and myself are failing and weakening fast. A few more days and this struggle for existence will be forever over. . . .

If, possessing the gift of divining the future, I should discover that I had yet another month of this terrible existence before me, I would at once end everything. When I shall have attained the age of three score and ten years, if fifty years from the best portion of my life were offered me as an inducement to endure again the agony of the past month, I would reject it as an insufficient reward.

In my daily journeyings across Cemetery Ridge, it was but natural at first that my reflections should be sad and gloomy. There lie my departed comrades, and to their left is the vacant space where, in a few days, my remains will be deposited, if sufficient strength remains to those who may survive me. The brass buttons on Lieutenant Lockwood's blouse, scoured bright by the flying gravel, protrude through the scanty covering of earth which our depleted strength barely enabled us to place over him. At first these dazzling buttons would awaken thoughts of those bright days so joyously spent with him at Fort Conger, and of the half-forgotten scene of his death and the universal sorrow that was felt at his departure. But later my own wretched condition served to counteract these feelings, and I can now pass and repass the place without emotion and almost with indifference.

Private Henry, still obviously the huskiest man in the party, somehow found the energy to write more of his high-flown prose, as if he could already picture himself triumphant on the lecture platform:

The majority of us 14 have given up all hopes of seeing our friends again, but a few have still a chance, after the conclusion of this terrible tragedy, to be welcomed with universal acclamation as worthy frontiersmen of Uncle Sam, and so men who have made themselves immortal by a splendid victory and innumerable sufferings hitherto incomparable in the annals of Arctic exploration, and against all laws of nature, as Tennyson freely sings:

"And there they lay, till all our bones were bleached,
And liken into color with the crags . . ."

Kept inactive by a driving storm the last two days of May, Brainard, still the dutiful supply sergeant, totaled up the shrimping figures and found them impressive. Before his fatal journey, Rice had brought in 143½ pounds of shrimp; Salor in early April had caught 42 pounds. Brainard himself had accounted for 450 from April 8 to the end of the month, and in May he had brought in 475 pounds—an average of 15 pounds per day. Further, he had raked up some 83 pounds of sea vegetation. This marine harvest had provided the margin by which they had so far maintained life.

When the storm ended early on June 1, those of the party still sleeping in the half-wrecked stone hut turned out to shake the snow from their sleeping bags and to warm some food. The meal was three ounces of shrimp and a cup of weak tea. Shortly after finishing it Kislingbury began to talk incoherently, then begged piteously for a drink of water. Dr. Pavy, believing that water at this stage was injurious, denied it to him. Kislingbury pulled himself halfway erect in his bag and in a clear, though feeble voice sang the "Doxology":

> Praise God, from whom all blessings flow,
> Praise Him all creatures here below . . .

then fell back unconscious and in a few hours was dead. Impulsive, proud, for the past three years desperately unhappy over being trapped with this expedition, he had found in death the release from sorrow that he had joined Greely to seek.

On June 2, a fine, clear day, his body was given a scant gravel cover on the ridge. No more burials were to be made there. The same day, Connell told Greely that he wished his diary to be sent to his former commanding officer as a token of his respect. Gardiner declared that his journal should go to his young wife, Minnie L. Gardiner, a North Carolina girl he had married two months before starting on the expedition. During the evening, Salor became delirious; at three in the morning he died.

> We were lying together in the same bag at the time [Brainard wrote later], and having neither the strength to remove the re-

mains nor the inclination to get up myself I slept quietly until 9 o'clock.

Now with twelve men left alive, half of them invalids, what all had been dreading began—the mental and physical breakdown of their doctor. For several days Pavy had been eating nothing, taking only tea at mealtimes. Biederbick had told Greely that the surgeon was taking various medicines, perhaps not fully certain which he was handling. Now he began talking incoherently to himself and making absurd prescriptions. Brainard, for one, no longer could take seriously Pavy's advice against eating the rock lichens and recorded the result on the 4th:

> During the last few days I have eaten a great many of the dark-colored rock lichens (tripe-de-roche) which abound here, and I have invariably found them quite palatable and not in the least injurious to the stomach, the experiences of Franklin and Hayes to the contrary notwithstanding. Lieutenant Greely and several others, including myself, are of the opinion that they possess considerable nutriment, and we seriously contemplate using them as an article of diet in the near future.
>
> Smith Sound is a beautiful sheet of water today. There is not a piece of ice in sight, and its surface is as smooth as glass and as clear as a polished mirror. How easily we could be reached by a relief vessel, & the whole party saved much suffering if not their lives if the supporters of the Expedition only knew of our situation & would send a vessel with the whalers when they pass Melville Bay.
>
> Not feeling strong enough to make a grave for Salor in the gravelly soil on Cemetery Ridge, we placed his remains where they will be inaccessible to the wild animals—in the tidal crack.

Long that day again killed a dovekie and Greely again ordered it shared by the hunter and shrimper. But Bender begged so imploringly for his twelfth of the bird that it was given him, amid expressions of contempt from the others.

> Henry stealing again from our shrimps [Greely wrote on the 4th]. Schneider and Bender also suspected. It will be necessary to take some severe action, or the whole party will perish. Our

condition grows more horrible every day. No man knows when death is coming, and each has long since faced it unmoved. Each man who has died has passed into the preliminary stages of mental, but never violent, wandering without a suspicion that death has marked him.

Henry, now under close surveillance as a result of Greely's whispered instructions to his most trusted men, wrote a cryptic note in his journal:

June 4. Brainard prepares cairn this A.M. and shrimp bait. N. Salor to be buried tonight, and Eskimo Fred to be. . . .

The strange entry, referring to a man who had been dead for two months, was left unfinished. Henry's hand was destined to return to this page no more. On the evening of the 5th Greely quietly handed Brainard a page torn from his pocket notebook. On it he had penciled these words:

Near Cape Sabine, June 5, 1884.
To Sergeants Brainard, Frederick and Long,
    Private Henry having been repeatedly guilty of stealing the provisions of this party, which is now perishing slowly by starvation, has so far been condoned and pardoned. It is, however, *imperatively ordered* that if this man be detected either eating food of any kind not issued him regularly, or making caches, or appropriating any article of provisions, you will at once shoot him and report the matter to me. Any other course would be fatal leniency, the man being able to overpower any two of our present force.

A. W. Greely
1st Lieut., 5th Cav., A.S.O. & Asst.
Comdng., Lady Franklin Bay Expedition.

During the afternoon Greely had accosted Henry with stolen sealskin in his possession and the man had readily acknowledged his thefts. Greely had tried to persuade the soldier that the only hope for life for everyone lay in fair dealing. Henry had acted as if he genuinely meant to reform, but the skeptical commander nonetheless wrote the secret order for his most reliable men.

Nor did they have long to wait before Greely's fears were justified. As Frederick's back was turned while preparing the morning breakfast, Henry dipped into the shrimp pot. Later he made two trips down the hill to the old hut. As he was returning from the second foray Greely called to him from the tent and asked what he was carrying. After slight hesitation Henry admitted that he had taken sealskin thongs from the hut, contrary to explicit orders, and that he had already concealed a bundle of sealskin somewhere nearby. The man was bold in his admissions and showed no contrition whatever. Greely dismissed him, then wrote a new order:

> Sergeants Brainard, Long and Frederick:
> Notwithstanding promises given by Private C. B. Henry yesterday, he has since, as acknowledged to me, tampered with seal thongs if not other food at the old camp. This pertinacity and audacity is the destruction of this party if not at once ended. Private Henry will be shot today, all care being taken to prevent his injuring anyone, as his physical strength is greater than that of any two men. Decide the manner of death by two ball and one blank cartridge. This order is *imperative* and *absolutely necessary* for *any chance* of life.
>
>

A. W. Greely
1st Lieut., 5th Cav., A.S.O. & Asst.
Comdng., Lady Franklin Bay Expedition.

Greely had forgotten that there was now only one reliable rifle in camp, the one with which Long was hunting. When Brainard received the fateful order from the commander's hand he read it, showed it to Frederick, and then the two moved casually in the direction from which they expected Long to appear. Somewhat later Greely, lying in the tent with the flap open, could see them meeting the hunter a few hundred feet away. For a while the trio seemed by their gestures to be engaged in a dispute. Then the commander was relieved to see two of the figures move downhill toward the abandoned winter quarters, while the third walked in another direction. Whatever their point of discord, they seemed to have settled it.

Henry was picking lichens from some rocks when the sergeant summoned him to help carry some wood from the old hut to the tent. Suspecting nothing, the big soldier went along down the hill. Turning the corner of the stone wall, he came face to face with the two men who were waiting for him. He saw that one of them held the hunting rifle. Coldly, he was told that he was to be shot for thievery, by order of the commanding officer. If he wanted a chance to say one last prayer he might do so now.

The doomed man threw himself upon his executioners in a desperate effort to foil their plan. There was a struggle. The rifle was fired twice. The first bullet struck Henry in the chest, the second in the head.

The dispute on the hill, Greely learned later, had been caused by the insistence of one of the men that he would not be party to killing Henry by stealth, no matter how much stronger he was than his executioners. They had then drawn lots to determine which of the three should fire the shot, and further, they had sworn then and there never to reveal the man's name.

At the sound of the two shots, the few members of the party who were not at the tent assembled there, and at Greely's request Biederbick read the two orders aloud. Every man agreed that the drastic punishment had been fully merited. Yet even as the group discussed the extreme provocation that had brought Henry to his fate, death was again reaching into their midst. By 6 P.M. both Private Bender and Dr. Pavy had breathed their last—the former perhaps in shocked reaction to the execution of his bag companion; the latter, according to Biederbick, partly poisoned by the ergot with which he had drugged himself while not in his right mind. Now they were nine.

Among Henry's effects were found stolen sealskin, tea, knives, and a valuable silver chronograph that Greely recognized as one he had packed away at Fort Conger before the retreat. Two days later, Biederbick recorded a new find:

> While picking tripe-de-roche for our dinner today I was fortunate enough to find about a pound of fresh bear meat put up in a small English tobacco bag and stuck into the top of a sock. It

had evidently lain there quite a time in the rocks in the snow, for it had either been cached there by one of the party (perhaps Henry?) or it had been cached elsewhere and had been blown there by the wind.

But the bear had been killed eight weeks before. The meat Biederbick discovered was apparently from another source.

Schneider, long a pathetic figure because of his weakness of body and spirit, managed to write a self-justifying account of his feelings and the conduct of others, as he saw them:

> *June 6.* During last night Henry was eating burned seal-skin and I asked him for some, yet he refused me it positively. . . .
> *June 7.* Upon searching the pockets of the dead, lots of burned and unburned seal-skin and thongs were found on the Doctor and Bender both, which showed how dishonest they was. . . .
> Although Henry has told before his death that I had eaten a lot of seal-skin, yet, although I am a dying man, I deny the assertion he made against me. I only eat my own boots and part of an old pair of pants which I received from Lieutenant Kislingbury. . . .
> I feel myself going fast, but I wished that it would go yet faster.

Though his limbs gave him great pain, Biederbick was unremitting in his care of the sick. On the 9th Elison asked the hospital steward to record, since he could not write himself, that he wished his limbs and bones to be given to the Army Medical Museum in Washington in the interests of science. Next to Elison, Schneider was now the most nearly helpless, with Gardiner also suffering greatly. Biederbick dutifully recorded the medical symptoms as carefully as he could:

> Gardiner is suffering very much. He has been caustic for a long time and now cannot make his stool, and I am afraid inflammation of the bowel has set in already from the irritation caused by the working of his fingers in the rectum. The last few days he suffered fearful pain. I have given to Gardiner for days past calomel in one and later in 2-grain doses, and have prepared suppositories for him, but without effect.

To Brainard, food and the search for it were still the main topics:

> Long and myself felt greatly refreshed by the portion of dovekie stew which was accorded us by the party in consideration of the severe strain which we undergo in hunting and shrimping. For dinner the lichens were prepared in the form of a stew, and I think they were generally well liked. After boiling them for a few minutes they became greatly swollen, and the water soon assumed the color of tar and the consistency of thick sirup. These will now become our staple article of food until the supply is exhausted. . . .
>
> Today I saw a bumble-bee flitting about among the saxifrage blossoms and was reminded that summer had come at last. Its approach has been so gradual that we can scarcely realize that it is here. After fishing for several hours, I gave up in despair, having caught only two pounds of shrimps.

On the 11th Long cheered the group by bringing two fine dovekies to the tent from the water's edge, where he had shot them. One was put in the general stew-pot, the other saved for the few doing the heavy work. Late that evening Brainard found that the spring tide had broken out the ice by his shrimp nets and swept away all his nets and bait. He returned despondent to camp after everyone else had bedded down for the night, not having the heart to tell them there would be no shrimps at all for the morning stew.

The afternoon of June 12 brought an end to the sufferings of Observer Sergeant Gardiner. For some hours before it came, he held up photographs of his wife and his mother, gazing fondly at them as he grew weaker. His last words were: "Wife! Mother!" Then he fell over and breathed out his life. His grave, like those of Salor, Dr. Pavy, and Bender, was of necessity the tidal crack three hundred feet from the tent, to which Brainard, Long, and Frederick barely had the strength to drag his remains.

On the day Gardiner died, Brainard was shocked to hear Connell openly propose to abandon the others. The first sergeant earlier had noted that "Connell still remains very strong & looks well. He takes good care not to do too much work & thus weaken himself."

Now, while Brainard was pushing himself to the limit, as were most of the others, for the sake of all, Connell was shirking:

> Connell this morning wanted to shift for himself, work & cook for himself alone—this is the first instance of this kind in the history of the expedition. He was quite abusive & used profanity in his conversation with the C.O.

On the 15th, the malcontent raised the issue again, and in a menacing way. The helpless Schneider wrote plaintively:

> Connell made a remark this morning about each one for himself now, which caused the commanding officer some uneasiness. Two of us, Elison and myself, are unable to do anything. . . . The guns are put out of reach of Connell, for he is very strong yet.

Brainard denounced him in vigorous terms:

> Connell who is now the strongest man amongst our number declared this morning that he intended to abandon the party and live by himself depending on his own resources for a living—this is the height of selfishness. He has done nothing during the winter & spring, has saved his strength & allowed himself to be provided for by his comrades & now wishes when they are all weak to abandon them.

How close they had approached the end of any organic matter with which to renew their starving bodies, to what animal level their tastes had been reduced, the first sergeant expressed with frank lucidity in his journal entry of the 15th:

> The oil-tanned seal-skin cover to Lieutenant Greely's sleeping bag has been removed and divided equally between Connell, Biederbick, Schneider and Elison. To the remaining members of the party will be issued the cover off Long's bag, which is identical with the one used today. . . .
>
> All sense of the feeling of hunger appears to have left us. We eat simply because we think it necessary to do so to insure the

prolonging of our lives, and not from the inclination which a healthy hunger would produce. All fastidiousness of taste has also departed. Crumbs of bread which are occasionally exposed at our winter quarters through the melting snow are picked from heaps of the vilest filth and are eaten with avidity and without repugnance. Henry at one time ate ptarmigan droppings. Bender ate caterpillars, worms & saxifrage blossoms. Lichens and other vegetation are considered delicacies.

How our stomachs will be surprised if they are ever again permitted to enclose civilized vegetables, choice steaks, ham, sausage, eggs in various forms, oysters, hot rolls, cakes, confectionery, preserves, fruit, &c.

Throughout the expedition, the men had been officially re-enlisted on the expiration of their five-year terms. Even now, when only eight men were left alive, the practice continued. On June 13th Greely noted:

Formally discharged Biederbick today, his term of service having expired. Having no regular blanks, I gave him a written certificate of discharge, to be replaced by a regular one. Was unable to give him "final statements."

Next day the dischargee joined the Army again:

Re-enlisted Biederbick as a hospital steward of the first class, subject to approval.

On the 16th the last grains of tea were used for breakfast. Shrimp, caught in an improvised net, and lichen formed the breakfast stew. There was no supper. As a tea substitute, saxifrage in hot water was found unpalatable. On the 17th the party could make out the many walrus bellowing and tumbling about in the water off the northern tip of the island, but there was no way to hunt them without a boat. The end of the edible skin was in sight, and Brainard for lack of bait abandoned his efforts at shrimping in favor of picking rock lichen as long as the supply should last. He contemplated their fate—death for all soon, about the same time, and none left to bury them as they had interred their comrades. Schneider, scarcely strong enough to hold his pencil, scribbled: "Connell is off a good ways picking lichens; he is very strong yet in his legs."

The next morning Schneider worried down a little stew, then lost consciousness; by 6 P.M. he was dead. The last man to be detailed to the expedition, Private Roderick R. Schneider had joined the group exactly three years before, June 18, 1881, and had arrived in Washington barely too late to be included in the group photograph that Rice made in his brother's studio. Far from the strongest of the eighteen of them who had died, either in physique or in will, he had nonetheless fought tenaciously to survive. His survivors could do no more for him, after Greely had read the burial service, than to drag his body a few yards toward the ice foot by the shore.

Seven men.

Biederbick had succeeded some days since in training Elison to urinate unassisted, using a pan which he held in his stumps of hands. On the 20th the medic tied a spoon to one of his patient's stumps and had him practice spooning the gelatinous lichen mess from his plate.

June 20th was the commanding officer's sixth wedding anniversary. To Greely, his marriage to Henrietta Nesmith in San Diego on this date in 1878 seemed something in another world. Recalling the date as he rose that morning, he pulled from his pocket the gold wedding band he had put away some weeks before when he felt his finger joints swelling. He slipped the band down over his first joint, then said to Frederick:

"I am putting my wedding ring back on today. I have the feeling it may bring us good fortune, just as it did to me six years ago."

It was just a sentimental gesture, but these men were now living almost in their minds alone. Connell, a few days ago relatively strong, had during the past two days turned alarmingly weak. His swollen face and limbs and the soreness around his mouth and gums gave Biederbick the impression that he was suffering from scurvy. Most of the men spent several hours

picking lichens. Long went out again with his rifle, still despondent over having been unable to reach four birds he had shot the
day before: they had been carried away by the ebbing tide. It
had been nine days now since he had brought in a bird. How
much those four birds would have nourished their wasted bodies!
The 20th ended with no luck for the hunter.

The summer solstice, June 21, came in with the wind blasting
from the south and the temperature hovering around the freezing
point. Connell was worse, complaining that his legs were now
useless below the knees; he could not rise from his sleeping bag.
Snow squalls blew over the tent. The men were too weak to
stake it down properly. They settled into their bags with a breakfast of lichen stew. In the afternoon they ate a few pieces of
boiled sealskin. By evening the howling gale had pushed the
front of the tent to the ground, flattening Greely, Brainard, and
Long in their sleeping bags.

12 JUNE 22, 1884

HELPED ON BY the following wind, the *Thetis* and the *Bear* plowed across Smith Sound in just four hours. By 7 P.M. the ships were anchored to the edge of the ice that still covered Payer Harbor, an indentation just south of the tip of Cape Sabine sheltered by tiny Brevoort and Stalknecht Islands. To Schley's way of thinking, it was most likely that Greely had either remained at Fort Conger or had retreated to its safety for the winter after learning of the *Proteus* disaster. That he had come as far south as Cape Sabine and had not crossed the sound to Littleton Island seemed highly improbable. But because Brevoort and Sabine had long ago been established as message depots, the rescue mission was obliged to make a thorough search here before heading northward into the Kane Basin.

Schley sent one search party headed by Ensign Charles H. Harlow to Stalknecht Island, where the big English cairn of 1875 could be plainly seen against the sky. Lieutenant E. H. Taunt was dispatched to Brevoort Island to examine the cairn that ice pilot Norman remembered Beebe's having set up in 1882. A third party was sent to scour the shore below Payer Harbor; a fourth, under Colwell, was to set out from the *Bear* in her steam tender, the *Cub,* to round Cape Sabine and proceed about three miles northwest to examine both Beebe's supply pile and the *Proteus* wreck cache, which Colwell had himself established eleven months before.

There was some delay in getting the *Cub* launched. Just as she was about to start, those aboard the *Thetis* thought they heard shouts coming faintly to their ears above the roaring wind. Then they spied Seaman George Yewell running toward them from the Brevoort Island search group. In his hand was a bundle of papers. As he approached over the ice, Yewell cried out the news that Greely was at Cape Sabine.

Schley took the papers from the breathless messenger. There were six records in the packet, five signed by Greely and the sixth by George Rice, outlining successively the geographic discoveries at Fort Conger, the retreat to Smith Sound with the party intact, the discovery of Garlington's note of the *Proteus* wreck, and the final, brief message in Greely's hand:

> My party is now permanently encamped on the west side of a small neck of land which connects the wreck cache cove or bay and the one to its west. Distant about equally from Cape Sabine and Cocked Hat Island. All well.
>
> *A. W. Greely*
1st Lt. &c, Commanding

To Schley, the date on this message was the most significant part of it—*Sunday, October 21, 1883*. Eight months had passed since Greely had written that his party was in good condition. These men had rations for scarcely forty days, even if they had stripped all the surrounding caches. For fuel they must have had next to nothing; and for shelter from the arctic winter—nothing. By now they must all be dead.

While Schley was skimming these papers, the officer of the deck reported that Harlow had just signaled by flag from Stalknecht Island:

> Have found Greely's records. Send five men.

So great was the excitement that the message was garbled in reception. Harlow had indeed waved that he had found Greely's scientific records and instruments, but instead of requesting help he was telling the ship that he was "sending news by man." The messenger was soon discerned, growing larger as he dodged among the pools, crossing the rough ice toward the *Thetis*. He bore to Schley the note written by Lockwood last October 23:

This cairn contains the original records of the Lady Franklin Bay Expedition, the private journal of Lieutenant Lockwood, and a set of photographic negatives. The party are permanently encamped at a point midway between Cape Sabine and Cocked Hat Island. All well.

J. B. Lockwood,
Ist Lt., 23d Inf.

There was no question now of what to do. Schley directed Colwell to put off in the *Cub* and steam around the point for the wreck cache with the two civilian ice pilots from St. John's, James Norman and Francis Ash, Engineer John Lowe, and a three-man crew. Condensed milk, biscuit, pemmican, spirits, and blankets were dropped into the launch on the chance that the searchers might find some survivors. The little boat was soon away into the choppy sea, while the *Thetis* steam whistle blew three long blasts—the general recall for all shore parties. Impatient to be off, Schley himself transferred to the *Bear,* which pulled its ice-anchor and set about to follow the launch. The *Thetis* waited impatiently to pick up the searchers. It was now close to 9 P.M.

As the *Cub* pitched and rolled in the choppy sea rounding Sabine, Lieutenant Colwell and James Norman excitedly pointed out one spot after another which they clearly recalled from their humiliating experience of the previous July. Revisiting now this stern, forbidding coast, on which patches of snow and ice at midsummer emphasized its inhospitality to humankind, both men believed that no one could possibly have survived a winter here. For three days at the height of summer it had been bearable. But through an entire winter?

On Sunday morning, June 22, the wind was blowing too hard for Frederick to light a fire on which to heat the mess of lichen and sealskin thongs in the pot. Heavy gusts made it impossible to straighten up the tent pole and secure the canvas with stones. The men lay in their bags most of the day waiting for the weather to clear, nothing passing their lips except a drink of water around noon. Connell had become so quiet, his face fixed, his eyes glassy, that his companions knew the sands of his life were about to run out.

Sometime in the gray of evening, a strange moaning sound broke in upon their consciousness.— It was a familiar sound, yet one that none of them had heard in nearly three years. It sounded like a steam whistle. Greely managed to pull himself together and clear the drowsy wandering from his mind. A signal? Could it possibly be a signal from a ship? No, no vessel had ever got through to Smith Sound this early in the season. Still—— Greely asked Brainard and Long if they could manage to go up to the ridge above the tent to look out into Buchanan Strait.

The two men crawled up to the ridge and looked out over the stormy sea. The water was breaking on the ice foot below them, very close to the rocks, and ice was drifting rapidly with the tide. But nothing they had not seen a hundred times before appeared to their gaze. Brainard turned back toward the tent to report, while Long went up to the knoll to raise the signal flag that Brainard had planted there some weeks since—a couple of pieces of underclothing tied to a broken oar. The wind had blown it down.

As the first sergeant approached the tent, he noticed that the wind caused a moaning sound when it blew across the openings of the empty water cans lying about. That must have been what they had heard a few minutes before, he told Greely. They had heard this faint sound nearby and imagined it came from afar. There was a short discussion of the noise; then the occupants of the tent settled down once more, disheartened, to wait out the gale.

A little after nine o'clock the *Cub* rounded the tiny neck of land near the site of the old wreck cache. Colwell, Norman, and the others looked up to see the ragged figure of Sergeant Francis Long against the evening sky.

The boat crew shouted and waved. Long, seeing the boat as if in a dream, picked up the broken oar with its ragged signal flag and waved back. Then he started slowly down the rocks toward the water's edge. The group in the boat saw him fall several times while they were working into the cove. Then Norman, Colwell, and Ash jumped out and rushed up to the man, who put out his skinny hand to grasp Colwell's. He was a ghastly sight—tattered, filthy, wild-eyed, smelling of body wastes.

"How many of you are there?" asked the navy officer.

"Seven—seven left alive!" croaked Long. He managed to wave his arm in the direction of the tent: "Greely's alive . . . over there. The tent is down. I'm Long, Francis Long."

Picking up some of the rations and stuffing them into their pockets, Colwell and the two pilots left this scarecrow of a man in Lowe's care and hurried over the rocky rise in the direction Long had indicated. Over the crest, in seconds they came upon the collapsed tent surrounded by a filthy scattering of refuse. It was a shocking sight. One man lay half inside, half out. From within came muffled sounds of activity, as if their approach were already known.

"Cut the tent!" The feeble voice came from inside the shelter.

In an instant Norman had pulled out his knife and ripped the end of the tent from top to bottom. When he threw back the flap, a horrifying sight met the eyes of the three rescuers. Six gaunt, shaggy men were inside, one of them stiff and staring as if he were dead, except that another man was holding his head up and forcing a spoonful of liquid between his lips. Biederbick, when he heard *running* footsteps, had realized that a miraculous rescue was at hand. He had reached for the medicinal spirits to give the dying Connell the next-to-last spoonful. He had then proffered the final few drops to Greely, but when the commander shook his head the faithful medic had sent the second dose in the wake of the first—to stimulate the man among them who was nearest death. This was his final office as medical orderly to the expedition.

Brainard and Frederick pulled themselves out of their bags and staggered to their feet. Biederbick tried to do the same in spite of his rheumatic pains. Greely, too weak to rise, reached his lean hand out for his spectacles, solemnly put them on, and peered at the new arrivals, a red skullcap on his head surrounded

JUNE 22, 1884   255

by a wild growth of black hair. Elison, his dark, shriveled and useless fingers a pitiable sight, still had the spoon tied to his right wrist. He seemed in body and mind the strongest of the lot.

Assuring the men that their rescue was truly at hand, the three newcomers set about raising the fallen tent pole, meanwhile urging the six survivors to remain quiet until blankets and food were ready. Sparingly they fed them pemmican and biscuits, trying to obey the doctors' injunction that the starving should not be permitted to overfeed. But as the ravenous survivors swallowed the food meted out to them in bits, the old visceral pangs returned and they implored their rescuers for more, mingling supplication with abuse when they were denied.

Within a few minutes Engineer Lowe and his crew had ferried Long out to the *Bear*, where he was hoisted aboard and helped to a comfortable chair in the wardroom. Schley, with a few questions, elicited the main facts of the party's condition, Long frequently shaking his head from side to side and interposing, as if the words were the refrain to his story:

"A hard winter, sir—a very hard winter."

Within another quarter-hour the little tent was surrounded by a score of active men from the *Bear* busy warming food over a fire, carefully feeding the men, gathering together the camp debris, and searching the area for recoverable property. To each of the rescue crew it seemed impossible that anyone could have lived through the winter in these dismal surroundings—and yet these pitiful skeletons had. Schley's official report to the Secretary of the Navy on the spectacle, penned some weeks later, can only suggest what he must have felt on the scene:

> Lieutenant Greely was in his sleeping bag, with his body slightly inclined and resting his head upon his hand. Notwithstanding he had been told who we were, he appeared dazed and asked if we were not Englishmen. Physically he seemed the weakest, except Connell; mentally, he appeared more vigorous than the others of his party. His mind wandered somewhat. His answers to questions appeared disconnected and at times incoherent; occasionally he would collect himself, apparently with

some effort, but would soon indicate that his memory was indistinct.

Pausing for a moment, as if reflecting, he would say, "I'm so glad to see you," and almost immediately afterwards, "Those lemons which your wife so kindly put up for us . . ." etc.

He had lain for weeks in his sleeping bag, on account of gradually failing strength; was unable to stand alone, and was almost helpless, except in a sitting posture; all pain of hunger had ceased; his appearance was wild; his hair was long and matted; his face and hands were covered with sooty, thick dirt; his form had wasted almost to a skeleton; his feet and joints were swollen; his eyes were sunken, and his body scantily covered with dirty and almost worn-out garments, which had not been changed for six or eight months.

Emotionally stimulated as they had not been since the bear had been killed in early April, nourished by warm food and beverages doled sparingly to them by Surgeons Green and Ames, the strongest of the survivors of the Lady Franklin Bay Expedition soon were ready for transfer to the ships. Frederick, Brainard, and even Biederbick at first insisted they could walk to the launch, but the latter two quickly accepted the stretcher. Only Frederick was able to keep his feet for a few steps, and he was supported by two husky seamen who towered above him on either side as they helped him down the rocky path.

By this time the *Thetis* had arrived from Payer Harbor. Schley ordered a man down to the ice foot to signal the ship for more help. On board, young Harlow, detailed to act as navy photographer along with his other duties, ran forward to read the message, of which he lost the first words:

". . . Harlow with photograph machine, doctor with stretchers. Seven alive."

Seven alive would mean that most of the party had been wiped out! Perhaps it should be *Seven dead.* The officer requested a repeat of the last two words.

S–E–V–E–N A–L–I–V–E waved plainly through the air. The men aboard the *Thetis* in this way learned the fate of the Greely party.

For weeks Harlow had dreamed of capturing on a photographic plate "Schley's Meeting with Greely," just as Stanley had with a phrase immortalized his meeting with David Livingstone in the depths of darkest Africa twelve years before. As ill luck would have it, he had missed the dramatic scene by half an hour.

Transferred to shore by boat, Harlow came upon Frederick walking with the aid of his two sailor escorts, a blanket draped over his head and shoulders, picking his way slowly toward the ice foot. As Harlow recalled later, these were the words that came to his mind: "How are you, old fellow?"

To which Frederick replied blankly: "Oh, I am all right, I guess."

Harlow hurried up the hill and over the crest to the tent, where he exposed five plates. One took in the tent interior with its occupants, two more were devoted to the outside of the tent, another to the abandoned winter hut, and the final one to the row of graves on Cemetery Ridge. The scene was now documented; the decampment on Schley's order could begin.

It was not alone the condition of the seven survivors that impressed Schley deeply, as he later recorded his thoughts for Secretary Chandler, but the misery of their location:

> The conditions of the surroundings of this wretched camp were in keeping with the scenes inside and about the tent— desperate, desolate and abandoned.
>
> The bleak barrenness of the spot, rarely visited by Arctic fowl or animal; the row of graves on a little ridge a hundred feet away, with protruding heads and feet of those later buried, were a sad and silent witness to the daily increasing weakness of the little band of survivors.
>
> The deserted winter quarters in the hollow below, with its broken wall, invaded by water from the melting snow and ice about it; the dead bodies of two companions stretched out on the ice-foot that remained; the wretched apology for cooking utensils, improvised by them in their sore distress, hardly deserving the name; the scattered and worn-out clothes and sleeping bags of the dead; the absence of all food, save a few cups full of boiled seal-skin scraps; the wild and weird scene of snow, ice

and glaciers overlooking and overhanging this desolate camp, completed a picture as startling as it was impressive.

The five other men followed Frederick on stretchers. They were put aboard the launches and after they took a splashing in the choppy sea, the boats delivered them all to the ships, where warm blankets in a berth awaited each of them. For the first time since Fort Conger they were resting as civilized men, secure from wind, wet, and the freezing ground.

While other officers and men cleaned up the tent site and re-covered every one of the neat bundles of personal belongings, each marked with the name of its owner, living or dead, Lieutenant Emory and a grave detail set about the removal of the corpses. The ten shallow graves on Cemetery Ridge were easily opened; each of the light, emaciated bodies was brought on board ship, where all ten were temporarily stored in two of the longboats on deck with a covering of ice as a preserving agent. Schneider's body, emitting a foul odor from the mouth, was recovered and wrapped, as was Henry's incomplete corpse, which had been exposed to the sun and to insect life for more than two weeks. The bullet holes did not escape the notice of Lieutenant Colwell, who quietly reported the matter to Schley. At this point, however, Greely was in no state, either physical or mental, to be questioned about it. The few who were aware of what Colwell had discovered were enjoined to remain silent.

By three in the morning the site of Camp Clay had been thoroughly cleared. The wind having not yet abated, Schley ordered the ships to sail through the gloom for the shelter of Payer Harbor, and later in the morning he sent a party to check the entire coast, from Cape Sabine all the way to Camp Clay to recover anything of value to the survivors, the families of their dead comrades, or the government. Another party visited Stalknecht Island. Starting on top with the case containing the pendulum, brought with such determination on the retreat from Fort Conger, they pulled aside the protecting rocks and recovered every one of the scientific records and instruments of the Lady Franklin Bay Expedition. Whatever else had befallen this group of abandoned men, the fruit of their two years' work had been recovered for science.

As the two ships steamed away from Cape Sabine toward Littleton Island on the afternoon of the 23d, Surgeon Edward H. Green believed that Greely had already turned a corner and would recover. His pulse, which had been only 52 per minute the previous evening, was now up to 60. His temperature was 98°, compared to 97.2° when it was first taken. On being brought aboard near midnight, Greely had fainted; carried below to the wardroom, he had vomited. Revived with aromatic spirits of ammonia, he was placed in a berth and given a teaspoonful of minced, raw fresh beef. His foul clothing was carefully cut from his emaciated body and heavy red flannels, previously warmed, were substituted.

On examination his body, like that of all the others, emitted a sickly, offensive odor as of stale urine. The skin hung from his limbs in flaps. The patient, Dr. Green noted, was excitable and irritable, at times not rational. His eyes were wild and staring. He insisted on talking, expressed a craving for news and for food, as was only natural. Yet at the same time, Green remarked, he complained of no pain.

As he examined his patient later in the day, Green realized that he had a subject for an extraordinary medical study of what hunger over a long period can do to the human body. He noted many details. Greely's tongue was dry and cracked, and was covered with a heavy, brownish-black coat. His hollow abdominal cavity was almost in contact with the vertebral column. There had been no movement of the bowels for six days. Respiration was at the rate of twelve times per minute, with no abnormal conditions of the lungs revealed by percussion. The skin was cold and clammy, shriveled and sallow. The surgeon recorded Greely's weight at 120 pounds, and determined later that Greely had lost 48 pounds since leaving Fort Conger.

As each day passed, the records of the two navy surgeons showed a steady improvement in the condition of all the rescued men except Elison, about whose full recovery they had serious doubts as soon as they had examined his stumps. The surgeons feared that warmth and revived extremity circulation might be followed by a renewed attack of gangrene, the final outcome of which would be extremely doubtful in a case where the body lacked basic strength to withstand the shock of operation. Concerning Greely, however, Dr. Green recorded on June 24:

> No sleep; mind more tranquil, but too active. Great desire to talk and read; less persistent in demanding food; complains of soreness in limbs; tongue presents a moister appearance; bowels slightly distended with gas, no stool; pulse 62, not so thready; heart sounds stronger; still a pronounced anemic murmur. . . .
>
> 25th. Marked improvement; mind more tranquil; talks quietly without excitement; slept two or three hours naturally, awoke refreshed; . . . pulse 65, some strength; respiration 14, principally costal; temp. 98°; muscles sore; ankles puffed.

On the 26th Greely was allowed to sit up in bed and read a little after he had slept six hours soundly during the night. Two days later he had gained enough strength so he could sit up for a couple of hours, then he felt exhausted and returned to bed. By now he was being fed five times daily at four-hour intervals on oatmeal, broiled steak, beef essence, soft-boiled egg, milk toast, raw minced beef and onions, and beef broth again as a 10 P.M. nightcap. On July 1 he felt quite refreshed on waking, since he had slept well during the night, and for the first time was content with his breakfast without asking for more. Since the sun was shining brightly, Greely was helped up to the deck, where he sat in the fresh air, well bundled up, for an hour.

As the days passed and the survivors gained strength they began to tell their story to the rescuers, so that its outlines were generally known by the time the ships met the *Alert* and the *Loch Garry* on June 30, struggling through the ice a short distance north of Upernavik. Four days earlier Schley had come upon five of the whalers he had left behind on the way north. They were in the North Water about a hundred miles short of Cape Sabine, and without doubt would have gone all the way to that point within a short while—though they would have been barely

Sergeant Joseph Elison.

Relief Squadron of 1884 at Godhavn, Greenland.

too late to save any of the survivors of June 22; Green firmly believed that none could have survived another forty-eight hours. Schley passed the news of the rescue to the whalers to prevent their taking further needless risk in hope of gaining the $25,000 bounty. Then, on July 2, the squadron left the ice zone for good and crept into Upernavik. When Schley reported his success to Governor Elberg, the populace quickly gathered around, some two hundred people in all, and the Governor repeated the news to them in Eskimo. Supposedly stoic by nature, these simple people of the Arctic showed deep compassion over the sufferings of the men they remembered from three years earlier, and many a tear was shed for their compatriots, Jens Edward and Fred Christiansen. At the Governor's suggestion the Americans decided to carry Christiansen's body south to Godhavn on Disko Island for burial.

July Fourth was celebrated during the voyage through the treacherous coastal waters with flying pennants, cannon salutes, and toasts. Six of the survivors were on deck, roaming about much as they pleased, and several recalled the baseball game at Fort Conger one year before as they awaited the ship that would effect their return home. But down below in his berth the seventh man, Joseph Elison, was sinking fast. Greely had named Elison sergeant at the end of winter as a tribute to his heroic fight for life; he had meant the promotion largely as a moral gesture, a salute to a doomed soldier. Yet the man had amazed him by pulling through into spring, then into May, then June. But in the warmth of the ship, as his system strengthened with life-giving nourishment, his extremities, from which the gangrenous tissue had been amputated by nature in the cold of January, became a purulent source of infection. As soon as the ship stopped off Godhavn early on July 5, Surgeons Ames and Green amputated the suffering soldier's ankles in an effort to save him from blood poisoning. The shock proved too much. In his weakened condition Elison never fully rallied from the operation. On the morning of July 8, after defying death for two thirds of a year, he breathed his last.

Six men were left of the original twenty-five who composed the Lady Franklin Bay Expedition. Fate was not to reach out for another among them for twenty more years.

Even as Elison lay dying aboard the *Bear,* a solemn procession of officers and sailors in their blue uniforms wound up the hill above Godhavn bearing Eskimo Frederik Thorlip Christiansen to his final rest. In the Christian chapel at its summit the Danish Inspector addressed his farewell to Fred in English for the benefit of those few who knew him well, and those who had brought him home:

"As head of the Danish Government in North Greenland, I have received your body, and in the name of all the Danish and Greenland people I will say you farewell. Your last master, Lieutenant Greely, has said you were a good and a brave man; he has promised me to send for your tomb a monument as a sign for your countrymen that he will never forget your service, nor will he ever forget the poor Eskimo who has lived and suffered as a comrade with the United States friends. . . ."

To Brainard especially, it was a moving experience to hear the Lutheran pastor of stolid Eskimo countenance deliver the funeral discourse before this mixed gathering for his comrade of the assault party that had attained the Farthest North. Delivered in the musical rhythm of his Eskimo dialect, the pastor's words were given to the Americans in translation before they sailed from Godhavn:

"No man knows the thought of God concerning us. He whose soulless body we today are to bury, and the other, his companion, who perished in a kayak in the northern regions, did not think their days were numbered when they took leave of the wives they loved and the children who were to be their support in their old age. They thought they would be better able to support their families when they returned, and they begged them to pray for a happy meeting. But they were never to be made happy by seeing each other's faces. . . .

"We pray to God that He will assist these strangers in the far country to whom the angel of death has also come. Peace be with their dust. In the name of Jesus, Amen."

Arctic Highlanders—Saunders Island Natives.

Lieutenant A. W. Greely and survivors 1884, on board ship. Clockwise from top to bottom: Long, Frederick, Connell, Biederbick, Greely, and Brainard.
— *Greely Papers* —

The rescue ships now set course for St. John's. Greely, though physically still weak, was mentally quite alert toward the close of the sea trip. Bit by bit, the relief commander had let Greely know the series of events that had taken place since his departure three years before—including the steps toward the relief of his party taken by President Arthur, Secretaries Lincoln and Chandler, General Hazen, various senators, and the American press. As Greely went carefully through his mail, both official and private, and conferred with Schley, the pieces of the picture fitting together in his mind led him to firm conclusions about the responsibility for the party's ordeal and the death of nineteen men.

Among the most precious letters Greely read on shipboard were the messages from Henrietta, breathing her love and hope and confidence in him. She had sent him photographs of herself, Toinette, and Adola with the letters, which she confided personally to Lieutenant Emory, whose deceased brother had been a close friend of Greely's in Washington years before. The brave lines she had written told him she had measured up to everything he had asked and expected of her during those long months of separation six and a half years ago, when he had written: "It will be hard—hard, but can be borne by stout hearts and strong wills."

On the morning of July 17 the rescue ships were poking warily along the Newfoundland coast in a dense fog, searching for the narrow entry to St. John's harbor, when a church bell from on shore clearly rang out eight o'clock. Thus oriented, Schley led the way into port. His arrival caused a great commotion. Three years before, the Lady Franklin Bay Expedition had sailed out to sea without causing a ripple of interest here, except among those, as Greely noted at the time, who stood to gain financially from supplying it. Today the entire world was awaiting word from St. John's, and all St. John's was electrified by the news that was shouted from the ships as soon as they had come within hearing.

A messenger stepped from the *Thetis'* launch and darted toward the telegraph office, a packet of dispatches in his hand addressed to Washington and many other points. Among them was one penned by the principal actor in the drama now moving to its denouement, which left a great measure of what was in the writer's heart unsaid:

> Mrs. A. W. Greely, San Diego, Cal.—Perfectly well but weak. Five men only survive, no officers. Remain here four days. Lockwood beat Markham latitude. Suit your convenience coming East. Shall take long sick leave.
>
> *A. W. Greely*

Reserved and practical as ever, aware that Henrietta would, within a couple of hours, be inundated with messages and visitors, congratulations and well-wishers, Greely wrote no words of affection for the gaze of strangers. And since his telegram to his wife was personal, not official, he marked it without question—*collect*.

13 "HOME AGAIN"

THE WIRES from Schley and Greely in St. John's swiftly turned the State-War-Navy building on Pennsylvania Avenue into a bedlam. Secretary Chandler was in West Point, New York, on a combined vacation and political trip, leaving Admiral Edward T. Nichols as Acting Secretary. Summoned to the telegraph room, Nichols stood anxiously by as Schley's detailed message clicked in over the receiver and was copied, page after hasty page. It recounted the resounding triumph of the Navy squadron in rescuing Greely without a casualty of its own. But only six of the Lady Franklin Bay Expedition members would return home. One sentence of Schley's dispatch seemed to Nichols to petition a special authority for which the commander in St. John's desired official sanction:

> I would urgently suggest that bodies now on board be placed in metallic cases here for safer and better transportation in a sea-way; this appears to me imperative.

As telephones jangled and the corridors of the ornate building filled with excited clusters of people, Nichols at once got in touch with General Sheridan, Acting Secretary of War in the absence of Lincoln, who was in New York. As soon as they had digested the first of the rescue news, the two acting department heads hurried across the street to the White House, where they surprised President Arthur with the news at breakfast. A short while later Secretary Chandler got word from Nichols. He thought over his answer for a time, then dictated his own reply to Commander Schley:

Receive my congratulations and thanks for yourself and your whole command for your prudence, perseverance and courage in reaching our dead and dying countrymen. The hearts of the American people go out with great affection to Lieutenant Greely and the few survivors of his deadly peril. Care for them unremittingly and bid them be cheerful and hopeful on account of what life yet has in store for them. Preserve tenderly the remains of the heroic dead; prepare them according to your judgment and bring them home.

At about the same hour in Newburyport, the first word of the rescue was received from Boston by John D. Parsons, editor of the Newburyport *Morning Herald* and local correspondent of the *Boston Globe.* A minute after he had been waked from his morning sleep to read the news, Parsons dashed out to the front porch in his nightgown and called his twelve-year-old brother Freddie to run with the telegram to the house of John Greely at Federal and High streets, then to Mrs. Greely, the explorer's mother, down on Prospect Street.

Parsons' account in the paper the next day described how the mother of the now world-famous explorer, "while overjoyed to learn that her son was alive and well, with true womanly sympathy expressed deep sorrow at the loss of the men who had accompanied him to the Arctic regions."

In San Diego at her father's house, Henrietta was soon surrounded by friends and sympathetic strangers, while telegrams poured in all day upon the happy wife for whom, at last, the long ordeal had come to an end.

In St. John's, as the hours passed, a steady flow of congratulatory messages flowed from the wires. From his friend and mentor, General Hazen, Greely first received a purely personal greeting:

Our hearts are overflowing with gladness and thanks to God for your safety and in sadness for those who without fault of yours are dead. Your family are well and in San Diego.

—and then one with an official air, also from General Hazen:

Your dispatches are most satisfactory and show your expedition to have been in the highest degree successful in every particular. This fact is not affected by the disaster later.

On July 18 every morning paper in the United States carried column after column on the rescue. It completely shut out any other news from the front pages of *The New York Times* and the *Chicago Tribune,* for example. Banks of terse headlines summarized the various parts of this latest epic of the North: the triumph of Commander Schley, Greely's return alive and well, the attainment of the Farthest North, the exploration of interior Grinnell Land—and, counterbalancing the good news, the death of nineteen men of the original twenty-five. The *Chicago Tribune* headlines:

> FROM THE JAWS OF DEATH—Lieut. Greely and Six Brave Companions Rescued in the Northern Sea—A Graphic Tale of Terrible Privation—Results Achieved by the Daring Explorers— GOOD NEWS—Commander Schley's Creates a Sensation.

James Gordon Bennett's *New York Herald,* exultant over the rescue and the accomplishments of Greely's party, nonetheless reported President Arthur's sour first reaction when informed by Nichols and Sheridan:

> The President said that he had never favored these explorations, as the geographical and scientific information secured could not compensate for the loss of human life. He could not see what had been gained so far that would justify any men, however ambitious and daring, in making another attempt. He was only too glad that any of the party had been rescued alive, as he had very little hope of the success of the relief expedition.

In view both of the calamity that befell the party during its final winter and the risk and expense of the rescue, no newspaper in America could afford to assert bluntly that the scientific results of the expedition were worth nineteen lives. Few, however, recognized in print the fact that those results could not be telegraphed in a few hours, but rather represented a huge mass of data to be analyzed by specialists in the months ahead. Most editors appeared to think that the science of arctic work was limited to sketching a few new lines into the blank spaces on maps and planting the American flag four miles closer to the North Pole than the British had. The *Chicago Tribune* editorialized:

> The original purpose of the colony has failed. . . . Arctic exploration has involved an immense waste of money and life, and entailed horrible sufferings upon those who have survived. It is time that it stopped. No bar can be placed upon private enterprise, but the Government should not authorize another dollar to be spent in sending men to certain death and for no useful purpose.

The *Philadelphia Inquirer* was blunt in its condemnation:

> With the rescue of the survivors of the Greely party there should come a surcease of the monstrous and murderous folly of so-called Arctic exploration.

The New York Times likewise took a dim view of arctic work, as dim as that Senator Ingalls had taken on the Senate floor the previous winter, and as President Arthur and its Philadelphia and Chicago confreres were taking now:

> Not even when it is played under favorable conditions is the game worth the candle. . . . Let there be an end to this folly.

Because its publisher-editor had a mind for arctic science, the *New York Herald* took a longer view. Anxious to turn the finger of culpability away from arctic exploration per se and toward those who had failed in their duty to the expedition, Bennett printed at length the expert views of George Kennan, the widely renowned veteran of a historic trek across northern Siberia—a man not bound by the self-protecting discretions of the political office-holder and therefore not one to cut his words into finely minced phrases. Greely's experience, Kennan said:

> . . . is a story of remarkable and heroic achievement in the field clouded by disaster due to incompetence in Washington. If

The six who survived. From left to right: Henry Biederbick, Private Maurice Connell, Sergeant D. L. Brainard, Lieutenant A. W. Greely, Sergeant Julius Frederick, and Sergeant Francis Long. Photo taken at Portsmouth Navy Yard in New Hampshire, August 1884.

— Collection Garland W. Patch —

Lieutenant Greely and his party had all returned in safety to the United States, as they might have done had they been properly supported, their Arctic record, in point of skillful management and success, would have been unparalleled.

No other Arctic expedition has ever spent two consecutive winters and part of a third in such high latitudes and achieved such results without a casualty or a single case of serious sickness. If Greely had found at the mouth of Smith Sound the shelter and food which he had a right to expect there he would probably have brought his entire party back to the U.S. in perfect health. . . .

To think that two ships on successive years, and probably a third, were in a position to land stores which would have saved the lives of those eighteen men! . . . But their commanding officers were not ordered to do so, and they did not think of it.

From England Sir George Nares sent a hearty "well done!" in a spirit akin to Kennan's:

I . . . felicitate Lieutenant Greely on his safety and success in making the longest stride yet made toward a knowledge of the Arctic mysteries. . . . Mr. Greely's achievement has placed America in the van of Arctic research up to the present moment.

Benjamin Leigh Smith, another experienced British explorer of the Arctic, echoed Sir George's views:

Greely has performed a feat unequaled in Arctic exploration, and one which stirs the blood like a recital of times of old.

The meteorologists of the London Balloon Society called a special meeting on the evening of July 19 at which the members discussed at length the cables carrying Greely's summary of the expedition work. The meeting voted a resolution congratulating him, extending him a lifetime membership, and ordering a gold medal struck in his honor. In Paris, the Société de Géographie at its semimonthly meeting on July 18 minuted

. . . its having learned with sorrow of the death of some of the members of the Greely expedition, and transmits to those who survived the expression of its sympathy. . . . The Secretary adds that the list of survivors unfortunately does not include that of our compatriot, M. Octave Pavy, who was a member of the expedition.

From Windsor Castle came a cable addressed to President Arthur, in which—

The Queen heartily congratulates the President and people of the United States on the rescue of Lieutenant Greely and the gallant survivors of the Arctic Expedition. She trusts that favorable reports have been received of the sufferers.

Arthur, in reply, cabled to Queen Victoria America's renewed thanks for the generous gift of the *Alert* to aid the rescue mission.

In St. John's, meanwhile, Schley impatiently awaited the completion of the dozen metal caskets he sought for the bodies before moving farther south in the heat of midsummer. Greely and his men stretched their legs ashore daily, but they found it almost impossible to escape the crowds which their presence in St. John's attracted. As strength slowly returned to their bodies they increasingly enjoyed the strolls, which afforded them the luxury they had not enjoyed for three years—to wander in the parks to admire the beauty of green trees and soft grass.

On one occasion Greely called at the home of Mr. and Mrs. Joseph F. Rice, parents of George Rice, who had moved to St. John's from Nova Scotia. For him it was a moving experience to recall for these grief-stricken people the unforgettable heroism of their sturdy son, his comrade and strong right arm. The symbolic meaning of the life and death of George Rice was the major theme running through an emotional sermon the Reverend David Beaton preached to an overflow crowd at Queen's Road Congregational Chapel on Sunday evening, July 20:

"There are two sustaining features in the record of the Greely party that enforce their truths: comradeship and self-sacrifice. . . . The strong men of the party were found willing and ready to sacrifice themselves for the weak. Darwinism did not obtain in that doomed ice-camp. Not the law of animal self-seeking, but the law of Christ; for there the strong man helped the weak, and so fulfilled the law of the Divine Master. I am doing no disparagement to the rest of that brave band when, in the words of its leader, I say that there was one man who conspicuously manifested this noblest trait of character. George W. Rice, whose family resides among us, was one of the strongest and most cheerful in that little company of brave men. He had one of the best chances of surviving the privations of that awful winter. . . .

"He perished on the ice-floe, and the memory of his heroism, his self-sacrifice and noble character was all that remained to cheer his companions under their great loss. We are left in no uncertainty as Christian men about the nature of such an action. Jesus Christ himself has named it for us: 'Greater love has no man than this, that a man lay down his life for his friend.' "

All flags in St. John's flew at half mast, private businesses as well as public buildings were draped in black crepe on the morning of July 26 as the four-ship squadron hauled anchor and pointed out of the harbor. Craft of all kinds saluted the Americans with shrilling whistles and fluttering pennants as they escorted the ships bearing the remnants of the Lady Franklin Bay Expedition out to the sea and toward home. The dead were now secure, in heavily bolted iron caskets below decks. Schley's orders from Washington had informed him to be prepared for a tremendous greeting at Portsmouth, New Hampshire, where the survivors were to be delivered to the Navy Yard, which lay opposite the town at Kittery, Maine.

Even if Schley had not made Greely and his men aware of the attention that would be paid them when they touched American soil, the expedition leader had caught an indication of it from the flood of messages he had received during his eight days in St. John's. One telegram from D. W. Leslie, impresario of the lecture circuit, almost ordered him to the platform:

A. W. Greely, St. John's.—Have managed nearly all leading lecturers for past twenty-five years successfully. Want you for one hundred or more nights. Make no arrangements until I see you. Write me at 11 Court Street, Boston, stating when and where we can meet. Confidential.

Two days later, having heard nothing, Leslie reiterated his plea, increasing his bait to attract the lion of the hour:

> Want you for two hundred lectures. See me at Portsmouth before making any engagements. Write. Confidential.

Harper & Bros., the publishers, also approached the celebrity, though in a slightly more genteel manner:

> Could you favor us with an .article with sketches for Harpers Weekly descriptive of your expedition? Do you propose a book? Answer at our expense.

The wind swung around to the east, blowing fair for home; Schley was able to sail most of the way to Portsmouth without using steam. He thus gained a day on his estimated schedule, which would have brought him to Portsmouth on Saturday morning, August 2. During the homeward run the heat and moisture increased markedly. Dr. Green noted that Greely under these conditions "felt much prostrated" and his muscles ached. His nervous system had calmed, however; his digestion was good and his heart murmur was disappearing. Like all the survivors he had put on considerable flesh quickly, most noticeably about the face. By the time the squadron approached Portsmouth, Greely's body weight had reached 169 pounds, a gain of 49 in six weeks. He had put on 9½ pounds the first week, gained a startling 15 pounds the second, then successively 8, 7, 5½, and 4 pounds weekly. He, Connell, and Biederbick were still less sturdy than Brainard, Frederick, and Long. Although all six survivors displayed common symptoms in varying degrees—sallow complexion, weak muscles, and swelling of the ankles—the health of each could be classified in navy medical terms as fair, fairly good, or good. It was obvious that they all would require several weeks of regular food and rest before they would be ready for normal work.

At daybreak on Friday, August 1, the squadron emerged from a dense fog. There, about ten miles ahead, stood the Isles of Shoals lighthouse, marking the picturesque cluster of sand, rock, beach grass, and white houses Greely had known from boyhood as an excursion spot. It was ironic, yet poetically just, that of all the great coastline of the United States he should be coming home today among landmarks familiar to him almost since his birth. As the sun mounted, the survivors stood on deck drinking in their first view of the beloved land, native soil to three and adopted home to the others, which a few weeks ago they had despaired of ever seeing again.

Greely, straining his eyes to the southwest, tried to make out the hills and spires of Newburyport, which lay some twenty miles off as the *Thetis* passed close by the Isles of Shoals on the port side. Here on the beaches of Appledore Island, Greely's friend, the poetess Celia Thaxter, had watched and written of the little sandpiper flitting before the incoming waves; here she had composed "A Tryst," her poem of fate, which Greely had often read aloud to the men at Camp Clay by the murky light of the seal-blubber lamp. To them the tryst between Celia Thaxter's doomed pleasure-ship and the fatal iceberg symbolized their own tryst with the ship they wanted to believe would come to their rescue at Sabine:

> For still the prosperous breezes followed her,
>   And half the voyage was o'er;
> In many a breast glad thoughts began to stir
>   Of lands that lay before.

Now to the south of Portsmouth town, high and proud on its green bluff by the sea, loomed the Hotel Wentworth, a mighty pleasure-dome with three towers dominating the horizon, twenty-six windows stretching across its broad front. Greely remembered it well, and often at Camp Clay had thought of the Sybaritic dinners served in its luxurious dining room while Lockwood, Brainard, Rice, and the others were invoking Delmonico's, the Parker House, and the fleshpots of Chicago.

Straight in toward Portsmouth harbor steamed the ships as the sun burned down on a calm sea. Dead ahead Whale Back Light came plainly into view. Beyond, in the estuary of the Piscataqua River, could be seen the spiny masts of dozens of ships riding at anchor. The entire North Atlantic fleet, including the Annapolis midshipmen on their summer training cruise, were assembled to greet the rescuers and their rescued. A message from the fleet flagship, the *Tennessee,* ordering him to proceed into the harbor was soon conveyed to Schley.

As the *Thetis, Bear, Alert,* and *Loch Garry* steamed home through the narrows past Whale Back Light into the haven of old Portsmouth, crewmen of the naval vessels climbed into the rigging and sent their resounding three cheers ringing out over the water. The cries were taken up aboard the other boats and ashore by the crowds massed on the banks. Hundreds of pleasure craft of every description surrounded the new arrivals, while ladies fluttered their handkerchiefs and waved their bright parasols. On board the *Tennessee* Secretary Chandler, General Hazen, and Henrietta Greely were proudly watching as the ship's band struck up "Home Again," the sentimental favorite of ocean voyagers and navy families. Soon, as eyes grew moist, thousands of voices were echoing from ship, boat, and shore:

> Home again, home again,
> From a foreign shore,
> And oh! it fills my soul with joy,
> To meet my friends once more;
>
> Here I dropp'd the parting tear,
> To cross the ocean's foam,
> But now I'm once again with those,
> Who kindly greet me home.

Only that morning Henrietta had reached Portsmouth after a long, tiring train journey from the West Coast. Adola and Antoinette, still thought to be infectious from their recent whooping cough, were left on shore while their mother was hastened aboard a waiting launch, on Secretary Chandler's order, to the *Tennessee.* In the main cabin she met the Secretary, his wife and mother; Admiral Luce, commanding the North Atlantic fleet; Admiral Wells of the Navy Yard; General Hazen; Mrs. Annie

Schley; and many others. The epitome of courtly kindness, Chandler gave Henrietta no chance to feel lost among all this rank and distinction. Taking her arm, he introduced her around the circle, then escorted her to the deck to watch the rescue ships come in. The most thoughtful touch of all, to Henrietta, was Chandler's announcing to the assembled company that no one, not even Mrs. Schley, would be permitted to board the *Thetis* until Henrietta Greely, escorted by her twin brothers Otto and Loring, should have been conveyed to Schley's flagship for a quiet reunion with her husband.

With such tact and care had the Secretary stage-managed it, through a message sent across the water to Schley, that no one was witness to the tearful embrace which reunited Henrietta and Dolph Greely in the privacy of Schley's cabin. Only after a discreet interval did others arrive—Mother Greely, Chandler himself, Hazen, and a host of others. Nonetheless, newspapers from coast to coast the next day described the intimate scene in detail, as though their correspondents had stood in the doorway, notebooks in hand. Some journals pictured Schley in engravings leaving the room and taking a furtive backward glance at the reunion, as Greely knocked over a chair in his eagerness to seize Henrietta in his arms. Others sentimentalized over the cries supposed to have been uttered by the principals ("Dolph!"—"Arthur!"—"Rettie!"—"Wife!"). On Sunday morning, when she found a spare hour, Henrietta wrote to her father in San Diego of the events of the big day:

Of course the published descriptions of our meeting were absurd, as there was no one anywhere about Capt. Schley's room when we met. . . .

Mr. Greely is improving perceptibly daily. His brain and nerves are in perfectly sound condition and his general physical health is good. The only trouble is with his muscles, which are weak. This prevents his walking far or standing long at a time. Sec. Chandler is taking the most active interest in Mr. Greely and all of us. Mr. Greely and myself are at Admiral Wells' residence (he is Commandant at the Navy Yard) where we could not bring the children because there are little ones here who have not had whooping cough.

Over the week end of August 2–3 Portsmouth was gay with a holiday atmosphere. Visitors flocked into town by cart, wagon, train, and boat to see the assembled fleet and to catch a glimpse of the hardy six who had come back alive from their arctic ordeal. Hundreds swarmed the decks of the relief ships on both Saturday and Sunday. The steamer *E. P. Shaw* of Newburyport came in with a load of excursionists and landed them at the Navy Yard. On her stern above her name, a banner proclaimed: "Newburyport Is Proud of Her Son." The steamers *General Bartlett* and *Startled Fawn* and a tugboat also came up the coast from Newburyport loaded, in the words of the *Portsmouth Chronicle,* "with parties as large as the law will allow them to carry."

While Greely remained secluded at Admiral Wells' home, Brainard and the other enlisted men were housed aboard the historic frigate *Constitution.* Old Ironsides was serving out her years now as a receiving ship at the Portsmouth Navy Yard. In town, the mayor and his citizens' committee busily prepared for the mammoth parade and celebration on Monday, August 4, which bade fair to attract more attention to Portsmouth than any other event in her long history.

From the earliest hour on Monday morning, the toll bridge leading into Portsmouth from Kittery was choked with pedestrians and carriages, while from other directions people poured in by train and highway from surrounding towns. By the time set for the start of the parade, the *Chronicle* estimated, "there were at least fifteen thousand strangers in the city."

As the parade was forming on Congress Street, Greely and his fellow survivors rode through the center of Portsmouth in a smart Tally-Ho lent by the owner of the Hotel Wentworth. Wave upon wave of cheers followed them as they were recognized. Greely was the easiest to spot, his spectacles and jutting black whiskers contrasting strongly with his white linen suit and panama hat worn against the glare of the summer sun. "Handsome Dave" Brainard of the high forehead and classic profile caused more than one feminine heart to flutter as the group passed by. Biederbick had trimmed his mustache to a thin line and cut his hair very short, whereas Connell had a heavy black mustache curling down at the ends. Long had added a goatee to his red mustache, and his shiny, round cheeks were beginning to take on their former apple redness. "Shorty" Frederick, his black hair plastered like patent leather on his head, looked as earnest as ever, despite the joy of the occasion. When the group appeared on a balcony above the door of the ornate red sandstone Rockingham Hotel, they produced a new wave of enthusiasm in the street below, making it difficult for the marshals to get the parade under way.

It was a long and colorful procession that wound from Market Square up State Street to Middle Street, left on Court Street down to the waterfront among its tightly packed frame houses, then looping back around the big homes of Middle, Cass, and Islington streets at the other end of town to terminate amid a blare of brasses and a waving of handkerchiefs at Market Square once more. There were bands and flags, contingents of sailors, fire companies, and United States Marines, the Naval Academy midshipmen, and dignitaries in carriages. But the show was stolen by the march-past of the relief-ship volunteers in their heavy blue uniform shirts and pants, blue cap on the back of the head and sheath knife at each man's belt. The *Portsmouth Chronicle* described the scene:

> Liberal applause greeted the bronzed and roughly-dressed men as they were recognized by the crowds, and when they arrived in front of the review stand the Greely survivors, who were seated at the front, rose and stood while their rescuers marched past.
>
> Longer processions have been seen in Portsmouth, but probably never before one in which there were so many trained organizations, or which attracted so much attention from the country at large.

And of the assemblage of ships in the harbor:

It is not likely that ever before were there so many government vessels in Portsmouth harbor at one time as since the arrival of the Arctic relief expedition.

On medical advice from Dr. Cleborne of the Navy Yard hospital and Dr. Francis Gunnell, the Navy Surgeon General, whom Chandler had brought from Washington to minister to the survivors, the midday parade and the afternoon reception on the courthouse lawn were considered all they could take for one day. They were therefore not present that evening when a throng of 1500 people jammed into Portsmouth Music Hall (then known in show business as "the biggest hall north of Boston") for a welcome-home rally. Everyone was there, and it seemed as if they all were seated on the platform, which was decked colorfully with flowers and draped with bunting—Secretary Chandler, very dignified with his pince-nez glasses attached to a ribbon and his short-trimmed beard touched with gray; Governor Samuel W. Hale of New Hampshire, General Hazen, Admirals Wells and Luce, Senator Hale and Representative Randall, who had steered the Greely relief bill through Congress—Schley, Emory, Coffin, the mayor, sheriff, aldermen, clergymen, and everyone else in town of any consequence. The relief-squadron crews made a gallant appearance when they marched down the main aisle and took their seats in front to a sustained roar of applause.

It was a night of glory for New Hampshire. Strangely absent from the rally, as he had been from the four days of festivities, was the head of the department which had dispatched the expedition to Lady Franklin Bay: Robert Todd Lincoln, Secretary of War. By the conspicuousness of his absence he hovered over them like an ominous shade, Banquo beside the table of Macbeth. Although Chandler and several other speakers mentioned Lincoln courteously in passing, there was not much they could say about his involvement in the cause of saving his own men. Chandler, who had hopes of becoming a U.S. Senator from the Granite State, was chairman and star performer of the evening. He performed his role to perfection and early in the program addressed the survivors with the sentiments that Lincoln should properly have come to Portsmouth to convey:

"With special tenderness we turn to Lieutenant Greely and his rescued comrades," Chandler said, and named each man. "They are the only survivors of an American Arctic exploration party which reached out farther toward the pole than any previous explorers, and whose observations were extended into the Polar Ocean. Their coast and land journeys were extensive, and have mapped out with increased exactness the shoreline of Greenland and the interior of Grinnell Land. Their scientific observations, made at fearful cost, have resulted in valuable additions to our knowledge of the lands within the Arctic Circle. For their labors and their endurance we honor them, for their sufferings we give them our pity and sympathy, and to comfort, cheer and encourage them we promise them the gratitude of their Government and their countrymen, as the sole survivors of a polar expedition which will always illustrate American enterprise and American heroism."

The message sent to the meeting by Secretary Lincoln, which Chandler read from the platform, seemed calculated to ignore the sufferers while hailing their rescuers:

War Department, Washington. August 1, 1884.—I regret that I am not able to accept your invitation to join at Portsmouth in the greeting to Commander Schley and his command on their return. I beg you to express to him my appreciation of the energetic and thorough manner in which everything possible was accomplished by his expedition, and to tender him the thanks of this Department for his inestimable services to the survivors of Lieutenant Greely's party.

From the Secretary of War to Greely and his men not one word. It seemed almost as if Greely had firmly resolved to reply to a slight with a slight. The message of greeting and thanks he had written at the Navy Yard on behalf of the survivors was read to the hushed throng by Henrietta's brother, Otto Nesmith:

No reason less serious than sheer inability from lack of strength and health could prevent the presence tonight of the living members of the Lady Franklin Bay Expedition. I am now unable to fittingly express how deeply we feel the honor done us by your assembling here to greet with kindly words of welcome the living, and to give voice to tender sympathy for the dead.

During our service in the North we tried to do our duty. If in our efforts aught is found of work accomplished or of actions done which touches the heart of the people, we shall feel that our labors and hardships are more than rewarded. . . .

Never for a moment in our darkest or gloomiest hour did we doubt that the American people were planning for our rescue, through their representatives, all that lay in human power and skill. From day to day, as food failed and men died, that strength and that certainty gave strength to us who lived. I need not tell you what you well know, how the Secretary of the Navy set heart and soul on our relief, and, by imbuing his subordinates with his own indomitable energy, started relief vessels in an unprecedentedly brief time. . . .

We thank you for your kind deeds, thoughtful consideration and tender sympathy to and for us all—the living and the dead.

Greely's message praised Chandler, Schley, and their navy associates of all ranks without stint. It did not even mention the name of the Secretary of War, to whom its writer clearly felt no debt.

On Tuesday, the fleet and celebrants melted away. Chandler, with an honor guard of U.S. Marines, escorted the body of Sergeant Winfield S. Jewell to the Concord railroad station, whence it was shipped to Lisbon, the tiny town in northern New Hampshire where he had been born and had willed to be buried. Schley led his squadron from Portsmouth harbor bound for New York, where the remaining eleven bodies were to be turned over to General Hancock on Governor's Island. Brainard, Long, Frederick, Biederbick, and Connell were installed in the hospital on the Navy Yard grounds, while Greely, Henrietta, and the two children moved into a small cottage framed by apple trees on the navy reservation facing the harbor mouth, as guests of Secretary Chandler. Now at last, with the excitement of the welcome past, they all had a chance to compose the mind as the body rested and grew stronger.

Messages continued to pour in. One enterprising Brooklyn, New York, theater manager wanted some of the men to appear as an extra added attraction for his melodrama "Storm Beaten." An exposition in the midwest offered Brainard and his comrades a thousand dollars a week if they would appear and lecture on their experiences. A wire to Henrietta from Fort Buford, Dakota, by its very tardiness in arriving, bespoke the anguish of its signer, whose name was linked in every printed article with the Cape Sabine tragedy:

> Mail just brought news of Greely's rescue. Thank God. Convey to him and those with him my heartfelt gladness and my extreme pain and sorrow at the fate of those poor fellows who so bravely died.
>
> *Garlington*

Greely was deluged with flowery testimonials—from gushing girls who tried their hand at poetic encomiums ("Wreathe the chaplet, twine the laurel, for our Heroes safe returned . . ."); from Annie Greely, a deaf-mute foundling girl in a Kansas institution, who sent a pathetic letter seeking to learn her identity ("Are you my father?"). From long time army friends scattered across the land they came, from schoolmates, relatives, strangers, from scientists who more than anything else valued his work in behalf of International Polar Year. One of the warmest greetings, beautiful in its simplicity, came from President William F. Warren of Boston University:

> A thousand welcomes to home & friends & life. Would that your precious contribution to the world's knowledge might have been secured at smaller cost.

Yet as he rested all was not serene within the commander's mind. He had reported privately to General Hazen the terrible responsibility he had undertaken in ordering the execution of

Private Henry, and had received the assurance of his friendly
superior that the matter would be presented to Lincoln in the
most favorable possible light. Convinced himself that he had
done the only practical thing under the grim circumstances obtaining at Camp Clay, Greely had no assurance that the Army,
officially, would see it the same way. He was somewhat relieved
when Hazen wrote him a few days later from New York of his
talk with Lincoln:

> ... he was a little uncertain as to what action would be best
> and thought that later you should call for a court of inquiry. But
> next morning, after having more maturely considered the matter,
> he said: "Tell Greely to rest perfectly easy about the matter; for
> it was in the nature of a mutiny and his action was not only thor-
> oughly legal and proper, but took place beyond any territorial
> jurisdiction, and no civil authority anywhere can touch it."

A comforting point for a political man, perhaps, but a slim
reed for a man of honor to lean on—that he could get away with
having a soldier shot because it was done beyond the geographical bounds of civilization! Hazen's letter continued:

> He did not think that even a court of inquiry would be neces-
> sary, but that in due time when you feel strong and ready, it
> would be proper for you to make a full report of the transaction
> for the file.
> He said further that he [the Secretary] being now in full pos-
> session of all the facts, no one in future could say that you had
> shown the least disposition to hold back any facts. The whole
> matter this far has not gone beyond the official who should know
> it, and we have full possession of the ground. The funeral which
> took place with the military honors can, if necessary, be explained
> in future by the then apparent propriety of silence.

Henry's body had been duly interred at Cypress Hills Cemetery on Long Island and the other remains were sent to their
families. Schneider's father, having ascertained that his wandering son was with the expedition only when he read of his death,
had his body shipped home to Germany. In every case the funeral

ceremonies attracted great local attention—Cross' burial in Washington; Elison's in Pottsville, Pennsylvania; Israel's at Kalamazoo, Michigan; Linn's in Philadelphia; Kislingbury's in Rochester, New York; and Lockwood's at the Naval Academy Cemetery, Annapolis.

Greely realized that the Henry execution could not be kept quiet forever. Members of the rescue party must certainly have seen the bullet holes, and one could not expect them or the other survivors to remain silent. On August 11 Greely wrote a careful report for his superiors, but already the air was beginning to buzz with rumor and suggestion that the expedition story was not yet fully told. Surgeon General Gunnell in a private note advised Chandler to get rid of all responsibility for the survivors by turning them over to army control. Something "very dirty," he hinted, was about to break. He had learned from Dr. Cleborne, he wrote, that hospital personnel were hearing an ominous tale from one or more of their patients. But Chandler, to whom Schley had confided certain extremely unpleasant news on the first day in Portsmouth, spurned the advice of his Surgeon General. On the morning of August 12 he sent Greely a note by private messenger:

> You will please remember that I have not taken my clutches off you yet. Tomorrow Dr. Cleborne must determine whether or not you are fit to go to Newburyport, and if so, the conditions on which you may go, and when you are to return.
> You will please consider yourself as in hospital until regularly discharged, and will on account of this very injunction believe me
> Sincerely your friend,
Wm. E. Chandler

To: Lieut. A. W. Greely
(not at) Lady Franklin Bay
        Grinnell Land
        (Thank God)

That same morning Charles R. Miller, the ambitious, energetic editor of *The New York Times,* gambled his reputation on the most sensational story of the year, with which he hoped to recoup the circulation of a newspaper which had slid downhill since the recent passing of its great chief, Henry J. Raymond. Henrietta's brother Otto Nesmith had earlier turned to Miller, an old classmate at Dartmouth, to help in the bounty-bill fight with an editorial, and at the time had written his sister of his success:

> Though I was told by a prominent newspaper man here that he wouldn't do it because the *N.Y. Tribune* had advocated it, I was not disappointed in my man.

But now, with Greely rescued, personal friendship was cast aside and Miller's big scoop was being telegraphed to the four corners of the country. Its black headlines were to scar the soul of Adolphus Washington Greely for the rest of his life:

> HORRORS OF CAPE SABINE—Terrible Story of Greely's Dreary Camp—Brave Men, Crazed by Starvation and Bitter Cold, Feeding on the Dead Bodies of their Comrades—HOW PRIVATE CHARLES HENRY DIED—The Awful Results of an Official Blunder.

14 SCANDAL

ACCORDING TO THE *New York Times'* article, everything about the Greely rescue fitted neatly into a sinister cover-up plot to hide the dastardly deeds done at Camp Clay by men "crazed by starvation." Cleverly compounded of certain selected facts mixed with suppositions, innuendo, and downright falsehood, the article was spread across the country in the columns of many other newspapers. Their editors were eager to inject new sensationalism into the Greely rescue-and-return story, since by now it had grown cold. *The Times* brought it back to life with a vengeance by asserting boldly:

> Written documents, now in the possession of the Navy Department at Washington, add to the record of miserable human suffering already published in connection with the finding of the Greely Relief Expedition the most shocking stories of inhumanity and cannibalism. All the facts have been in the possession of Secretary Chandler for nearly three weeks, but so closely have they been guarded, and so strictly have the naval officers and sailors maintained the silence imposed upon them, that not even an inkling of the true and horrible condition of affairs has yet reached the public ear.
>
> The sufferings and privations of the men in their canvas hut during the long, bitter winter of 1884 have not half been told. It has been published that after the game gave out early in February they lived principally on sealskins, lichens and shrimps. As a matter of fact, they were kept alive on human flesh.

Thus *The Times* dismissed, as if they never existed, the rations, meager as they were, that lasted until the middle of May,

the bear shot on Good Friday, the seal, and the dovekies brought
in by Long. All these facts had been in prominent print, but *The
Times* ignored them all. The evidence of cannibalism, the article
stated, lay in the condition of the bodies exhumed by the rescue
party from Cemetery Ridge. The corpses were wrapped in
"blankets" (conjured up by the newspaper), the contents of
which were described as follows:

> Most of the blankets contained nothing but heaps of white
> bones, many of them picked clean. The remains could be identi-
> fied only by the marks on the blankets. By inquiries Commander
> Schley discovered that many of the seventeen men who are said
> to have perished by starvation had been eaten by their famished
> comrades.

To many readers, living on the flesh of those already dead
might be a necessary, though unpleasant, last resort; but this sentence pointed to something quite different—and much more horrible. So also did *The Times'* description, almost as if its own
reporter had been present, of the way one of the rescued is supposed to have reacted to the approach of the navy deliverers:

> One of them, a German, was wild in his delirium: "Oh," he
> shrieked as the sailors took hold of him to lift him tenderly,
> "don't let them shoot me as they did poor Henry! Must I be
> killed and eaten as Henry was? Don't let them do it! Don't!
> Don't!"
> The sailors were horrified.

The shooting of Henry, according to the article, was "particularly tragic" because the victim was basically a good man who
had merely given in to momentary temptation and stolen just a
little food, which gave the others a pretext for killing him as a
thief. Then, the story declared, they ate his body. And the cannibalism had been on a large scale, the article continued:

> It is reported that the only men who escaped the knife were
> three or four who died of scurvy. The amputated limbs of men
> who afterward perished were eagerly devoured as food.

On its editorial page *The New York Times* soberly asserted that the men at Camp Clay

> ... were led by horrible necessity to become cannibals. The facts hitherto concealed will make the record of the Greely colony ... the most dreadful and repulsive in the long annals of Arctic exploration.

As the story spread, public reaction varied.

A complete falsehood from beginning to end, said some. But others asked: What if they were forced to use the dead bodies for food? Who among us, well-fed and comfortable here at home, can put ourselves in the place of those men dying of slow starvation? Is the mortal human shell sacred after the spirit is gone? Is it wrong to use it to sustain the divine spark in those still alive?

Earnestly, heatedly, the issues were discussed from the Atlantic to the Pacific, in pulpit, parlor, saloon, and business office. The moral and practical issues became hopelessly entangled, and disputants who read different newspapers were often at a loss for agreement on the facts of what had actually happened at Camp Clay. Was any of it true? readers asked themselves. If true, was it wrong? What, exactly, did happen? Did they really kill in order to eat human flesh? Or did they simply make use of cadavers? Why was Henry shot, anyway? Because he was a thief, or for another reason? Was it true, as some of the papers said, that the party had been divided into two factions, one headed by Greely and the other by Lieutenant Kislingbury—and that the latter had been deprived of their share of the food?

In spite of the accusations of cannibalism reprinted in the Portsmouth and Boston newspapers, however, the big celebration at Newburyport on the 14th went off serenely, rivaling in size, color, and enthusiasm that in Portsmouth ten days earlier. Greely had already issued a statement from the Navy Yard, available to all the papers that wished to use it, that he knew of no cannibalism at Cape Sabine. He and Henrietta with their two little girls returned to the town of his birth for a day of tribute unmarred, at least on the surface, by the unpleasantness which had by this time been spread into almost every community in the United States. One of the notable exceptions, for understandable reasons, was the press of his home city.

In Newburyport that day Greely had at least one devoted follower with his own peculiar motive for trailing his new hero. The *Portsmouth Chronicle* noted:

> During the passage of the Greely procession in Newburyport on the 14th inst. six houses were entered by burglars, and small amounts of money taken. Officer Bagley arrested on suspicion Charles Ewlings, who was taken to be photographed. He was recognized by Charles H. Goodwin of Malden, Mass. as being the man who stole a gold watch valued at $200 from him in this city on the 4th inst. on the occasion of the civic reception to Greely here.

To General Hazen, who had returned to Washington, the entire scandal seemed the result of a desperate attempt by *The New York Times* to take his scalp. Ten years earlier, as inspector of army posts in the West, Hazen had risked his career by exposing wholesale graft within the War Department in awarding franchises to private trading companies operating as suppliers to the western posts. The investigation that grew from Hazen's charges led all the way up to the office of William W. Belknap, President Grant's Secretary of War, who had been forced to resign and was tried by the Senate. For some reason Hazen did not fully understand, the business manager of *The New York Times* and his editor, Charles R. Miller, had taken the part of Belknap and of his business friends in New York. They consequently developed a deep hostility toward Hazen. Now, he insisted, they were using the Greely expedition tragedy against him in every way they could. No sooner, for example, had the rescue news arrived in July, than *The Times* laid the blame for the suffering and death at Sabine to "the carelessness and stupidity . . . the miserable blunders" of the Chief Signal Officer. One day after another, as the newspaper carried the reports from St. John's, spelling out the tragic story of the expedition, its editorials blasted away at Hazen and called for his ouster and court-martial. It seemed as if that were the only conclusion drawn by *The Times* from Greely's arctic ordeal. Now, with the cannibalism sensation, the paper seemed to Hazen to have scored a dangerous point and he was deeply disturbed. As soon as he had read the first article, with its accompanying editorial attack on him, he wrote to Greely:

> You see the N.Y. Times has raked out and published what it has been after all the while, adding all the lies it has seen fit. You had better now make a short statement to me in writing of the Henry matter. Put it about as you did verbally, which the Secty. will probably publish, putting a stop to gossip in that direction. It appears his name was not Henry at all, but Buck, and I have no doubt, a desperate vagabond.
>
> As to the talk of eating human flesh, you can say just what you are prepared to. I have no sentiment about it, and readily perceive where it might be necessary.

Still smarting under the rebuff administered to him by the *Proteus* court of inquiry, Hazen also asked Greely to forward to him a statement summarizing the events of the past year for inclusion in his annual report, trusting that it would tend to vindicate him:

> You may also say whatever you see fit about the failures of last season. As you know, there has been a strong effort to shift the responsibility for the failure of others to me. No man can do so much to set this right as you, and a few words will do it.

On Thursday, August 14, while Greely and his family were going through the welcome-home ceremonies at Newburyport a ghastly scene was being enacted behind closed doors in the chapel of Mount Hope Cemetery in Rochester, New York. At the vigorous instance of the management of the *Rochester Post-Express,* the three surviving brothers of Lieutenant Kislingbury had signed an agreement under which they would permit the newspaper to pay for the exhumation of their brother's corpse in order, they were persuaded, that their minds might be relieved of anxiety on the state of his remains. In return, the *Post-Express* was to have exclusive access to the exhumation story.

It turned out as well as the editors could have hoped. Before a select group consisting of the brothers and their attorney, a few public officials, two medical examiners, and the *Post-Express* reporters, cemetery workers opened the coffin, then the inner casket, and exposed the unpreserved remnants of the man, dead for nearly eleven weeks. According to the medical report published the following day, signed by Charles A. Buckley, M.D., and Frederick A. Mandeville, M.D., both of Rochester, large pieces of tissue had been cut from the thighs and trunk of the dead officer.

Here was a new sensation, a "proof from the grave," on which those editors with stomach for this sort of thing (the great majority) could leap with eagerness. Greely, shocked at the Rochester dispatch, then gave his side of the story from Portsmouth. But only a handful of papers, such as the *New York Daily Tribune,* quoted his statement on the result of the Kislingbury exhumation:

> I say that it is news, and horrible news, to me. All these later disclosures and terrible charges come upon me with awful suddenness. I can truthfully say that I have suffered more mental anguish these last few days than I did in all my sojourn in the North. . . .
>
> I can but repeat that if there was any cannibalism, and there now seems to be no doubt about it, the man-eating was done in secrecy and entirely without my knowledge and contrary to discipline. I can give no stronger denial. . . .
>
> The body of the last man dead, Schneider, was not mutilated in any way, and the fact that we kept Elison alive in the hopeless state we were in ought to convince anybody that we were not cannibals. . . .
>
> Every man of the survivors has called upon me. They came in a body, and assured me separately that they knew nothing about the condition of the bodies of their fallen comrades, and each man solemnly swore that he was innocent of the deed. I cannot tell whether they told the truth or not, and I doubt if an investigation will reveal who are the cannibals. Perhaps those who died

last fed upon the bodies of those who died before; but all this is supposition. I can but answer for myself and for my orders to the party.

Hazen was dispatching notes daily to Greely now, assuring him of support in Washington. Immediately upon learning of the Kislingbury exhumation he penned a hasty vote of confidence to the subordinate whose help he felt he needed:

> Your course all the way through can't but be sustained in every particular, and with great credit and admiration. Only get strong, and don't be worried.... Secty. Chandler told me the story of mutilation at Portsmouth before I left. But he was your friend all the way through....
>
> Ever your friend,
> *W. B. Hazen*
>
> P.S. Everybody in the Army & Navy sustains you.

The dead Kislingbury, even though a detailed description of his stripped body had been paraded before the nation's gaze, had still not met his full debt to those who had paid to raise him from the grave to accuse. It was not enough for the press to describe in sickening terms how his remains had been used, as if the public might not fully appreciate the meaning of the Latin anatomical terms in the doctors' report. On the 16th the *Free Press* in Detroit, where Kislingbury had lived for a time, quoted "dispatches from Rochester" offering "proof that Lieutenant Kislingbury also fed on the flesh of his comrades." The accuser had himself been accused. In addition to moss and bits of sealskin in the "fecal matter removed from the large intestine," the newspaper claimed that "when placed under a powerful magnifying glass" the debris showed "bits of muscle and tendon." This, the *Free Press* asserted,

> ... points very conclusively to the fact that Kislingbury himself was forced to partake of the flesh of his dead comrades, as he later on became food for the survivors.

In New York, *The Times* did not quite go this far, but limited itself to hinting that the fecal matter contained human flesh, without directly saying so:

> It is composed of several substances [including] muscle and flesh. The muscle has the appearance of the end of a severed tendon. This fact is quite suggestive.

Amid this disgusting orgy of a nation's free press running riot, other journals suddenly discovered a "source" on which to base their own shocking sensations. The *New York World* on August 16 produced an unnamed "junior naval officer" of the rescue squadron, who told a *World* reporter the "confession" of cannibalism exactly as he had heard it from an unnamed "survivor" aboard ship. The survivor was described as wild-eyed and staring like Coleridge's Ancient Mariner, nor could he rest until he had told his tale. The *Chicago Tribune* pinned substantially the same story more exactly to "one of the junior officers of the *Thetis*," who cited the same restless survivor. In Philadelphia, the *Inquirer* flatly attributed the same story (headlined "Anthropophagy—Some of the Survivors Acknowledge that They Consumed Human Flesh") to a "Third Officer Kelly on the *Bear*" as well as to "one of the cooks on the *Bear*"—not the slightest daunted by the fact that no man named Kelly, either officer or crewman, was on any ship of the rescue mission.

For several days these and other imaginative newspapers seemed to vie with one another to reach the extremes of shock-value without regard at all for the truth. "One of the survivors" was quoted in the *Chicago Tribune* as having held the still-anonymous naval officer and his companions

> ... spellbound through all one night telling, if words can tell, of his first taste of human flesh. Waking or sleeping he seemed to feel his lips pressing the smooth, flabby meat that must be choked down somehow if he would live.... The little beaten path, worn smooth between the graveyard and the wretches' tent, told its own tale.

Perhaps the most revolting story of all was that extracted from an alleged "second interview" with the unnamed junior officer, who this time came forth with a new horror story on the death of Dr. Pavy, even worse than that of Henry. The doctor was done to death, he said, by that half of the party which was outside the Greely clique, and therefore hungrier than the rest. As to the unfortunate doctor, "he died by his own hand and was devoured by the survivors." There followed an account of Pavy's being driven mad by the vulturelike gaze of the hungry men hovering over him, waiting for him to expire, his death of a heart attack while running from them, then his being cut apart "while yet the muscles quivered with the life that had just gone out." The ravenous men barely passed "the ghastly dripping morsels" through the flames, impaled on sticks, then devoured them almost raw!

While the worst of these horror stories generally did not use the names of survivors, the living were still not spared direct accusation. On Sunday, August 17, *The New York Times* headline read:

Every Man for Himself.—Brutal Selfishness of Sergts. Long and Frederick.—Hiding Food from Others.

Without a shred of documentation to back it up, the article stated that when the rescue launch approached Camp Clay on June 22, Long was discovered munching on a raw duck, with blood dribbling down his beard. The rescuers found two other ducks which Long and Frederick, acting in selfish collusion, had secreted, the article declared. The *Philadelphia Inquirer* extended this tale by adding that Sergeant Brainard had shown a suspicious lack of hunger when taken aboard ship, for he was said to have refused a piece of hardtack handed to him. This was the same newspaper that at first had castigated its confrere in New York for having started the entire nasty business which, in the interest of competitive journalism, it felt bound to emulate. The *Inquirer* had said editorially:

There is a difference between printing an unpleasant piece of news and making a disgusting sensation of it. The *New York Times* made a sensation, and a most disgusting one, of the so-called cannibalism of Lieutenant Greely's men, and after it had printed the story, reputable papers felt obliged to copy it.

Although they were not related, and their names were spelled differently, the spirit of the late Horace Greeley must have hovered over his beloved *New York Daily Tribune* during this week of trial for Lieutenant Adolphus Washington Greely. The newspaper Horace Greeley had built was one of a handful of journals that conducted themselves with decent restraint. The *Tribune* reported briefly that the cannibalism claim had been made, but playing the story in a very low key, referred to the papers that shrilled it from the headlines as: "the vultures who have been gloating over these exaggerated and revolting stories."

From London the *Tribune* quoted the comment of Clements R. Markham, Secretary of the Royal Geographic Society:

> The accusation of murder and cannibalism made against the Greely party is a disgrace to American journalism. Decency would have suggested silence until Lieutenant Greely had submitted his report to the government.

The *Tribune* might have pointed, though it did not, to the strange contrast between the way its New York competitor broadcast the cannibalism sensation and on the very same day printed an editorial pleading for a suppression by the nation's press of the charges that both Grover Cleveland and James G. Blaine, Democratic and Republican nominees for President, had, each in his own unguarded moment, sired an illegitimate child. While expressing painful regret over any such indiscretion by either man, *The Times* had said:

> We hope that all decent and reputable journals and all decent and reputable men in both political parties will do their utmost to prevent the further use and spread of these scandalous stories. . . . Only harm, and not good, can come from the present agitation of these scandals.

Meanwhile in Washington, General Hazen found himself acting as messenger between Greely and Secretary Lincoln, and
rather precariously balanced between the two. On August 16 he
wrote to Greely:

> It seems that someone has reported to the Secty. that the rec-
> ords and journals had been mutilated for the purpose of covering
> up certain things, which evil people hoped might be true, and the
> Secty. was going to have it investigated at once. I think he was
> inclined to believe it.

A couple of days later Hazen seemed much relieved at the
turn matters had taken for the better, as the press uproar began
to show signs of abating. He was desperately anxious to bring
together, if he could, the superior and the subordinate whose
mutual hostility made his own position extremely difficult:

> I have yours of the 16th and am glad to have it, and your em-
> phatic denial of any knowledge of the mutilation.
> This was not necessary for me to have, but I took it at once to
> the Secty., who positively denied having at any time believed a
> word of it. As to the living, I do not believe any of them has mu-
> tilated any of them at any time. . . .
> The Secty. is firm friend now, no matter what the past may
> have been, and so are all good men everywhere.

Nor was this turn in Greely's favor mere wishful thinking on
Hazen's part. Greely did have the sympathy and trust of most
thoughtful people, whose minds were not turned against him by
the headlines of the week. His mail at Portsmouth Navy Yard
was filled with kind notes of friendship and support. Indeed, some
of the messages were based on the assumption that Greely had in
fact kept the party alive by using the bodies of their dead comrades. One post card, signed simply *Humanity,* declared:

> I am living in the most intelligent community and have re-
> peatedly heard it said, just as often indeed as it has been spoken
> of: "If I had died of their number I would have been glad to
> have them eat me." Be sure that this is the language of all intelli-
> gent humane people all over the world. Every man on this ques-

tion thinks for himself & don't ask the newspapers. God be with
& comfort you and all who were with you.

A sympathizer in New York, perhaps fortified by a drink or
two, urged upon Greely an act of old-fashioned righteous vengeance in defense of his good name:

> My poor suffering fellow countryman—that you should suffer
> more at the hands of the *New York Times,* that dirty sheet.
> Shame has long since deserted that paper & it sticks at nothing.
> There is only one course, of stolid indifference to all that comes
> from that paper, except that you should get hold of that Jones &
> give him a sound flogging.

—the same George R. Jones from whose newspaper Otto Nesmith had secured willing cooperation in favor of the bounty
bill, by grace of his Dartmouth College friendship with Editor
Miller!

By the 20th of August, eight days after it had burst, the cannibalism bombshell had been reduced to a mere splutter. Although it had lasted but a short time compared to the ordeal in
the Arctic, it had been one of the most miserable weeks in the
lives of the six survivors. It came as a distinct anticlimax to the
affair, yet in a sense it was a relief to those personally involved,
when Commander Schley on August 22 issued a brief statement
to the press and public. When the bodies of the twelve deceased expedition members had been examined aboard ship
upon being placed in a tank of preserving alcohol, six—and only
six—were found to have parts missing. These were the corpses
of Kislingbury, Jewell, Ralston, Whisler, Henry, and Ellis. The
others, Schley stated emphatically, were intact in every way. This
was all the Navy knew—there were no "confessions," no other
evidence. Simply six bodies with flesh cut away.

As to precisely what had happened in the final weeks at Camp
Clay, each man among the six was left to his own thoughts—to
his memory of who among the party had been alive and physically
able to move about on occasions when dismemberment of the
dead might have been possible. More important, every man

knew the moral stature of each of the others, and could judge for himself what he chose to think about his companions of those last bitter weeks near Cape Sabine.

Who had inspired the scandal in the first place? Several among those who were on the rescue voyage thought the finger pointed to ice pilot James Norman, whom Schley had felt obliged to discharge at Portsmouth for habitual intoxication. In the spring *The New York Times* had engaged Lieutenant Harlow to act as its correspondent with the rescue fleet, and he had supplied a firsthand account by wire when the ship had docked at St. John's. But in this era of intensely competitive journalism the editors wanted stronger meat, and they found a source for it in the disgruntled Norman in his cups. The man had a flair for the dramatic that he had revealed back on July 17.

When the squadron pulled into St. John's on that date Norman had gone directly to the newspaper offices and told a story that puffed up his own role in the rescue, and from his home ground in Newfoundland it was flashed to the outside world. He, Norman declared, had been the first man to leap from the *Cub* to greet Sergeant Long, he had first reached the dismal tent site, and he had called out: "Greely, are ye there?" From within, he said, joyful voices had at once cried: "It's Norman! It's Norman!" After three years they had recognized his voice as the mate aboard the *Proteus* in 1881!—or so went Norman's story, sent out to the world over the wires from St. John's on that first hectic day. But now he was out of the limelight, and unhappy about his discharge. It was almost inevitable, therefore, that he should be drawn toward a newspaper reporter, and it is surprising that it took so long for his elaborate tale to break into print.

Some time after the scandal had subsided, Greely penned the final word in the official army service records of the Camp Clay dead. For most of them the wording was the same as that he had written in pencil during the bitter cold of the previous winter:

Died at Camp Clay, Ellesmere Land, on south shore of Buchanan Strait, halfway between Cape Sabine and Cocked Hat

Island, [date], from action of water on the heart induced by insufficient nutrition.

Appropriate distinctions were made in the cases of Cross (who was thought to have been touched with scurvy in addition to starvation), Rice, Jens, Henry, and Elison.

It was in fitting tribute to the spirit of the remnants of his decimated command that Greely could, some months after the furor had died down, make public a note which paid it an authoritative accolade:

> My dear Greely:
>
> On the occasion of your rescue on the evening of June 22nd last, by the relief expedition under my command I saw no indications of insubordination nor of division among your party. On the contrary I was much impressed by the salutes of Brainard, Frederick and Biederbick when I approached your camp.
>
> This one slight feature bore its own testimony to the condition of your command.
>
> Very sincerely yours,
W. S. Schley

Late in 1885, with the publication of his two-volume account of the expedition, *Three Years of Arctic Service,* Greely gave his final statement on the dreadful scandal which had marred his homecoming and which brought to him and to his fellow survivors such deep anguish in August 1884:

> As to other matters which have engaged an undue share of public attention, while having no official knowledge of the facts in the case, yet the responsibility for all action in connection with such an expedition rightfully and properly rests on the commanding officer. In assuming that responsibility I know of no law, human or divine, which was broken at Sabine, and do not feel called on as an officer or as a man to dwell longer on such a painful topic.

15 AFTERMATH

As THE SURVIVORS gradually regained their health they were released from the hospital at Portsmouth Navy Yard to go their several ways on extended leaves. By the end of August, Biederbick had returned home to New York, where Messrs. Shook & Collier, producers of "Storm Beaten" at the Union Square Theatre, had worked him into the show. But the medical soldier was hardly a thespian at heart and was only putting his time to profitable use while waiting for War Department approval of his application for a hospital steward's rating. Greely had heartily backed his candidacy on the strength of Biederbick's devoted life-saving work with the arctic party. When, within a few weeks, Biederbick was awarded the rating he sought, he bade show business good-by and reported for duty to the Medical Department of the Army.

Brainard had fought off Collier's entreaties to appear in "Storm Beaten," explaining to Greely that he thought exploiting his adventures on the melodrama stage might be an impediment to receiving a commission. He did agree, however, to appear in public with Long, Frederick, and Connell at an exposition in a Cleveland museum under auspices and amid surroundings, he soberly wrote to Greely, which were "dignified and respectable." So great was public interest in the lectures the four men delivered to their audiences that they were paid a thousand dollars a week simply to recite a factual account of the arctic adventures through which they had come—against an imaginatively painted backdrop. But it was too good to last. Early in September someone in Washington reported disapprovingly to Secretary Lincoln that the soldiers were being exhibited "like freaks in a carnival" and were "disgracing the uniform." Without inquiring into the truth of these whisperings, Lincoln summarily ordered the men to withdraw from the exhibition and report for duty. By the time Brainard could appeal to Greely to intercede it was too late to reverse the order.

Despite the acclaim with which the arctic heroes had been greeted in July and August, the Army could find neither the space nor the flexibility in its table of organization for the Signal Corps sergeants' ratings to which Greely had promoted Long and Frederick. They found themselves back on duty as privates once more. Greely himself, a lieutenant for eighteen years, had missed his regular turn for promotion to captain while on duty with the expedition and was therefore passed over. But the matter of rank was unimportant now, compared to the satisfaction of being alive and at home with his family. He spent a substantially happy, though somewhat hectic, summer recuperating at the little frame house amid the apple trees on Seavrey's Island within the Navy Yard confines, and he felt his mental and physical strength slowly returning to him.

The end of the expedition brought in its train a mass of paper work ranging from the all-important labor of putting the expedition's scientific report in shape for publication, to the most trivial —such as formally notifying the Army quartermaster whether one of the dead had been careless with a lost garment (which should therefore be charged against the pay owed to his estate), or had legitimately lost it in line of duty. Both at Portsmouth and later in the year in Washington, Brainard spent weeks assisting Greely in piecing together all the details of the three years in the Arctic which now seemed worth recording, on which their notes at the time were more sketchy than they should have been. There were gaps in diaries to fill, nearly illegible scrawlings to decipher, aid to render the stenographer struggling over transcription of Lockwood's precious shorthand journal, details to interpolate into the story of their life and scientific observations in the North.

There were at the same time personal kindnesses and duties toward the families of their dead comrades which fell to the commander and the first sergeant, since both Greely and Brainard had been named executors in most of the men's wills. Correspondence never seemed to end, and Greely especially found himself cast in the role of friend, counselor, and consoler to faraway families, whose members he had never met. A close friend of General Lockwood's in Washington, for instance, wrote to Greely asking that he send a personal assurance to the old gentleman, now greatly broken in spirit, that his son had died properly. The friend wrote that the elder Lockwood's mind had shown signs of giving way over the grief of losing his beloved James, his second son to die. He wanted very much to be comforted with the knowledge that the young lieutenant had died a believing Christian.

The forlorn Minnie Gardiner, young widow of Observer Hampden Sydney Gardiner, wrote from Magnolia, North Carolina, pleading for some personal keepsake of her husband, who had left her for the Arctic only two months after their marriage. Since he had been one of the last to die and his body had been buried in the tidal crack and swept away, she did not even have his remains over which to weep. Deeply touched, both Greely and Henrietta corresponded frequently with Minnie Gardiner and through the years she came to rely on them both for help in securing government appointment as postmistress in Magnolia. She remained their loyal friend for life.

From the Imperial German Consulate General in New York came a letter in behalf of Alfred Schneider of Chemnitz. The father was still unwilling to accept the reported death of his long-missing son without proof, and the Consul asked "whether the soldier who joined your Arctic expedition under the name of Roderick Robert Schneider is the same whose photograph is enclosed." Greely was forced to report with regret that he was.

On the letterhead of W. H. Ralston, "Dealer in General Merchandise, Grain and Seeds—Howard, Ohio" came an inquiry typical of several:

Will you please inform me what my Bro. David C. Ralston done with his personal property? I mean, did he direct to whom you should turn them over to? He had a gold watch & other small articles.

Most of the men's families were cordial to Greely and Brainard as they performed their executors' offices. But the brothers Kislingbury remained distant, understandably so in view of the falling-out between Lieutenant Kislingbury and his superior and the unpleasantness following the exhumation of his body. The behavior of Lilla Mae Pavy, however, was distinguished almost from the first by the most bitter hostility. Although she was aware from her husband's attitude, expressed in 1880 when he sailed for Greenland and in letters he sent her by the *Proteus* in 1881, of his inordinate desire to lead the expedition and his conviction that he was Greely's superior, she had urged him to be content with a secondary position. But now that he was dead, his body not even returned to her, and with the brutal lies about what had been done to him at Camp Clay broadcast across the land, she fought to preserve his image as she had idealized it. Her mission in life seemed to become the destruction of her late husband's colleague and commander, and to this end she used every weapon on which she could lay hand.

While Pavy's scattered personal notes were at the War Department being copied for the expedition record, she cried that this was a "plot to suppress the truth." When she finally received the papers from Washington, she sought outlets in print for her own selected extracts from them to "prove" the incompetence of the expedition leader—little caring whether this meant also besmirching the good name of the others who lived, such as Brainard, or the memory of the dead. With the publication of Greely's official report, in which he was obliged to take note of such facts as Pavy's failure as expedition naturalist, his refusal to turn over his journal, and his ignominious state of arrest in the summer of 1883, the widow Pavy turned more venomously against him than ever. In her campaign she even circulated printed copies of the testimonial to Dr. Pavy's medical skill written in Edward Israel's hand, which the doctor had dictated and most of the men had signed. For a number of years certain editors found her fulminations against Greely worth printing, as did members of Congress who later opposed some of Greely's projects in the Signal Corps and found her convenient to use as an expert witness before their committees.

As if one Widow Pavy were not enough, Greely found himself besieged from another side by the woman calling herself Mme. Alice Pavy (*née* Loiseau), whom the medical man had left in Paris with their child in 1871, promising his faithful devotion and support. For several years Alice Pavy penned one appeal after another to Greely, begging that he use his great influence, as she put it, to obtain some financial support from the generous American government for the child of the man who had died in its service on the Lady Franklin Bay Expedition. In every second paragraph she cursed the American woman who was the legal widow and heir of the man they both had known. Greely, hopelessly caught in a difficult position, helped Alice Pavy in a modest way from his own pocket. But where the United States government found no way to honor the request of the Frenchwoman, on the ground that Pavy was not an American citizen, the *Société de Géographie* in Paris chivalrously came to her aid and raised a large subscription for the destitute orphan of their lamented compatriot and colleague.

Greely's official report on the expedition, which included all the scientific records and observations, page after page and column after column of figures, along with a narrative account of the three years in the Arctic, ran to 1300 pages in two heavy volumes. It was printed in 1888 as a document of the House of Representatives, Forty-Ninth Congress, First Session. It included George Rice's photographs—a notable first in arctic documentation—Lockwood's topographical sketches, maps of the expedition discoveries in Greenland and Ellesmere Island, accounts of every sledge journey made from Fort Conger, parts of several diaries (most notable those of Brainard, Lockwood, and Schneider), official orders and correspondence touching on the expedition. Francis Long contributed an account of his spring exploration trip west from Camp Clay during his futile search for game. Frederick wrote a report of his last journey with Rice and the death of the heroic Canadian in the storm on Baird Inlet. Biederbick carefully summarized the health problems the men faced in their final bitter months and the measures taken by Pavy, Greely, and himself to keep the party alive as long as possible.

Altogether, the voluminous report was the culmination of the expedition's effort. It represented the purpose for which the venture had been undertaken and it met, in every respect, the requirements of the Hamburg International Polar Conference. The two volumes remained for many years one of the most important source books of arctic data available to the world of science—in meteorology, astronomy, physics, oceanography, biology, anthropology—as well as to the adventurous amateurs who dreamed of reaching the North Pole. In it they read, to the surprise of a great many, that over the two years at Fort Conger precipitation totaled only 7.77 inches. Instead of the heavy snowfalls usually thought characteristic of the high latitudes, it was rather a case of its being "too cold to snow," and that snow which did fall remained in place for a long time. The records showed that February was the coldest month, with a mean temperature of 40.1 degrees below zero Fahrenheit, and July the warmest, with a mean of 37.1 degrees. July likewise was the month of minimum barometric pressure—29.725 inches of mercury—whereas April showed the maximum, 30.175 inches. The narrative account pointed to the need for improved weather-recording instruments, particularly the mercury and alcohol thermometers, which frequently solidified and thus could not perform adequately at sustained temperatures of −40 degrees and lower.

Expedition records of the height and intervals of 1314 consecutive tides at Fort Conger, when compared with tidal gauge data taken on sledging trips at other points, enabled Greely to work out a cotidal curve, or tide schedule, for Kennedy and

Robeson Channels. Combined with data from other International Polar Year stations, the tide-gauge figures brought back by Greely helped establish the general tide pattern in arctic waters. Tidal records combined with the attainment of Lockwood Island, 83°24′ North, convinced Greely that Greenland was an island—a point in dispute when the expedition set out. The records of the declination of the magnetic needle at Fort Conger (averaging about 100°13′ West) and the dip-circle, which inclined down toward the center of the earth at about 85 degrees, played their own valuable part in the international effort to probe the mysteries of the earth's magnetism—mysteries still not fully unfolded to science. They became benchmarks for the observations of the second International Polar Year in 1932–33 and for their lineal descendant, the International Geophysical Year of the late 1950s.

The collated data from all I.P.Y. stations remained the fundamental data library for arctic science through several decades. At last, random observations by many arctic explorers had been replaced by a systematically organized body of information based on common standards. Of all the conclusions drawn from the Lady Franklin Bay Expedition, however, perhaps the most interesting to explorers was its proof that a properly equipped party could spend two years and more safely and comfortably in the Arctic without incurring scurvy, up to that time the scourge of every extended arctic venture. While the exact nature of scurvy as a deficiency disease was not made clear to medical science until some years later, Greely and Dr. Pavy by careful study of the experiences of past expeditions and by remarkably successful empirical methods managed to keep the party free from this ailment, which had done great damage to the excellently equipped Nares expedition only five years earlier. The fresh musk-ox meat, pemmican treated with lime juice, and the lemons from the *Proteus* wreck cache certainly played an important part in the first significant triumph over scurvy in arctic history. Greely subsequently learned that the measures he had insisted on at Conger —clean floors, aired bedding, sunlight, recreation, and the use of hot water and soap, while they had other values, were not anti-scorbutic. Likewise, the discoveries of Lister and Pasteur, which were made public shortly after the expedition returned, led the survivors to wonder how they had managed to escape infection amid the filth of Camp Clay. On occasion they joked that such microbes as there were at Sabine must have starved or frozen to death.

During the months that saw Greely bent over his desk at work on his official report and on his two-volume narrative of the expedition General Hazen precipitated one more crisis in the long drama. An incautious man who sometimes stubbornly insisted on a fight when forbearance and compromise might have caused him less difficulty, Hazen felt compelled to take a final jab at Secretary Lincoln, who was due to leave office for the business world with Grover Cleveland's inauguration as President on March 4, 1885. Hazen thought he had been badly treated by the *Proteus* court of inquiry and resented implications in the press that he should be saddled with the blame for all that had been disastrous in the Greely affair, when he had really been heart and soul with Greely and his men during their suffering. He particularly resented the implication in Lincoln's annual report of the year before that the tragedy at Sabine could be laid to his, Hazen's, bungling.

A few days before the change of administration, Hazen took Rudolph Kauffman of the Washington *Evening Star* into a quiet corner of the Ebbitt Hotel and poured out to him the entire history of his frustrating difficulties with Lincoln—a Cabinet member who never cared about the expedition from first to last, as Hazen put it. Kauffman's article reflecting these views appeared on March 2. In it Hazen was made to appear the true friend of Greely and his men, eager and willing to do anything within his power to save them, including the dispatch of a ship in September 1883. Secretary of War Lincoln, on the other hand, was painted as a do-nothing bureaucrat. This was too much even for the phlegmatic Lincoln. With a scant forty-eight hours before his authority as Secretary of War would expire, he leveled formal charges of insubordination against Hazen, specifying "conduct to the prejudice of good order and military discipline, in violation of the 62nd Article of War." Then he left office, with the responsibility for prosecuting Hazen resting on the incoming administration.

The result of the Hazen court-martial could almost be predicted. The country was emotionally with Greely and therefore sympathetic to Hazen. But at the same time no responsible official, either civilian or military, could brook the General's course in fighting a battle with his civilian superior through the public prints. Hazen was found guilty of the insubordinate, unsoldierly conduct with which he was charged. But the new Commander-in-Chief—first Democratic President in twenty-four years—Grover Cleveland, had no desire to humiliate Hazen for the benefit of Lincoln, now gone from the political scene. In an announcement closing the book on the Hazen court-martial, Cleveland declared that the professional American soldier must never subvert the principle that he is the subordinate of the Secretary of War:

> In losing sight of this principle the accused has brought upon himself the condemnation of his brother officers, who examined the charges against him, and seriously impaired his own honorable record of previous conduct. It is to be hoped that the lesson will not be forgotten. General Hazen will be released from arrest and assume the duties of his office.

The outcome amounted, therefore, to a verbal spanking. But in retaining his post as Chief Signal Officer Hazen felt he had scored a moral victory for himself, the Signal Corps, and the expedition.

After months of delay, Long and Frederick obtained ratings as Signal Corps sergeants and were given observer duty in the cities in which they settled down and married. Frederick became established in Indianapolis, where he married eighteen-year-old Laura Kettler in 1885. Two daughters were born to the couple, whom Frederick named Thetis and Sabine. Industrious, quiet, and modest as he had been in the Arctic, he was usually diffident about recalling his experiences for those who inquired. Long went into the employ of the Weather Service in New York City, where he also married and raised a family. Unlike Frederick, he permitted his Baron Munchausen streak to lead him into telling ever-taller tales of the North. With each newspaper interview, the Good Friday bear, for example, got closer to the water's edge before Long dropped him with his fatal shot—the rations got thinner, the barrel staves used for fuel were whittled to matchstick size. And Long's fantasies were not confined to the Arctic. By the time he was middle-aged, it had become common knowledge in New York (though it was news to his arctic comrades) that Long was the dispatch rider who had carried General Custer's futile appeal for help to Major Reno in 1876, just before the massacre at the Little Bighorn.

Biederbick resigned from the Army after a short while to become an inspector in the U.S. Customs Service at the port of New York. He lived with his wife and daughters in Brooklyn and later in Jersey City. With some gratification and amusement, a couple of years after beginning this new employment, he found himself on the dock one day face to face with Greely, who was standing by his baggage for inspection on his return from a trip to Europe. After a friendly reunion, just a word from his old commander that he had nothing to declare was all Biederbick required to pass him through customs without opening his baggage.

Greely and General Hazen both tried hard to obtain the Army commission they agreed Brainard had a right to expect on the strength of his exemplary leadership and service in the North. At one point Hazen assured Greely that President Arthur had positively promised to make Brainard an officer. But his application became so hopelessly snarled in red tape that Greely at length took his case to the public. In *Three Years of Arctic Service*, which was based largely on his own diary entries, he had this to say about Brainard:

It is inevitable in most great undertakings that the subordinates should be relegated to secondary places, but I cannot believe that our great nation, which spent money so lavishly to save these men, will allow their heroic endurance and manly virtues to pass unrewarded. Lieutenant Lockwood and the Eskimo Christiansen have unhappily passed away, but Sergeant Brainard, who strove with them successfully to gain for the country the honors of the Farthest North, yet remains, after eight years of stainless and extraordinary service in the ranks, a sergeant. His manhood, courage and self-sacrifice, displayed on the polar sea and at Sabine, would have gained him a commission at once in any other service in the world.

Shortly after the publication of Greely's book, President Cleveland took action to commission Brainard in the cavalry, making him not only an officer and a gentleman but also, as the former sergeant happily wrote to Greely, "a Democrat for life." Brainard's eyesight suffered somewhat following his return from starvation, but this did not prevent his becoming one of the Army's outstanding riflemen. He rose in rank and responsibility through the years, serving later in the Commissary Department of the Army, as military attaché in the United States embassies in Buenos Aires and Lisbon, retiring in 1918 with the rank of brigadier general.

While his relations with the other four men remained cordial, Greely's contacts with Maurice Connell were for a few years marred by friction. Although in his formal report and his book on the expedition Greely spared embarrassment to others as much as possible by softening references to persons and incidents not measuring up to the level of heroism and sacrifice that was the common virtue of the arctic party, Connell could sense that he had put himself outside the fraternity into which their ordeal had bound the others. He was employed by the Weather Service in San Francisco for a time, then dropped for cause. In the summer of 1886 he wrote to Greely asking his old commander to intercede in his behalf with General Hazen, to the end that he might reenlist with the grade of first class private and remain at the same station for health reasons. In its first paragraphs it was a typical boon-seeking letter—but the end contained an ugly hint:

> Perhaps if you was aware of the pressure brought to bear on me to talk on certain subjects and which pressure I have so far resisted as far as I was able to resist them under the circumstances you would think different of my conduct. I know you have blamed me for several things said against you but leave me inform you for the first time that I am no more responsible for them than others who you do not suspect. I merely mention these facts to show I am not so black as I am painted.
>
> Hoping in the mean time that you can and will procure for me this favor, I remain yours very respectfully,
>
> *Maurice Connell*

The threat did him no good. Greely, Brainard, and the other survivors had good reason to mistrust Connell, because he had already been reached by newspapermen who every once in a while enjoyed raking over the coals of their Camp Clay misery, to plant in the minds of the public the notion that "the full story has not yet been told." Once Connell's misstatements of fact were so flagrant that all the other men wrote letters to their local newspapers in rebuttal. James Norman, the Newfoundland ice pilot whose tongue could be loosened by a couple of whiskies, also played this game on occasion. To the annoyance of the expedition survivors, editors for some while continued to print such exaggerated recollections from these two as fact.

Greely's friendship with William E. Chandler, formed and cemented with the rescue, lasted through Chandler's long service in the U.S. Senate and years of retirement. In 1886, after Greely's promotion was blocked by a political fight in Congress, the former Secretary of the Navy wrote to him:

> Of course, the "Greely expedition" gave me more real satisfaction than any other of my naval work; and I shall always look upon you as belonging to me. I much regret that you do not get the recognition and help you need and are entitled to. But it will come. I hope your health is such that it will not come too late.

Early in 1887 recognition came in a spectacular way when General Hazen suddenly died. Almost at once, voices were raised in many quarters in favor of putting Captain Adolphus Washington Greely, forty-two, into his place as Chief Signal Officer— with the rank of brigadier general. There was a flurry of opposition, as could have been expected, from the opponents of the rescue effort and defenders of former Secretary Lincoln. They brought Lilla Mae Pavy, not altogether unwillingly, to Washington to air her old complaints against him. But before Greely's obvious talents and qualifications for the post the resistance faded and Greely was soon confirmed by the Senate. Army historians could find no previous record of a soldier's reaching general-officer rank after starting out as a volunteer private.

From 1887 to 1906 Greely held the post of Chief Signal Officer, a longer term than any other C.S.O. before or since. Under his leadership the Corps modernized its weather-reporting service, which it eventually lost to the Department of Agriculture in a government reorganization move. Under Greely the Signal Corps developed military photography, pioneered in the use of aircraft for military purposes, laid telegraphic cable to Alaska and strung wires across its wild interior, bought and used the first military radios and the first gasoline-powered trucks for the Army. In an era of rapid technical development Greely was the direct opposite in temperament and behavior of the professional soldier who prepares to fight the next war on the previous war's terms. He was a seeker, an innovator, who constantly strove to keep the American Army and government abreast of events in science and the mechanical arts. After leaving the Signal Corps early in 1906, Greely was in command at the Presidio in San Francisco when the great earthquake and fire devastated the city. He directed the troops keeping order during the recovery and gained a reputation as a firm yet humane public administrator.

But he remained true to the New England heritage which led him to inquiry and to books as a youth, and was not a narrow technician. When he noticed that Washington offered nothing to the youngster eager to learn from books although it had splendid specialized libraries for privileged people like himself in the Capitol and the Smithsonian Institution, he started the local campaign that set up the first free public library in the District of Columbia. He was either a founder, an officer, or an active member of many cultural, scientific, and patriotic groups, including the Cosmos Club and Literary Society of Washington, the National Geographic Society, the Explorers Club in New York (its first president), the Sons of the American Revolution, Knights Templar, Grand Army of the Republic, and the Longfellow Memorial Association. Henrietta Greely was a founder of the Daughters of the American Revolution.

Known as a tough, demanding superior intolerant of carelessness and sloth, Greely could be kindly and compassionate to those who sought his aid. When Biederbick once wrote to ask for a personal loan, Greely supplied his needs without quibble. Again, when Biederbick asked Greely whether he could take time to write a letter to straighten out Francis Long, who had fallen into dissolute habits, Greely lectured his former sergeant and expedition hunter like a Dutch uncle, by mail, appealing to his pride as one of the marked men of the nation whose every move could reflect on his old comrades and become grist for the newspapers. The treatment worked.

After he had earnestly appealed for his men's rights to compensation through one bureaucratic snarl after another, it was distressing to Greely to learn that the surviving enlisted men had been compelled to hire a professional Washington lobbyist to push through Congress "a bill for the relief of David L. Brainard and others. . . ." Thanks to oiling the machinery of a grateful government through a 10 per cent contingency fee paid to one Allen Rutherford, the five men late in 1888 were paid at last what they were owed for clothing and personal property abandoned at Fort Conger, for rations, fuel, and quarters which had not been supplied by the Army in their bitter extremity at Sabine. Three times before, their relief bill had failed for want of support. Brainard reported to Greely, "so I deemed the employment of an attorney or agent, whose fee was conditional, as the only sure and safe method. And it seemed to work very well."

Not a human being disturbed the lonely peace of Fort Conger until January 1899, when Robert E. Peary, his feet badly frozen, welcomed the abandoned house as a refuge. After sixteen winters its windows were broken and its tarpaper ripped by the wind. The house not only saved Peary's life that winter but also, repaired, served as his base for subsequent assaults on the North Pole. The 83°24′ Farthest-North record of Lockwood's party was unbroken for thirteen years, until the spring of 1895, when the Norwegian polar enthusiast Fridtjof Nansen, aided by Hjalmar Johansen, sledged northward over the ice to reach 86°13′. Among the first to congratulate Nansen when he returned to civilization were Greely and Brainard.

The geographic names given by the Greely expedition to the new points they discovered still mark arctic maps printed in all languages. On his own initiative Greely expunged Garlington's name from the island on which Camp Clay was located. He inserted in its place the name of the noted Canadian explorer, Sir Bedford Pym. He likewise discreetly removed Capt. Henry Howgate's name from a fiord on the maps Lockwood had sketched. Robert Todd Lincoln himself asked that his own name be removed from the cape which Lockwood and Brainard had seen beyond their Farthest; Greely readily acceded and named the point Cape Washington instead.

From time to time, the fugitive Howgate was reported at various points in the United States, but Alan Pinkerton's men never seemed able to catch up with him. Occasionally he sent a letter to Greely through his daughter Ida, asking for help in a new money-making scheme, but his former protégé would have nothing to do with Howgate so long as he remained a fugitive from justice.

Greely's bitterness toward Garlington and Lincoln he carried through the years, and to his final days he could not forgive what he considered their culpable negligence, which led to the needless death of his men.

The marble likeness of John J. Ingalls, who nearly blocked Greely's rescue from the floor of the United States Senate, today looks coldly down on Capitol visitors from his pedestal in Statuary Hall, Kansas' tribute to her statesman-orator.

Frederick died of cancer of the stomach in January 1904, at fifty-one, and was buried in Crown Hill Cemetery, Indianapolis. Biederbick died in Jersey City in March 1916. Long was felled by an apoplectic stroke less than three months later, at work in the Weather Bureau building in New York. Connell lived five years longer, until June 1921, dying at San Diego. He had long since shown clear signs of regretting his old ways and both Brainard and Greely were convinced of his genuine contrition. In his later years Connell frequently spoke with affection of "my old commander."

For more than half a century following their return from the Arctic, Greely and Brainard maintained a cordial friendship. But the younger man, always junior in rank to his former chief, kept a respectful reserve between them. His letters never contained Greely's first name; they always began: "My dear General . . ." Whenever possible, the two dined together on June 22, the anniversary of their rescue, repairing for the occasion to the Cosmos Club or the Army-Navy Club in Washington, where they sat down to one of the menus Lockwood had so much enjoyed detailing in the hut at Camp Clay.

Retired with the rank of major general in 1908, Greely by temperament could never stay inactive. Travel, writing magazine articles on science and adventure, speaking engagements, and study kept him constantly busy and alert. Since 1884 his family had grown to six children, his social life with Henrietta in the capital was demanding, and his personal and scientific correspondence was voluminous. Indeed, it seemed that he was personally acquainted with almost everyone of consequence who had lived in Washington for any length of time from the Civil War

Major General A. W. Greely in full dress uniform, date unknown.
— *Author's Collection* —

1844—GEN. A.W. GREELY—1935

Cartoon from the Washington, D.C., *Evening Star,* by C. K. Berryman (originator of
the Teddy Bear), March 27, 1935, on the awarding of the Congressional Medal of
Honor to Greely on his ninety-first birthday.

— Greely Papers —

onward, as well as the scientists of a score of countries. And while he spoke and wrote frequently, and was aware of the fees he was worth, he would never speak for payment on the subject of the tragic winter at Cape Sabine, in deference to the memory of those who did not come back.

One of Greely's warmest admirers from the time of the Spanish-American War onward was a much younger man whom Greely had persuaded to undertake the construction of the Alaska telegraph line and later to learn how to pilot a flying machine, then still a dangerous innovation. To the young officer, William Mitchell, Greely became a kind of second father, and a good deal of Greely's outspoken manner rubbed off on Billy Mitchell. Not until early 1935, as Greely was approaching his ninety-first birthday, did General Billy Mitchell realize that the United States government had never paid Greely any special tribute or honor, as had the Commonwealth of Massachusetts and the governments and learned societies of numerous other lands. Mitchell promptly saw to it on Capitol Hill that a bill was introduced and passed awarding Greely the Congressional Medal of Honor. On March 27, his birthday, at the home in Georgetown where the lean, bewhiskered old soldier was living with his daughters Rose and Antoinette, the medal was pinned on his lapel by Secretary of War George Dern. Standing by Greely's side, as he had fifty-one years before at Sabine, was the erect, still-handsome David L. Brainard. Awarded, as the citation read, "for his life of splendid public service," Greely's Congressional Medal of Honor was the second such medal ever given for peacetime service (Charles A. Lindbergh received the first).

When Greely died on October 20, 1935, *The New York Times* had only words of praise to sum up his career. His grave in Arlington National Cemetery, beside that of Henrietta, lies near the historic Lee Mansion on a hill commanding a magnificent view over the capital of the country he served. Since 1946 his comrade Brainard has been near him on that same hill, as close now in final sleep as in their long winter of trial, abandoned at Sabine.

SELECTED READING

The Arctic Grail, by Pierre Berton. New York: Viking Penguin, 1988.

Ghosts of Cape Sabine: The Harrowing True Story of the Greely Expedition, by Leonard F. Guttridge. New York: G.P. Putnam's Sons, 2000.

Icebound, the Jeannette Expedition's Quest for the North Pole, by L. F. Guttridge. Annapolis, Maryland: Naval Institute Press, 1986.

The Outpost of the Lost, by David L. Brainard. Indianapolis: Bobbs-Merrill Co., 1929. See also his *Six Came Back: The Arctic Adventure of David L. Brainard,* Bobbs-Merrill Co., 1940.

Polar Journeys: The Role of Food and Nutrition in Early Exploration, by Robert E. Feeney. Fairbanks: University of Alaska Press, 1997.

The Rescue of Greely, by W. S. Schley. New York: Charles Scribner's Sons, 1886.

The Search for Franklin, by L. H. Neatby. New York: Walker and Co., 1970.

Three Years of Arctic Service. An Account of the Lady Franklin Bay Expedition of 1881–84, by Adolphus W. Greely. New York: Charles Scribner's Sons, 1886.

Unsolved Mysteries of the Arctic, by Vilhjalmur Stefansson. New York: Macmillan Co., 1972 (reprint).

INDEX

ABOUT THE AUTHOR

NOW A RESIDENT of Anchorage, Alaska, where he is a member of the Library Advisory Board, Alden Todd was born in Washington, D.C. A graduate of Phillips Exeter Academy and Swarthmore College, he had been a school and university teacher, shipyard machinist, parachute infantryman, and news reporter before he turned to freelance writing. *Abandoned* (1961) was the first of his seven books of history, biography, reference, and instruction.